The Law as It Could Be

The Law as It Could Be

Owen Fiss

NEW YORK UNIVERSITY PRESS
New York and London

NEW YORK UNIVERSITY PRESS
New York and London
www.nyupress.org

Library of Congress Cataloging-in-Publication Data
Fiss, Owen M.
The law as it could be / Owen Fiss.
p.   cm.
ISBN 0-8147-2725-5 (cloth : alk. paper)
ISBN 0-8147-2726-3 (pbk. : alk. paper)
1. Constitutional history—United States. 2. Constitutional law—
United States—Cases. 3. United States. Supreme Court—History—
20th century.   I. Title.
KF4541.F575 2003
342.73'029—dc21   2003004400

New York University Press books are printed on acid-free paper,
and their binding materials are chosen for strength and durability.

Manufactured in the United States of America
10 9 8 7 6 5 4 3 2 1

To John Doar
the embodiment of law itself

Contents

Preface

The essays in this book advance a position that once seemed self-evident but today is unfashionable: Law is an expression of public reason and provides structure to our public life. Judges are instruments of the law and embody that reason. Their function is to measure practical reality against the values made authoritative by the law and then seek ways to bring that reality into accord with these values.

The roots of this view of law can be found in the 1954 decision of the Supreme Court in *Brown v. Board of Education*. In that case, the Supreme Court declared "separate but equal" unconstitutional and then sought to transform Jim Crow school systems into unitary, nonracial ones. The Court's concerns did not stop with the public schools but in later cases extended to the police, housing, hospitals, prisons, and employment agencies and soon reached the whole of the modern state. During this age of American law, which is usually identified with the tenure of Chief Justice Earl Warren, the Supreme Court sought to make good on the Constitution's promises and used all the authority it possessed (and then some) to achieve that purpose. Equality was at the center of this program of reform, but the Court's vision extended to the full ambit of the Bill of Rights.

Today it is difficult to conceive of law in such terms. Faith in public reason has been shattered, and so has the belief that the judiciary is able or willing to use reason to give concrete meaning to constitutional values. Many point an accusing finger at the Supreme Court's December 2000 decision in *Bush v. Gore* as the cause of this sorry state. That decision barred a manual recount of thousands of Florida ballots and, in so doing, transcended the most elementary legal principles. Yet, as I explain in the final chapter of this collection, there was nothing unique about *Bush v. Gore*. It came, rather, as a culmination of twenty-five years of Supreme Court history that sought to repudiate the legacy of the Warren Court and to block the progressive realization of the Constitution. During this period the Justices paid homage to *Brown v. Board of Education* but, in fact, turned the law upside down to deny *Brown*, and the many cases to which it gave rise, most of their practical meaning.

In the face of these developments some in the legal academy, from both the Right and the Left, have turned from law altogether. Proponents of Critical Legal Studies portrayed "law as politics" and thus denied the integrity of law and its unique claim to public reason. The work of Critical Race Theorists and the branch of the Law and Literature Movement that reduced law to a form of storytelling had a similar import. The Civic Republicans of the Burger-Rehnquist era expressed their disenchantment with the Court in more nuanced ways. They turned their backs on the judiciary and placed their trust in the more political agencies, including Congress, to give specific content to our public values. The jurisprudential Law and Economics Movement had a very different political orientation. It exalted the market, and it proclaimed "law as efficiency." It achieved its greatest successes in the 1970s and 1980s, and, though it was more conservative in its outlook, it was nourished by the same disenchantment with the High Court that gave rise to Critical Legal Studies, Critical Race Theory, Law and Literature, and the legal branch of Civic Republicanism.

The essays in this book offer yet another alternative. They seek to identify the rightful place of adjudication in American society and systematically defend a conception of the judge as the paramount instrument of public reason. I wrote all these essays during the twenty-five year period of retrenchment in order to respond to the disheartening developments in Supreme Court doctrine under the chief justiceship of Warren Burger and then William Rehnquist. In that respect, these essays begin with the same concerns as many of the jurisprudential movements of the period. Yet, in the end, they offer a basis for believing in the enduring power of reason in public life.

A number of the essays—"Objectivity and Interpretation" (chapter 9), "Judging as a Practice" (chapter 10), "The Death of Law?" (chapter 11), and "Reason vs. Passion" (chapter 12)—directly engage the jurisprudential movements that emerged in response to the doctrines of the Burger and Rehnquist Courts. These essays identify the theoretical underpinnings of these various jurisprudential movements and explain how they contradict the most elemental understanding of law. I urge a return to law and present a general theory of adjudication so that return might become possible. The authority of judges, I contend, arises not from any unique moral expertise, of which they have none, but from the limits on the office through which they exercise power. In my view, judges command our respect because they are insulated from politics and engage in a special dialogue with the public. Judges are required to hear grievances they might otherwise prefer to ignore, to assume personal responsibility for their decisions, and to justify those decisions on the basis of publicly acceptable reasons. This is the source of their appeal.

The grounds of judicial authority may be clear enough, but they are often contested. "The Right Degree of Independence" (chapter 3) gives specific content to the ideal of judicial independence and explains how difficult it is to reconcile the judicial demand for political insulation with democratic principles. We seek to achieve both justice and democracy. In a similar spirit, "The Bureaucratization of the Judiciary" (chapter 4), describes how the increasing bureaucratization of the judiciary—the proliferation of decision centers and the diffusion of responsibility among these centers—threatens the integrity of the dialogical process on which the judiciary's authority rests. Bureaucrats rule by fiat, not by public reason. Accordingly, I propose new institutional arrangements to reduce the transformation of judges into bureaucrats and thus to strengthen judicial authority.

The notion that judges do not sit to resolve disputes but rather to give concrete meaning and expression to the public values embodied in the law underlies my theory of adjudication. Judges seek justice, not peace. Two of the essays in this collection, "The Forms of Justice" (chapter 1) and "The Social and Political Foundations of Adjudication" (chapter 2), develop this conception of the judicial function. While acknowledging that a dispute between two neighbors might create the occasion for the exercise of judicial power, and that the resolution of that dispute might be a happy consequence of a judicial decision, I emphasize the essentially public character of adjudication. These initial two chapters introduce a model of adjudication that I call "structural reform." Drawn from the school desegregation experience and more recent prison litigation, this model of judicial function is premised on the notion that the primary threat to constitutional values in contemporary society arises from the operation of bureaucratic organizations, and charges the judge with the duty of directing the reconstruction of these organizations. In contrast to the broadside against school desegregation remedies that Justice Thomas issued in his concurrence in the Kansas City case (*Missouri v. Jenkins,* 1995), I present structural reform as the defining triumph of public reason.

Structural reform places an emphasis on the injunction; the traditional remedy of injunction becomes the primary vehicle through which the judge directs the reconstructive endeavor. Other remedies, such as damages or criminal prosecutions, have played a lesser role than posited in traditional accounts of adjudication. The reasons for this shift are explored in "The Awkwardness of the Criminal Law" (chapter 8). This essay was originally written for an international audience primarily concerned with the protection of human rights, and it has special relevance in that domain. As exemplified by the truly remarkable developments of the 1990s, specifically the establishment of the Ad Hoc Tribunals for the former Yugoslavia and Rwanda and, more recently, the International Criminal Court, progress in protecting human rights at the global level tends to be measured almost exclusively in terms of establishing a criminal jurisdiction. However, experience in the United States during the civil rights era, which gave a primacy to the injunction and recast it in structural terms, might offer reason to doubt that tendency.

In addition to giving a primacy to the injunction, the structural model contemplates a reconfiguration of the party structure of the lawsuit, making it less individualistic and more group-oriented. Both "The Political Theory of the Class Action" (chapter 7) and "The Allure of Individualism" (chapter 6) analyze this feature of the structural suit and seek to reconcile it with the ideal that each individual must have his or her day in court. Admittedly, adjudication aimed at the protection of group rights seeks to further the interests of the individuals who comprise that group. Sometimes, however, a judge's decree has the opposite effect and endangers those interests, and efforts need to be made that reconcile the interests of the individual and of the collectivity.

The assault on judicial power that began in the closing decades of the twentieth century has taken many forms. One has been a program to substitute for adjudication a wide variety of devices of a more private character—bargaining, mediation, and arbitration. All these alternatives presuppose that dispute resolution is the primary purpose of adjudication. This movement, originally spearheaded by Chief Justice Burger but currently enjoying wide political support, has come to be known as Alternative Dispute Resolution (ADR) and reflects many of the same impulses that gave life to the program of the Burger and Rehnquist Courts to repudiate the activism of the Warren Court. In "Against Settlement" (chapter 5), I analyze the forces that gave rise to the ADR Movement and provide reasons to resist that movement. To my mind, the proponents of ADR mischaracterize the purposes of adjudication and slight the importance of public reason in our social life. In recent decades ADR has achieved great successes in professional circles, but I take that to be a further indication of our present predicament.

These essays are published today because I believe that the present malaise cannot last forever. Sometime soon, as the new century unfolds, we will once again turn to law and accord the judiciary the respect it is due. We must, however, not allow that wait to degenerate into idle nostalgia; we must resist, in action and spirit, the retrenchment of rights now afoot. To inspire that effort and to recharge a new generation, we should recall that the twentieth century began with a similar disenchantment among Progressives with the uses of the judicial power. They rebelled at Supreme Court decisions of their day—one invalidating a New York statute setting a ceiling on hours worked in bakeries, another sustaining the use of injunction to break a strike of the American Railway Union, and still another declaring unconstitutional the first peace-time federal income tax.

Disheartened with these decisions and many others, Progressives first turned away from the courts and toward the legislature, and put their store in administrative agencies as an alternative to adjudication. In the end, however, this position proved unsustainable. After the trying times of the New Deal, Progressives came to realize the unique authority of law in the American political order. They battled the Court, and, once the Court capitulated ("the switch in time that saved nine"), they wrote a new charter for the judiciary. This charter was embodied in the most famous of all footnotes, namely, Footnote Four of *United States v. Carolene Products Co.*, which ultimately came to fruition in *Brown v. Board of Education* and the many decisions that it inspired. Progressives realized that they had to distinguish between substance and procedure, and that a strong and active role for the judiciary in preserving constitutional values might indeed be proper, even if the courts of the Gilded Age had used their power to advance misconceived substantive ideals.

Whatever their disappointment with the decisions of the current Supreme Court, lawyers and the public in general will eventually come to realize that the reason of the law is necessary in order to make real our constitutional ideals. Defending the legacy of *Brown v. Board of Education*, in these essays I ask the reader to imagine, once the cycle of reaction turns yet again, what the law can deliver once it is fully understood—justice.

1

The Forms of Justice

After having worked for two years in the Civil Rights Division of the Department of Justice, in September 1968 I began my teaching career at the University of Chicago. I was asked to teach what was then the traditional course on equity. Not surprisingly, I responded to this first teaching assignment by trying to make sense of my rather extraordinary professional experience at the Department of Justice.

The teaching material for this first course consisted of five volumes of photocopied material (one of the many excesses of a brand-new teacher). By 1972 I had managed to cull the best of that material, and Foundation Press published the first edition of *Injunctions*. In this book, as well as in its earlier temporary editions, I explored the injunction in a wide variety of contexts—antitrust, labor, nuisance, and ordinary commercial litigation—but it was the civil rights cases of the 1960s that formed the heart of the book. These cases provided the most demanding test of traditional equity jurisprudence.

A casebook is a luxury. It allows a new teacher to collect material that he or she senses is important but does not fully understand. This was true for *Injunctions*. Although I made choices in the way I organized the material and decided what to include, and spoke to the substance in my scattered textual notes, for the most part my thoughts about the role of the judiciary in civil rights litigation only took shape as I prepared each day for the next class and reflected on the previous class.

In 1974 I moved to Yale. This exploratory process continued there, and in 1974 took a dramatic turn when I delivered the Addison C. Harris lectures at Indiana University. These lectures were published in 1978 as *The Civil Rights Injunction*. The process continued when I published "Dombrowski" in the 1977 *Yale Law*

Journal (volume 86, page 1103), which drew heavily on my classes at Yale. Following the publication of "Dombrowski," I was invited to write the foreword to the Supreme Court issue of the 1979 *Harvard Law Review*, and I used the opportunity to theorize even further. The result was "The Forms of Justice" (volume 93, page 1).

In the course of the decade in which my thoughts were developing, the use of the injunction took new and varied forms and achieved increasing prominence. The scope of school desegregation remedies became more ambitious, and lower federal judges broadened the scope of their injunctions to reform all manner of state institutions. It was a period of time in which, just to mention two examples discussed in the chapter, Judge Jack Weinstein announced his bold plans to desegregate the Coney Island schools and Judge J. Smith Henley began his program to restructure the Arkansas prisons.

Oddly enough, during this very same period the Supreme Court launched its attack on the civil rights injunction, particularly its structural variant. The decisive turn occurred in the 1976 decision of *Rizzo v. Goode*, which set aside lower court orders that sought to curtail the abuses suffered by blacks at the hands of the Philadelphia police. The Supreme Court opinion was written by William Rehnquist, who was then only an Associate Justice but already clearly a driving force among the group of Justices that had recently been appointed by President Richard Nixon. See "The Rehnquist Court," published in *The New Republic*, March 10, 1982, and written with Charles Krauthammer.

~ THE Constitution establishes the structure of government. It creates the agencies of government, describes their functions, and determines their relationships. The Constitution also identifies the values that will inform and limit this governmental structure. The values that we find in our Constitution—liberty, equality, due process, freedom of speech, no establishment of religion, property, no impairments of the obligation of contract, security of the person, no cruel and unusual punishment—are ambiguous. They are capable of a great number of different meanings, and they often conflict.

There is a constitutional need to give them specific meaning, to give them operational content, and, where there is a conflict, to set priorities.

All of us, both as individuals and institutional actors, play a role in this process. In modern society, where the state is all-pervasive, these values determine the quality of our social existence—they truly belong to the public; as a consequence, the range of voices that give meaning to these values is as broad as the public itself. The legislative and executive branches of government, as well as private institutions, have a voice; so should the courts. Judges have no monopoly on the task of giving meaning to the public values of the Constitution, but neither is there reason for them to be silent. They, too, can contribute to the public debate and inquiry.

Adjudication is the social process that enables judges to give meaning to public values. Structural reform—the subject of this essay—is one type of adjudication, distinguished by the constitutional character of the public values and, even more important, by the fact that it involves an encounter between the judiciary and the state bureaucracies. The judge tries to give meaning to our constitutional values in the operation of these organizations. Structural reform truly acknowledges the bureaucratic character of the modern state, adapting traditional procedural forms to the new social reality.

Structural reform is premised on the notion that the operation of large-scale organizations, not just individuals acting either beyond or within these organizations, affects the quality of our social life in important ways. It is also premised on the belief that our constitutional values cannot be fully secured without basic changes in the structures of these organizations. The structural suit is one in which a judge, confronting a state bureaucracy over values of constitutional dimension, undertakes to restructure the organization to eliminate a threat to those values posed by the present institutional arrangements. The injunction is the means by which these reconstructive directives are transmitted.

As a genre of constitutional litigation, structural reform has its roots in the Warren Court era of the 1950s and 1960s and the extraordinary effort to translate the rule of *Brown v. Board of Education*[1] into practice. This effort required the courts to radically transform the status quo, in effect to reconstruct social reality. The courts had to overcome the most intense resistance, and, even more problematic, they had to penetrate and restructure large-scale organizations, namely, public school systems. The imagery was rural and individualistic—the black child walking into an all-white school—but the reality, especially by the mid-1960s as the focus shifted to the urban centers and the nation at large, was decidedly bureaucratic.

Brown was said to require nothing less than the transformation of "dual school systems" into "unitary, nonracial school systems," and that entailed thorough organizational reform. It required new procedures for the assignment of students; new criteria for the construction of schools; reassignment of faculty; revision of the transportation systems to accommodate new routes and new distances; reallocation of resources among schools and among new activities; curriculum modification; increased appropriations; revision of interscholastic sports schedules; new information systems for monitoring the performance of the organization; and more.[2] In time it was understood that desegregation was a total transformational process in which the judge undertook the reconstruction of an ongoing social institution. Desegregation required a revision of familiar conceptions about party structure in litigation, new norms governing judicial behavior, and new ways of looking at the relationship between rights and remedies.

No one had a road map at the outset. No one had a clear vision of all that would be involved in trying to eradicate the caste system embedded in a state bureaucracy, or how the attempt would transform the form of adjudication. Having received their mandate from the Supreme Court, lower federal judges discovered what the task required and adjusted traditional procedural forms to meet these requirements. Legitimacy was equated with need, and, in that sense, procedure became dependent on substance. It was the overriding commitment to racial equality that motivated the procedural innovation and that was seen as the justification for the departures from tradition.

At critical junctures the Warren Court stepped in. The Justices emphasized their continuous commitment to *Brown* and acknowledged the comprehensiveness of the reform required: The dual school system would have to be eradicated "root and branch."[3] The process continued and, in time, the lessons of school desegregation were transferred to other contexts: to protect the security of the person and home from police abuses, to realize the ideal of humane treatment in prisons and mental hospitals, to ensure procedural due process in the welfare administration, and to equalize expenditures in state educational systems. In that way, school desegregation became a vitally important occasion for procedural innovations that transcended the substantive claim, for the emergence of a whole new conception of adjudication, one that was particularly suited to cope with a new unit of constitutional law—the state bureaucracy.

By the mid- and late 1970s, however, a new position had formed on the Supreme Court, led by Chief Justice Warren Burger. A strong bloc of Justices, sometimes obtaining support from the center of the Court, sought to reverse the processes that were still afoot in the lower courts. The major assault occurred, ironically enough, in the school desegregation cases of the mid-1970s. In other cases, in racial areas and elsewhere, the pattern was mixed: In a police case the Burger Court was sharply critical of structural reform;[4] in a prison case it was strongly supportive;[5] and so on.[6] In most cases the Court was deeply divided; even when structural reform survived, there was usually a high-pitched dissent.

The Burger Court counterassault—sniping is probably a more accurate description—changed our vision of structural reform. In the midst of the Warren Court era, the procedural innovations implicit in structural reform were almost invisible. Each step was small and incremental; each seemed unquestionably correct—and in the 1970s that confidence was destroyed. The counterassault brought into focus the changes in adjudication that had occurred in the 1960s and called them into question. We were forced, as perhaps we should have been, to examine the legitimacy of those changes.

Adjudication and Public Values

As a type of adjudication, structural reform is distinguished by the effort to give meaning to constitutional values in the operation of large-scale organizations. This organizational aspiration has important consequences for the form of adjudication, raising new and distinct problems of legitimacy. But much of the criticism of structural reform, and what I begin with, focuses on that characteristic common to all forms of injunctive litigation: the fact that so much power is vested in judges.

The great charter for ordering the relation between judges and other agencies of government is Footnote Four of the *Carolene Products* case.[7] The greatness derives not from its own internal coherence, nor any theoretical insight, but from its historical position. The footnote codified the hard-fought victory of the Progressives and seemed to provide a framework for the judicial activism about to transpire. The Progressives, and their 1930s successors, the New Dealers, fought their battles in the legislature, and the footnote reflected the terms of their victory: It posited the supremacy of the legislature. The role of the courts, even on constitutional questions, was defined in terms of "legislative failure": The courts should defer to the legislative branch, the footnote proclaimed, unless there is some reason for assuming that the processes of the legislature are inadequate. The footnote identified two instances of legislative failure: abridgment of the right to vote and victimization of a discrete and insular minority, a group disabled from forming coalitions and thus from effectively participating in majoritarian politics.

Although *Carolene Products* involved a challenge to a statute, it has been taken, as perhaps it was intended, to be a more general statement on the role of courts in our political system. The theory of legislative failure should be understood as a general presumption in favor of majoritarianism: The legislature should be seen as standing for those agencies of government, whether the chief executive of the polity or the local school board or the director of corrections, that are more perfectly tied to majoritarian politics than the courts are. *Carolene Products* and the theory of legislative failure thus have important implications for structural reform; they provide a basis, invoked with increasing frequency since the 1970s, for criticizing the strong judicial role implicit in that mode of adjudication.

Structural reform arose in a context that did not test the limits of the theory of legislative failure. The early school desegregation cases, concentrated as they were in the South, could be conceptualized as a compounded type of legislative failure. The normal presumption in favor of majoritarianism clearly did not apply. The group being victimized was a discrete and insular minority; indeed, it was the paradigmatic discrete and insular minority. Blacks were unable to form coalitions and, at the time of *Brown*, were also denied formal participation in the electoral process. They were denied the ballot. It should be recognized, however, as a first attempt to assess the theory of legislative failure, and to understand its implications, that by the 1970s the politics of race changed, and, as a consequence, *Carolene Products* and its commitment to majoritarianism today pose significant challenges to structural reform even when it seeks to secure the value of racial equality.

By the 1970s the disenfranchisement of blacks had been brought to an end. In some communities throughout the nation, particularly the large cities, blacks today represent a sizable portion of the electorate. On a national level blacks represent a numerical minority, but that circumstance alone would not entitle us to assume that the legislative process has failed. The footnote does not entitle any group to have a voice that exceeds its numbers—quite the contrary. Account must also be taken of the fact that blacks are now in a position to form coalitions. They are no longer insular, and their discreteness, their cohesiveness, may, in fact, give them a certain edge in forming coalitions, especially compared to other groups of their size. True, poverty, or more precisely the absence of large concentrations of wealth in the black community, stands as a barrier to effective political participation of that group. But poverty was not identified by Footnote Four as a category of legislative failure, and for good reason. The absence of wealth is so pervasive a handicap and is experienced by so many groups in society, even the majority itself, that to recognize it as a category of legislative failure would stand the theory of the *Carolene Products* footnote on its head—it would undermine the premise of majoritarianism itself.

I might also add that it seems increasingly important for structural reform to move beyond the bounds of racial justice, and in these new domains the usefulness of Footnote Four in explaining and justifying the judicial role is also unclear. Structural reform of total institutions—institutions such as prisons and mental hospitals that house and take control of every aspect of an individual's life—may be understood in terms of legislative failure or, more aptly, legislative neglect.[8] These institutions are intended to remove people from the body politic, and judicial intervention might be seen as the catalyst of majoritarianism rather than its enemy. Similarly, a few of the other state bureaucracies—for example, the public housing authority and the welfare department—might be seen as posing threats to distinct subgroups that are politically powerless. But when the focus shifts to the broad-based bureaucracies that typify the modern state —the police, the state university, the taxing authorities, the health maintenance organizations, the state-owned industries, and so forth—the theory of Footnote Four is of little use. The victim of these organizations is the citizenry itself.

With respect to these broad-based organizations, majoritarianism and judicial intervention might seem reconcilable on the theory that bureaucratization causes unique distortions of the legislative process; bureaucrats have special incentives and means for insulating their practices from public scrutiny.[9] But such an approach would expand Footnote Four far beyond its original scope and, given the large role of these broad-based state bureaucracies in our social life today, would undermine the premise of legislative supremacy itself. The commitment to majoritarianism would be a sham. Alternatively, the emphasis may be on egalitarian values and the threat posed to those values by these broad-based organizations. Yet the relevant subgroup invoking the claim of equality against these organizations—

women, the aged, or the lower and middle classes—is not likely to be one that is disadvantaged in terms of majoritarian politics. Footnote Four can be twisted and turned, and expanded, to accommodate these groups and their claims[10] but only at a price: incoherence. Such an accommodation would require us virtually to assume that whichever group happens to lose the political struggle or fails to command the attention of the legislature or executive is—by that fact alone—a discrete and insular minority.

It is not just a question of usefulness; it now seems clearer than ever that Footnote Four is radically incomplete, as is the theory of legislative failure it announces. The incompleteness derives from two sources. First, the footnote gives no account of the judicial function even in the acknowledged cases of legislative failure. It never explains why legislative failure is to be corrected by judicial action. Second, the footnote never justifies its major normative premise, the one positing the supremacy of the majoritarian branches even when constitutional values are at stake. I believe that at the root of both failings is a denial of the special character of our constitutional values.

The theory of legislative failure identifies occasions for a strong independent use of judicial power, but it does not prescribe what should be done with that power. If there is an abridgement of the right to vote, the judicial function may be clear enough: restore the vote. Majoritarianism is thereby perfected. But there is no simple way to understand the judicial function when failure arises from other causes, say, from the fact that a discrete and insular minority is being victimized. In such a situation the legislative decision may not be entitled to any presumption of correctness, at least as it affects that group, but the task still remains to determine, as an affirmative matter, what the group is entitled to, either by way of process rights or substantive rights.[11] Even if the legislative resolution is not entitled to a presumption of correctness, there is no reason to assume that the opposite resolution would prevail if the legislative process were working perfectly or that the discrete and insular group would win rather than lose. Nor would it make much sense in terms of professional norms to view the judge as a representative of, or as a spokesperson for, the otherwise voiceless minority. The judge is not to speak for the minority or otherwise amplify its voice. The task of the judge is to give meaning to constitutional values, and he or she does that by working with the constitutional text, history, and social ideals. The judge searches for what is true, right, or just.[12] He or she does not become a participant in interest group politics.

The function of a judge is to give concrete meaning and application to our constitutional values. Once we perceive this to be the judicial function in cases of admitted legislative failure, then we are led to wonder why the performance of this function is conditioned on legislative failure in the first place. What is the connection between constitutional values and legislative failure? If the legislative process promised to bring us closer to the meaning of our constitutional values, then the theory of legislative failure would be responsive to this puzzlement. But just the opposite seems true. Legislatures are entirely of a different order. They are not ideologically committed or institutionally suited to search for the meaning of constitutional values; rather, they see their primary function in terms of registering the actual, occurrent preferences of the people—what they want and what they believe should be done. Indeed, the preferred status of legislatures under Footnote Four is largely derived from this conception of their function. The theory of legislative failure, much like the theory of market failure,[13] ultimately rests on a view that declares supreme the people's preferences.

How might such a view be reconciled with the very idea of a Constitution? There is, to be certain, another part of Footnote Four, one I have not yet described. It concerns not legislative failure but textual specificity—highly specific prohibitions of the Constitution. The Free Speech Clause is the example.[14] Footnote Four is prepared to recognize these provisions as a limitation on legislative supremacy; they stand as a qualification of the view that postulates the supremacy of the people's preferences. It is assumed that these prohibitions are small in number. The more important point to note, however, is that, with respect to these textually specific prohibitions, Footnote Four does not condition judicial intervention on legislative failure but instead looks to the courts as the primary interpretive agency. Here the judicial function is to apply these provisions or, to put the same point somewhat differently, to give the values implicit in these provisions their operative meaning.

This view of the judicial role in the domain of the textually specific, plus an understanding of the judicial function in cases of legislative failure, is sufficient to call into question the theory of legislative failure itself. This combined understanding implies a view of the judicial function that is not easily limited. It suggests that, in fact, courts are not default institutions and that their rightful place is not determined by the failure of another institution (the executive or the legislature). Rather, courts should be seen as a coordinate source of government power with their own sphere of influence, one that is defined in terms which unify both the occasion and function of the exercise of power. The judicial role is limited by the existence of constitutional values, and the function of the judiciary is to give meaning to those values.

The values that lie at the heart of most structural litigation—equality, due process, liberty, security of the person, no cruel and unusual punishment—are not embodied in textually specific prohibitions. The Equal Protection Clause—no state shall "deny any person within its jurisdiction the equal protection of the laws"—is as specific as the Free Speech Clause— "Congress shall pass no law abridging the freedom of speech"—but neither is very specific. They simply affirm public values that must be given concrete meaning and harmonized with the general structure of the Constitution. The same is probably true of all the other provisions of the Constitution (e.g., the Commerce Clause) that have been central to constitutional litigation for almost two centuries. The absence of textual specificity does not make the values any less real, nor any less important. The values embodied in such non–textually specific prohibitions as the Equal Protection and Due Process Clauses are central to our constitutional order. They give our society an identity and an inner coherence—its distinctive public morality. The absence of a textually specific prohibition does not deny the importance of these values but only makes the meaning-giving enterprise more arduous. Less reliance can be placed on text.

Of course, the further one moves from text, the greater the risk of abuse; it is easier for judges, even unwittingly, to enact into law their own preferences in the name of having discovered the true meaning of, say, equality or liberty. It was just this risk, elaborated by the Legal Realists, that haunted the Progressives, and that helped sell the theory of legislative failure as the principle governing the interpretation of those values not embodied in textually specific prohibitions—better the preferences of the people than the preferences of the judges.[15] But the Progressives never explained why one set of preferences was a more appropriate basis for a constitutional judgment than the other; both seem inappropriate. Nor did they explain why the risk of abuse, any more than the risk of mistake, was itself a sufficient basis for denying altogether the intelligibility of the process of giving meaning to constitutional values. The judges of *Brown* may have, as critics of the Right and Left keep reminding us, enacted into law their own preferences, peculiarly reflecting their privileged social position. However, it is also possible—indeed, I would say eminently probable— that these judges had given a true account of the constitutional value of equality. The judges involved in contemporary prison litigation may have enacted into law their own preferences, peculiarly reflecting their social background, their squeamishness, when they proscribed the use of torture in all its varieties—the teeterboard; the Tucker telephone; the strap; the failure to provide medical care; the heavy use of armed, mounted, and undisciplined trusties to supervise field labor; and the housing of anywhere from 85 to 150 inmates in a single dormitory room, leaving the weak and attractive to spend each night terrorized by the "creepers" and "crawlers."[16] It is also possible, however—again I would say eminently probable—that these judges had given a true account of the constitutional ban on cruel and unusual punishment.

This conception of the judicial function, which has the judge trying to give meaning to our constitutional values, expects a lot from judges—maybe too much. The expectation is not founded on a belief in their moral expertise or on a denial of their humanity. Judges are most assuredly people. They are lawyers, but in terms of personal characteristics they are no different from successful businesspeople or politicians. Their capacity to make a special contribution to our social life derives not from any personal traits or knowledge but from the definition of the office in which they find themselves and through which they exercise power. That office is structured by both ideological and institutional factors that enable and perhaps even force the judge to be objective—not to his or her preferences or personal beliefs, or those of the citizenry, as to what is right or just, but constantly to strive for the true meaning of the constitutional value.[17] Two aspects of the judicial office give it this special cast: the judiciary's obligation to participate in a dialogue and its independence.

Judges are entitled to exercise power only after they have participated in a dialogue about the meaning of the public values. It is a dialogue with very special qualities: (1) judges are not in control of their agenda but are compelled to confront grievances or claims they would otherwise prefer to ignore; (2) judges do not have full control over whom they must listen to; they are bound by rules requiring them to listen to a broad range of persons or spokespersons; (3) judges are compelled to speak back, to respond to the grievance or the claim, and to assume individual responsibility for that response; and (4) judges must also justify their decisions.

The obligation to justify a decision has given rise to never-ending debates as to the proper sources of judicial decisions—text, intentions of the framers, general structure of the Constitution, ethics, the good of the nation, and so on. The notion of justification, as opposed to explanation, implies that the reasons supporting a decision be good reasons. The reason cannot consist of a preference, be it a preference of the contestants, of the body politic, or of the judge. The statement "I prefer" or "we prefer" in the context of a judicial rather than a legislative decision merely constitutes an explanation, not a justification.[18] Moreover, the reason must somehow transcend the personal, transient beliefs of the judge or the body politic as to what is right or just or what should be done. Something more is required to transform these personal beliefs into values worthy of the status "constitutional" and all it implies—binding on society as a whole, entitled to endure, not forever but long enough to give our public morality an inner coherence, and largely to be enforced by courts.

Judges are required to listen and to speak, and to speak in certain ways. They are also required to be independent. This means, for one thing, that they not identify with or in any way be connected to the particular contestants. They must be impartial, distant, and detached from the contestants, thereby increasing the likelihood that their decisions will not be an expression of the contestants' self-interest (or preferences), which is the antithesis of the right or just decision. The norm of impartiality also requires that judges be independent from politics, understood in this instance as the process of expressing the preferences of the people. Judges must not view their job as one of registering those preferences. Independence is clearly the norm in the federal system with its promise of life tenure, but independence is present also in those state systems in which judges are elected. Judges might be vulnerable to the body politic when they stand for election, but that does not determine the judicial task or how the body politic should use its power.

For these reasons the judicial task should be seen as giving meaning to our public values, and adjudication should be seen as the process through which that meaning is revealed or elaborated. The question still remains of how to determine the relationship between the courts and the other agencies of government, because structural reform places the courts in the position of issuing directives to other agencies of government. The judiciary's essential function is to give meaning to our constitutional values, but many of these other agencies can perform that function in addition to that of registering the preferences of the people. The legislature or the school board or the warden of a prison is entitled to express the preferences of the citizenry, a function not entrusted to the courts, but these agencies can also strive to give meaning to equality or to work out the complicated relationship between liberty and equality or to decide whether the punishment meted out is cruel and unusual. The status quo cannot be taken as a reflection of the considered judgment of another branch of government on the meaning of a constitutional value, particularly since we know that in bureaucracies policy is often determined by internal power plays and default.[19] On the other hand, there can be genuine conflicts. Situations—school desegregation is probably a good example—have arisen where the courts and other agencies of government have come to the opposite conclusion as to the meaning of a constitutional value, and it became necessary to work out the relationship between the branches.

To simply postulate the supremacy of the more majoritarian branches, the legislative or the executive, as the promoters of Footnote Four do, is no answer, for, as we saw, the people's preferences are not the standard, and there is no discernible connection between majoritarianism and the meaning of a constitutional value. Courts may have their difficulties in giving a constitutional value its correct meaning, but so would the other branches. History is as filled with legislative and executive mistakes as it is filled with judicial ones. Admittedly, adjudication will have its class and professional biases, simply because so much power is entrusted to lawyers, but the legislative and executive processes will have their own biases—wealth, dynasty, charisma. It is not clear which set of biases will cause the greatest departure from the truth.

One may be tempted to invoke the democratic ideal to resolve this conflict, but it is far from dispositive. There are many places at which the people bind the adjudicatory process, even in the federal system; they elect the officers who appoint the judges, they can pass statutes controlling procedural matters, and they even have the power to overrule a constitutional judgment by amending the Constitution. Of course, it is hard to amend the Constitution, harder than it is to revise the work of common law judges through the passage of statutes, but democracy is not a fixed rule that always prefers a simple majority, as opposed to a special majority, any more than it deifies the subjective preference. Democracy, as an ideal of our constitutional system, allows a role for both subjective preference and public value, and the special majority requirement of the amendment process may well be seen as a way of preserving the delicate balance between those two domains in our political life.

I suspect that the relationship between the branches in the constitutional domain—in giving meaning to the values that are not textually specific as well as the others—is a more pluralistic or dialectical relationship than Footnote Four permits: All can strive to give meaning to constitutional values. The theory of structural reform, like every other form of constitutional litigation, does not require that courts have the only word or even the last word. It requires that they be allowed to speak and to do so with some authority. Process is the measure of that authority. The right of judges to speak, and the obligation of others to listen, depends not on the personal attributes of judges nor even on the content of their message, but on the quality of their process—on their ability to be distant and detached from the immediate contestants and from the body politic yet fully attentive to grievances, and responsive in terms that transcend preferences and that are sufficient to support a judgment deemed "constitutional." There may be other processes or methods for giving meaning to constitutional values, though what they are is not clear to me, but the process I have just described—the core of adjudication—is the only one open to a judge. This process is a limitation on the judge's legitimacy, and, even more important, it has a close conceptual connection—not just a contingent or instrumental one—to the very act of giving meaning to a constitutional value. We impute function to the judiciary largely on the basis of process and at the same time use function to shape the judicial process. Others may search for the true meaning of our constitutional values, but when they do, they will have to mimic—if they can—the process of the judge.

In the 1960s the courts played a central role in our social life because they saw that the ideal of equality was inconsistent with the caste system implied by Jim Crow laws. In the decade that followed they struggled to give meaning to a broader range of constitutional values and perceived the threat to those values in a wide variety of contexts—the barbarisms of prisons and mental hospitals, the abuses of the police, the indignities of welfare systems. Starting in the late 1960s we began to have doubts about the role of courts, and, just as we rediscovered the market, we quickly resurrected Footnote Four and the claim of legislative supremacy. This development cannot be wholly explained in terms of increasing doubts as to the competency of courts. Without a belief in the conceptual connection between function and process, without a belief in the capacity of courts to give meaning to our constitutional values, even the subscribers to the theory of *Carolene Products* and its famous footnote are at a loss to explain the judicial function in cases of legislative failure or why the void left by legislative failure should be filled by the judiciary.

The resurgence of *Carolene Products* during the 1970s, and the triumph of the theory of judicial review propounded by John Ely in *Democracy and Distrust* (1980), does not stem from doubts about the special capacity of courts to move us closer to a correct understanding of our constitutional values; rather, it stems from the frailty of our substantive vision. We have lost our confidence in the existence of the values that were the foundation of the litigation of the 1960s and, for that matter, in the existence of any public values. All is preference. This, and not the issue of relative institutional competence, seems to be the crucial issue. Only when we reassert our belief in the existence of public values, our belief that values such as equality, liberty, due process, no cruel and unusual punishment, security of the person, or free speech can have a true and important meaning, one that must be articulated, implemented—and yes, discovered—will the role of the courts in our political system become meaningful or even intelligible.

Form and Function

The judicial effort to give meaning to our public values forms the core of structural reform. This allocation of power raises questions of legitimacy common to all types of adjudication, but the structural model raises additional and distinct issues of legitimacy because of the organizational setting of the structural suits. The judge is responding to a threat posed to our constitutional values by a large-scale organization. The judge seeks to remove the threat by restructuring the organization, and this ambition has important implications for the form of the lawsuit.

The structural model is most often attacked on the ground that it involves a departure from an ideal form of lawsuit. This criticism obviously presupposes a prototypical or model lawsuit, against which all lawsuits will be measured. The usual standard of comparison, the dispute resolution model, is triadic and highly individualistic. In this model, the lawsuit is visualized—with the help of the icon of justice holding the scales of justice —as a conflict between two individuals, one called plaintiff and the other defendant, with a third individual standing between the two parties as a passive umpire, to observe and decide who is right, who is wrong, and to declare that the right be done. Admittedly, from this perspective, structural reform is a breathtaking departure.[20] One must be clear, however, about the specific terms of the formal transformation from the dispute resolution model to structural reform before wondering whether the dispute resolution model can properly be considered an ideal.

The Transformation

The Focus of the Suit: Incident of Wrongdoing vs. Social Condition

The dispute resolution model presupposes a social world that is essentially harmonious. A set of norms confers rights and duties on individuals. Individuals make arrangements within those norms, but sometimes incidents occur that disturb the harmony; for example, the farmer may not honor his promise to sell the cow. The aggrieved individual then turns to the courts, either to implement or enforce one of the norms, or, possibly, to fill out the meaning of the norm. The focus of the evidentiary inquiry will be the incident or, in the language of pleading rules, the "transaction" or "occurrence."[21]

In contrast, the focus of structural reform is not on particular incidents or transactions but rather is on the conditions of social life and the role that large-scale organizations play in determining those conditions. What is critical is not the black child turned away at the door of the white school or the individual act of police brutality. These incidents may have triggered the lawsuit or may constitute evidence of a "pattern or practice"[22] of racism or lawlessness. But the ultimate subject matter of the lawsuit or focus of the judicial inquiry is not these incidents, conceived as particularized and discrete events, but rather a social condition that threatens important constitutional values and the organizational dynamic that creates and perpetuates that condition.

Party Structure: The Plaintiff

The concept of a plaintiff consists of three distinct analytic components: (a) victim, (b) spokesperson, and (c) beneficiary. The individual who claims that a contract has been breached is the victim of the wrongdoing. This person is also the one to gain primarily, or maybe even exclusively, from the action of the court. There is every reason to assume that this very same person is the best judge of his or her self-interest and thus a fully competent spokesperson. The ethic of the market is simply transferred to the courtroom. In structural reform, the unity implicit in the concept of party disintegrates, the components become separate, and the exclusively individualistic perspective shifts to one that includes social groups and institutional advocates.

The victim of a structural suit is not an individual but a group. In some instances the group is defined in terms of an institution, such as the inmates of the prison or welfare recipients. Or the victim may be a group that has an identity beyond the institution: In a school desegregation case, for example, the victims are not the pupils but are probably a larger social group, for example, blacks.[23] In either instance, it is important to stress two features of the group. First, it exists independently of the lawsuit; it is not simply a legal construct. Wholly apart from the lawsuit, individuals can define themselves in terms of their membership in the group, and that group can have its own internal politics, struggles for power, and conflicts.[24] Second, the group is not simply an aggregation or collection of identifiable individuals. We understand the plight of the inmates of an institution subjected to inhuman conditions without knowing, or, in the case of future inmates, without even being able to know, who they are in a particularized sense. The group exists, has an identity, and can be harmed, even though all the individuals are not yet in existence and not every single member is threatened by the organization.

Once we acknowledge that the victim can be a group, it also becomes clear that, in this case, the spokesperson need not—indeed cannot—be the victim. A group needs people to speak on its behalf. An individual member of the victim group can be a spokesperson, but there is no reason why individual membership should be required or, for that matter, even preferred. An individual must be a minor hero to stand up and challenge the status quo. Imagine the courage and fortitude required to be the spokesperson in a school desegregation suit or, even worse, the spokesperson challenging the administration of a total institution such as a prison. Individuals are in such a vulnerable position and have so much at risk that it is cruel to insist, as some have done on occasion,[25] that the spokesperson be a member of the victim group, for example, someone personally brutalized by the prison guards. Institutional advocates, some governmental (e.g., the Department of Justice), others private (e.g., the National Association for the Advancement of Colored People [NAACP] or the American Civil Liberties Union [ACLU]), are often needed to play this key role, to be spokespersons for the victim group.[26] Spokespersons such as these may even be preferred. They may introduce their own biases, but, on the whole, they are likely to present a fuller picture of the law or of the facts than the individual victim could.

The relation between the victim and the spokesperson in the structural context is instrumental, rather than a relation of identity. As an affirmative matter, this means that the court must determine whether the interests of the victim group are adequately represented. This inquiry is not without parallel in the dispute resolution context, though, in that setting, individuals, not groups or interests, are being represented. In either context, it is an extremely difficult inquiry. At the same time, the instrumental character of the relationship between spokesperson and victim group, the separation of the two, means that certain technical qualifications for the victim—that he or she is subject to a risk of future harm or exposed to irreparable injury— need not be satisfied by the spokesperson. For the structural suit, it is sufficient if the victim group as a whole satisfies these requirements. What the court must ask of the spokesperson is whether he or she is an adequate representative. Though that question is difficult, technical requirements such as irreparability or the risk of future harm do not have any important bearing on it. They do not make the question any easier because they are neither necessary nor sufficient conditions of adequacy.

The instrumental connection between spokesperson and victim also tolerates, even invites, a multiplicity of spokespersons. In the dispute resolution model, where the victim is an individual and is identified with the spokesperson, the typical party structure is binary: A single plaintiff vies against a single defendant. In a structural lawsuit the typical pattern is to find a great number of spokespersons, each perhaps representing different views as to what is in the interest of the victim group. Moreover, it would be wrong to assume that the relationship between all those on the plaintiff side is equally antagonistic to all those on the defendant side. The physical image of the antagonism is not binary but an array grouped around a single issue. Various spokespersons may favor different remedies. The multiplicity of spokespersons does not create these differences. The differences exist in the real world, and the court must hear from all before it can decide, for example, what the ideal of racial equality requires.

Paralleling this separation between victim and spokesperson, the structural mode of litigation also contemplates a distinction between the victim and the group who will benefit from the remedy. In a suit for breach of contract, the remedy is aimed at making the victim whole, whether the remedy is damages or specific performance. In the structural context, however, the victims and the beneficiaries need not be coextensive. Though the beneficiary of structural relief is necessarily also a group, it could have a different membership and a different contour than the victim group. Consider, for example, a police brutality case. Let us assume that the concern is with lawless conduct by the police directed at members of racial minorities in the city. The court believes an internal disciplinary procedure should be established within the police department to lessen the threat to constitutional values. The court could make that machinery available only to members of the victim group, say blacks and Latinos, but it need not. The court may decide that such a limitation would be both inefficient and counterproductive —indeed, might even raise its own problems of fairness and constitutionality (reverse discrimination)—and, for that reason, the court may extend the protection of the decree to a much larger group—the entire city.[27]

The separability of victim and beneficiary derives in part from the group nature of the victim, since, at best, the limits of that group can only be approximated. More fundamentally, it derives from the instrumental nature of the remedy. The whole judicial enterprise, as is true of any exercise of governmental power, is constrained by considerations of efficacy and fairness. In the context of structural reform, these factors may lead the court to structure the beneficiary class so that it is not coextensive with the victim group. There is no reason why the shape of the benefited class is to be determined by one factor and one factor alone, namely, a guess as to the approximate shape of the victim group.

Party Structure: The Defendant

As might be imagined, the disaggregation of roles I have just discussed on the plaintiff's side is repeated on the defendant's side of the lawsuit. The defendant envisioned in the dispute resolution model is expected to perform three different functions: that of (a) spokesperson, (b) wrongdoer, and (c) addressee (or the person who must provide the remedy). The dispute resolution model assumes that all three functions are unified or, put another way, combined in the same individual, for example, the farmer who breaches a contract. In the structural context the functions are separated, and, even more significant, one function, that of the wrongdoer, virtually disappears.

The concept of wrongdoer is highly individualistic. It presupposes such personal qualities as the capacity to have an intention and to choose. Paradigmatically, a wrongdoer is one who intentionally inflicts harm in violation of an established norm. In the structural context there may be individual wrongdoers, for example, the police officer who hits the citizen, the principal who turns away the black child at the schoolhouse door, the prison guard who abuses the inmate. They are not, however, the target of the suit. The focus is not on incidents of wrongdoing but on a social condition and the bureaucratic dynamics that produce that condition. In a sense, a structural suit is an in rem proceeding where the res is the state bureaucracy.[28] The costs and burdens of reformation are placed on the organization, not because it has "done wrong," in either a literal or metaphorical sense, for it has neither an intention nor a will, but rather because reform is needed to remove a threat to constitutional values posed by the operation of the organization.

From the perspective of certain remedies, such as damage judgments and criminal sanctions, this conclusion may seem startling. Those remedies are retrospective in the sense that a necessary condition for each is a past wrong; they require some evaluative judgment as to the wrongfulness of the defendant's conduct in terms of preexisting norms. The remedy at issue in a structural case, however, is the injunction, and it does not require a judgment about wrongdoing, as is required in a damages suit or criminal prosecution. The structural suit seeks to eradicate an ongoing threat to our constitutional values and the injunction can serve as the formal mechanism by which the court issues directives as to how that is to be accomplished. The injunction speaks to the future. The prospective quality of the injunction, plus the fact that it fuses power in the judge, explains the preeminence of the injunction in structural reform.[29] Only at later stages of structural reform, after many cycles of supplemental relief, when the directives have become very specific, do criminal sanctions or even damage judgments become available (in an independent proceeding or as part of the contempt process).[30] Then the wrongdoing largely consists of disobedience of judicial orders.

In the course of the reconstructive process, the judge must ultimately penetrate the institutional façade, that is, take the lid off the so-called black box, in order to locate critical operatives within the institution to whom the reconstructive directives must be issued. These directives seem addressed to individuals but, in truth, they are addressed to bureaucratic offices, not to the persons who happen to occupy those offices at any single point in time. These directives are not predicated on the view that the present or even the prior occupants of the office are guilty of wrongdoing in the individualistic sense but, rather, that the judicially prescribed action—with all its attendant burdens, financial and otherwise—is necessary to eliminate the threat that the institution as a whole poses to constitutional values.

The Posture of the Judge

The dispute resolution model envisions a passive role for the judge. He or she is to stand as umpire or observer between the two disputants, relying on their initiatives for the presentation of the facts and the law, and the articulation of the possible remedies. The judge's task is simply to declare which one is right. The appropriateness of such a passive pose is called into question by many factors, not the least of which is inequalities in the distribution of resources, both wealth and talent. These inequalities give the judge every reason to assume a more active role in the litigation, to make certain that he or she is fully informed and that a just result will be reached, not one determined by the distribution of resources in the natural lottery or in the market. These concerns are present in structural litigation and indeed may intensify when the organization has a clientele that predominantly comes from the lower economic classes, such as a prison or a welfare agency. But structural litigation introduces other, quite distinct reasons for abandoning a purely passive judicial posture. They stem from the special character of the parties, which makes exclusive reliance on their initiatives even more untenable.

In the structural suit, the named plaintiff and his or her lawyer speak not just for themselves but also for a group, for example, the present and future users of the institution. There is no basis for assuming they are adequate representatives of the group, for they simply elect themselves to that position. Similarly, there is no reason to assume that the named defendant and his or her lawyer are adequate representatives of the organization's interests. Here it is not a matter of self-election but election by an adversary.

The spokespersons for the state bureaucracy usually have a formal connection to the organization. For example, the superintendent of schools may be appointed by a school board, which, in turn, is duly elected; the warden of the prison may be appointed by the governor, and both may be represented by the attorney general, who, in turn, may be elected. The existence of these formal connections, however, should not obscure the fact that the initial choice of the person who must speak for or represent the organization in the proceeding is made by forces standing in an antagonistic or adversarial relationship to the organization: the named plaintiff and his or her lawyer. The risk is always that they may choose an inappropriate officer or have too narrow a conception of the institutional framework that accounts for the condition. The plaintiff, for example, may see the segregated schools as the responsibility of the school board alone, when, in truth, both housing and school policies are implicated.

The presence of an improper representative on either side of the lawsuit may have consequences that far transcend the interests of the participants. The court may be led into error. The named plaintiff may also wittingly or unwittingly compromise the interests of the victim group in a way that cannot easily be rectified in subsequent proceedings. Remember that the defendant speaks not just for himself or herself in a personalized sense but for all occupants of the office, past and future; all the other offices within the hierarchy of the institution; and all those who stand outside the institution but who are nonetheless directly affected by any reorganization of the institution, including the taxpayers who finance it and those who depend on the institution to provide some vital service.

Starting from this perspective, it seems almost absurd to rely exclusively on the initiatives of those named plaintiff or defendant. The judge must assume some affirmative responsibility to assure adequate representation, but how might that responsibility be discharged? It would seem foolish for the judge to assume a representational role; indeed, it would compromise the very ideal of impartiality, which is an important predicate of judicial legitimacy. The more appropriate response, and the one typically employed in the structural context, is for the judge—often acting on his or her own—to construct a broader representational framework. This might be done in a number of ways that are consistent with the judge's commitment to impartiality.

First, a notice can be sent to many of those who are purportedly represented in the litigation. The notice would explain the litigation, and invite a contest to the fullness and adequacy of the representation. Even here, the judge cannot rely exclusively on the named parties to insist on notice or to formulate its content. Extensive notice requirements might compound the adversary's costs of continuing the litigation. Alternatively, neither party has much of an incentive to make certain that his or her adversary is the best representative.

Second, the judge may invite certain organizations or agencies to participate in the lawsuit, as an amicus or as a party, or as a hybrid—the litigating amicus. Of course, ever mindful of the conditions of his or her legitimacy, the judge should not limit the invitation to those who would say what he or she wants to hear, nor has that been the practice. The concept of a litigating amicus first took root in school cases where trial judges invited the United States to participate; the intent was to obtain the Executive's commitment to enforce the decree, and also to broaden the representational structure.[31] Later, this practice was transferred to the context of total institutions, such as prisons and mental hospitals, where it is even more urgently required, given the relative absence of private institutional advocates and the distortion likely to flow from exclusive reliance on complaints from individual victims.[32]

Third, the trial courts have sometimes found it necessary, perhaps when they could no longer rely on the Executive or on private institutional advocates, to create their own agencies, such as special masters, to correct any representational inadequacies. The special master is an institution with many roles, as we will see, but one of them is representational.[33] Although a delegate of the judge, a special master sometimes acts as a party, presenting the viewpoints about liability and remedy that participants in the lawsuit are not likely to express.

The Remedial Phase

The focus in the dispute resolution model is the incident, that is, the transaction or occurrence, and the remedial phase is largely episodic. The remedy is designed to correct or to prevent a discrete event, and the judicial function usually exhausts itself when judgment is announced and the amount of damages calculated or when the decree, aimed at some discrete event, is issued. Under these assumptions, the lawsuit has an almost Aristotelian dramatic unity, with a beginning, middle, and end. In some cases involving a recalcitrant defendant, there may be more to the remedial phase—for example, seizure and sale of assets or a contempt proceeding.[34] These struggles with the recalcitrant defendant are the exception, however, and, in any event, they are not considered an integral part of the first proceeding. They often involve a collateral proceeding handled by different personnel, such as the sheriff or special master, to enforce the remedy given in the initial proceeding.

The remedial phase in structural litigation is far from episodic. While it has a beginning and maybe a middle, it has no end—well, almost no end. It involves a long, continuous relationship between the judge and the institution; it is concerned not with the enforcement of a remedy already given but with the giving or shaping of the remedy itself. The task is not to declare who is right or who is wrong, nor to calculate the amount of damages or to formulate a decree designed to stop an isolated act. The task is to remove the condition that threatens the constitutional value. In some instances, where deinstitutionalization is conceivable, as in the mental health field, closing the institution may be a viable option. For the most part, as in cases involving schools, prisons, welfare agencies, police departments, and housing authorities, that option is not available. Then the remedy involves the court in nothing less than the reorganization of an ongoing institution, so that it may remove the threat the institution poses to constitutional values. The court's jurisdiction will last as long as the threat persists.

Limitations on our knowledge about organizational behavior, coupled with the capacity of organizations to adapt to the interventions by reestablishing preexisting power relationships, invariably result in a series of interventions—cycle after cycle of supplemental relief. A long-term supervisory relationship develops between the judge and the institution. Performance must be monitored and new strategies devised to ensure that the operation of the organization is kept within constitutional bounds.[35] Judges may even create new agencies, such as the special master, to assist in these tasks. In doing so, the judge displays either doubt about the capacity of the existing parties to discharge the necessary tasks or an awareness of the magnitude of these tasks.

The Significance of the Transformation

Assume that the structural lawsuit has the formal features I have just described and also that it can be sharply differentiated from the dispute resolution model in these particulars. The two lawsuits do not look alike. Gone is the triad, the icon of justice holding two balances, and in its place a whole series of metaphors are offered to describe the structural suit. Some, emphasizing the distinctive party structure, speak of town meetings;[36] others, emphasizing the activism of the judge, speak of management or the creation of a new administrative agency. Of course, these metaphors decide nothing; they merely express a feeling that something is different. The question still remains as to the significance of the distinctive form of the structural suit. Differences do not provoke doubts as to legitimacy unless a normative priority can be established for the dispute resolution model. This seems to me precisely where the standard critique of structural reform fails.

The ultimate issue is whether dispute resolution, particularly in the individualistic sense just described, has a prior or exclusive claim on the concept of adjudication. Even beyond that, the dispute resolution model can be faulted for its account of the judicial function. Dispute resolution is not an adequate description of the social function of courts, which, to my mind, exist to give meaning to our public values, not to resolve disputes.

Constitutional adjudication is the most vivid manifestation of this function, but it also seems true of most civil and criminal cases, certainly now and perhaps for most of our history as well.[37]

Most accounts of the judicial function begin with the same story. Two people in the state of nature are squabbling over a piece of property. They come to an impasse, and then, rather than resorting to force, they turn to a third party, a stranger, for a decision. Courts are but an institutionalization of the stranger. This story, much like the story of the social contract, operates in the ill-defined land between the normative and the descriptive. It does not purport to be an accurate portrayal of social history, of how courts actually came into being; nevertheless, it is supposed to capture or express the underlying social logic of courts, even though no attempt is made to reconcile this story with the underlying social reality.[38] It seems to me, however, that once full account is taken of the role of courts in modern society, in ordinary criminal, constitutional, and statutory cases (e.g., antitrust, environmental, or securities law), and perhaps also in the traditional common law cases, it becomes clear that the familiar story fundamentally misleads. It does not capture the social logic of courts and thus could be replaced by another story: The sovereign sends out his or her officers throughout the realm to speak the law and to see that it is obeyed.

Disputation has a pervasive role in litigation. Disputes may arise as to the meaning of a public value or as to the existence of a norm, and thus provide the occasions for judicial intervention. Also, courts may rely on the antagonistic relationship between various individuals or agencies for the presentation of the law and facts. The desire of each party to win provides a motivating force. I will also concede that the judge's decision may bring an end to the dispute; dispute resolution may be one consequence of the judicial decision. But as pervasive a role as disputation may play in litigation, it is equally important to recognize that the function of the judge, which is both a statement of social purpose and a definition of role, is not to resolve disputes but to give the proper meaning to our public values. Typically, the judge does this by enforcing and thus safeguarding the integrity of the existing public norms or by supplying new norms. These norms may protect the fruits of one's bargains or labors; they may regulate the use of automobiles or determine responsibility for compensation; they may preserve the integrity of markets by curbing fraud or monopolization; or they may impose limits on the use of state power. In the structural suit, the judge reorganizes the institution as a way of discharging this very same function.

Of course, some disputes may not threaten or otherwise implicate a public value. All the disputants may, for example, acknowledge the norms and confine their dispute to the interpretation of the words of the contract or the price of a bumper. Such disputes may wend their way into court, and judges may spend time on these purely private disputes—private because only the interests and behavior of the immediate parties to the dispute are at issue. That seems, however, an extravagant use of public resources, and thus it seems quite appropriate for those disputes to be handled not by courts but by arbitrators (though courts may have to act as background institutions enforcing or maybe even creating obligations to arbitrate).[39] Arbitration is like adjudication in that it, too, seeks the right, the just, and the true judgment.[40] There is, however, an important difference in the two processes arising from the nature of the decisional agency—one private, the other public. Arbitrators are paid for by the parties, chosen by the parties, and enjoined by a set of practices (such as a reluctance to write opinions or generate precedents) that localizes or privatizes the decision.[41] The function of the arbitrator is to resolve a dispute. The function of the judge, on the other hand, must be understood in wholly different terms: The judge is a public officer, paid for by public funds, chosen not by the parties but by the public or its representatives, and empowered by the political agencies to enforce and create society-wide norms, and perhaps even to restructure institutions, as a way, I suggest, of giving meaning to our public values.

Wholly apart from whether the dispute resolution model confuses arbitration with adjudication and gives an adequate account of the judicial function, the question remains whether it has a prior normative claim on the office of the judge. Is dispute resolution the ideal against which structural reform should be judged, and, if so, how might that priority be established? Three different tacks have been taken in attempting to answer this question—one is instrumental, another is historical, and the third is axiomatic.

The instrumental critique, first systematically presented by Donald Horowitz in *The Courts and Social Policy* (1977), emphasizes the high risk of error in structural reform as opposed to dispute resolution. The argument is that the judiciary should be limited to doing what it does best—dispute resolution. Under the instrumental critique, dispute resolution becomes the ideal simply because it is what courts can do best.

Some of the empirical premises underlying this position seem plausible enough. The task of structural reform is fraught with danger, not just in defining the rights but also in implementing them within the operation of the state bureaucracy. It may also be true—note I only say "may"—that the risk of judicial error in dispute resolution is not nearly as great as it is in structural reform. In many instances there is virtually nothing to the remedial phase in dispute resolution; it simply requires declaring whether plaintiff or defendant wins. This does not compare to the difficulties inherent in the reorganization of an ongoing social institution, such as a public school system, a welfare department, or, worse yet, the institution we know least about, a prison. All this we may safely concede, without, I am certain, accepting the normative conclusion that idealizes dispute resolution.

In the first place, it is not clear why any social institution should be devoted to one and only one task, even the one it does best. Each of the different divisions of government may have several different functions. The performance of one function may interfere with another, and failures in one domain may impair its capacity to perform in others. Still, there is no reason to believe that the relationship between the structural and dispute resolution modes of discharging the judicial function is one of interference or that involvement in the structural litigation will compromise the judiciary's capacity to resolve disputes. The functions may be independent or even complementary.

Furthermore, even if a choice must be made between the two functions, the instrumental critique assumes too limited a criterion for choice by insisting that we preserve the function the institution performs best. Success rate is important in evaluating institutions, but two further factors must be introduced into the analysis: the value of a successful performance and the success rate of alternative institutions performing comparable tasks. Structural reform fares quite well under both criteria.

The hypothesized low success rate of structural reform is amply compensated by the promise of greater social returns. Suppose the choice is between resolving a dispute between two individuals, such as that between a citizen and a policeman over some alleged incident of wrongdoing, or trying to eradicate conditions of lawlessness through the reorganization of the police department. The claim that the first is more likely to be successful clearly does not make it the more socially worthwhile enterprise, in terms of either the breadth of the corrective action or its durability. Success may come more rarely or less perfectly in a structural case, but a structural success, even if it is only partial, could dwarf all the successes of dispute resolution. It may greatly reduce the need for dispute resolution by eliminating the conditions that give rise to incidents of wrongdoing, and it may even compensate for all its own failures.

The instrumental critique might have more appeal if it were clear that alternative institutions could better perform this worthwhile but perilous activity. Just the opposite, however, is true. Dispute resolution might be diverted to arbitration, but obviously such a diversion is not available for structural reform. It is among the most public of all forms of adjudication because it involves constitutional values and the state bureaucracies. Some have suggested administrative agencies as the alternative, on the theory that these agencies might have special expertise in the reorganization of ongoing social institutions not otherwise available to courts. But, as I will explain, this suggestion also seems without basis.

The claim for diversion is largely predicated on the view that these administrative agencies possess some expert knowledge, yet I, for one, fail to see the evidence to support that position. The instrumental critic makes a comparative argument about the superiority of administrative agencies but only attempts to document half that argument. The critic typically points to failures of the courts but never considers the failures of the administrative agencies, of which there are many. The literature is filled with evidence of administrative failures and teaches us to be wary of the claim of administrative expertise, also voiced at earlier times by the Progressives. Admittedly structural reform is a perilous and arduous activity, but the problem is largely one of knowledge: knowing how large-scale organizations operate, not the distribution of that knowledge among various agencies. I doubt there is some special body of knowledge relevant for such a remedial undertaking, but, even if there were, it remains to be seen why it could not be made available to the judge, either through expert witnesses or through auxiliary structures such as special masters.

The evidentiary process of the administrative agency has long promised to be more open, broader, and more freewheeling than that available to the judiciary, but it is not clear to me that this promise has ever been fulfilled, that such a liberated process would be consistent with rudimentary notions of due process, or even that such a process is needed for structural reform. Although the focus of a structural suit is necessarily broad, concerned with social conditions and organizational dynamics instead of discrete and particularized incidents of wrongdoing, the judicial process is capable of that breadth. Some might, I realize, emphasize the insight that comes from accumulated experience rather than a body of knowledge that can be communicated to a decision maker; yet it is hard to see how this reformulation of the claim of expertise advances the criticism of structural reform. Some judges have been engaged in the reconstructive enterprise over a long period of time, say, a decade, and though, as we will see, this involvement creates its own problems, it probably dwarfs all the experience administrative agencies presently possess on how to reconstruct ongoing social institutions.

The argument for diversion to administrative agencies thus seems to rest on exaggerated claims of expertise, a recurrence of a myth of Progressivism, but even more fundamentally it reflects a misunderstanding of why courts are involved in the first place. Courts are not entrusted with the reconstructive task on the theory that they possess some expertise (either in the form of knowledge or experience) on how best to perform that task. In the domain of instrumentalism, of means-end rationality, courts have no special claim to competency. Their special competency lies elsewhere, in the domain of constitutional substantive rationality or deciding what some constitutional value means or, put differently, in declaring rights, and that expertise is derived from the special quality of the judicial process —dialogue and independence. The reconstructive endeavor, calling for instrumental judgments, should be seen (for reasons to be elaborated later) as but a necessary incident of that meaning-giving enterprise, as an attempt by the judge to give meaning to constitutional values in practical reality. Thus, even if one were to assume, as the instrumental critique suggests, that administrative agencies possess an expertise in the domain of instrumental rationality, the diversion argument would still be deeply problematic because administrative agencies lack any special competency in this particular domain of substantive rationality. They lack the independence so essential to giving expression to our constitutional values.

The specialized jurisdiction of administrative agencies may lend support to the claim of expertise, but it also poses a threat to the independence of the agency: The regulators may become too closely identified with the regulated.[42] More fundamentally, administrative agencies are more tied to majoritarian politics than are courts, both because of ideology (they are sometimes allowed to make their judgments on the basis of the preferences of the body politic) and institutional arrangements (appointment for short terms, subject to removal when administrations change). The so-called independent regulatory agencies of the federal system might be seen as standing somewhere between the courts, on the one hand, and Congress and the Executive, on the other, but surely their relationship to the majoritarian branches is sufficiently close to make us wary of any claim, such as that embodied in the instrumental critique, that would charge these agencies exclusively, or even primarily, with the task of giving meaning to our constitutional values. I venture to say that the truth of this assertion would be conceded in most contexts. It seems no less true—maybe even more so—when it is bureaucracies of the modern state that threaten those values and structural reform is needed to remove that threat.

A second method for establishing the priority of the dispute resolution model is historical: Dispute resolution is traditional, and structural reform is new. Support for this position comes, oddly, from Abram Chayes,[43] who identified a mode of adjudication quite similar to the structural one (though he attributes its formal characteristics to the public character of the rights, whereas I see them linked more to the organizational setting—all rights enforced by courts are public). He celebrates the new model, but, rather than centrally dealing with the questions of legitimacy, he emphasizes the positivistic or descriptive dimensions of his enterprise. He presents himself as a "biologist" describing the "evolution" of a new form of adjudication, which will, he adds secondarily, legitimate itself by winning the assent of the people, provided it is given a chance to work.

I have doubts as to whether the historical claim is wholly accurate as a purely descriptive matter. To my mind, the form of adjudication has evolved but not the function. The function of adjudication has never been to resolve disputes between individuals but, rather, to give meaning to our public values. What has changed is social structure, the emergence of a society dominated by the operation of large-scale organizations, and it is these changes in social structure that account for the changes over time in adjudicatory forms. Such changes should hardly be a cause for concern. What would, in fact, provoke a genuine crisis of legitimacy would be to insist on procedural modes shaped in a different social setting, to assume that adjudicatory forms created centuries ago should control today.

But even assuming for a moment that the dispute resolution model has a claim to historical priority, it remains to be seen what that has to do with legitimacy, which is essentially a normative judgment. Nothing in the Constitution constricts the federal courts to dispute resolution. Even in the late eighteenth century, during the heyday of the common law, the function of courts was paradigmatically not dispute resolution but to give meaning to public values through the enforcement and creation of public norms, such as those embodied in the criminal law and the rules regarding property, contracts, and torts. The courts created our law and were then the central lawmaking institution. The judicial function implied by contemporary constitutional litigation, of which structural reform is a part, is continuous with, and perhaps even identical to, that of the common law. The issues have changed and so has the social setting; that has required a change in the form of adjudication, though not its function.

Alternatively, it may be thought that the historical critique derives its normative power not from the Constitution but from the application of a theory that sees the people's consent as the basis of legitimacy. This argument equates "implied consent" with "actual consent," interprets the people's acceptance of the status quo as implying a consent to the existing institutional arrangements, and then locates the dispute resolution model —but not the structural one—in the status quo. Such an argument might seem capable of transforming a historical priority into a normative priority, but, in truth, the argument fails on a number of grounds.

First, one can take issue with the interpretation of the status quo that privileges the dispute resolution model over the model of structural reform. Some historians, for example, Theodore Eisenberg and Stephen C. Yeazell, find antecedents for contemporary institutional litigation in the nineteenth-century equity and receivership cases as well as the antitrust and bankruptcy cases of the early twentieth century.[44] Indeed, following this line of thought, one might also argue that the very existence of the structural mode in constitutional litigation for the past several decades is sufficient to place it within the status quo—it, too, implicitly has received the people's consent.

A second response, primarily exemplified by the work of Professor Chayes, is to table the question of legitimacy and to suggest it has arisen prematurely. Assent by the people need not be given prospectively, in the way the social contract metaphor might suggest. Instead, all the people come together at one historic moment and decide whether they wish to have a particular social institution. Consent can also be earned. But that takes time, and thus structural reform should be given a chance to operate—a so-called trial run (assuming the past decades have not been sufficient). If it survives, it will then be given the same claim to legitimacy as the so-called traditional model: The institution will have legitimated itself.

A third response—and the one most appealing to me—would be to question consent theory itself. The problem with the theory is, in part, its ambiguity. What is it that one consents to when one accepts the status quo in adjudication? Is it the form? Or is it the function? Or is it the substantive results? Consent theory fails to answer these questions or even to suggest a procedure for working toward answers and, as a consequence, transforms the historical argument into an endorsement of the status quo. It might well work a colossal collapse of "is" and "ought." Beyond that, however, one can question the very premise on which this critique of structural reform rests—the identification of consent with legitimacy. Institutions can seek their justifications in domains other than consent, even in a democracy.

A democratic political system is one ultimately dependent on the consent of the people, but the authority of each and every institution need not be founded on consent. Consent goes to the system, not the particular institution; it operates on the whole rather than each part. The legitimacy of particular institutions, such as courts, depends not on the consent—implied or otherwise—of the people but rather on their competence or, put differently, on the special contribution they make to the quality of our social life. Legitimacy depends on the capacity of the institution to perform a function within the political system and its willingness to respect the limitations on that function. Legitimacy does not depend on popular approval of the institution's performance, nor does it depend on popular approval of the processes through which that performance is rendered. In a democracy, it is the legitimacy of the political system as a whole that depends on the people's approval.

The people have the power to express their disapproval of how courts are discharging their function. Presumably they can pass statutes to curb procedural innovations, or they can adopt constitutional amendments for overturning particular outcomes. Some might argue that the failure of the people to exercise this power is "implied approval" of all that the courts are doing today, but such an argument would be mistaken (this is surely a situation when inaction is not tantamount to action), and, more important, it is unnecessary. The existence of the power of the people to express disapproval should be understood as the means by which institutions such as courts can be integrated into a system ultimately founded on the people's consent. Some institutions—the legislature, the school board, the police chief—may have a tighter, more direct connection to consent in the sense that particular incumbents serve at the pleasure of the people. To insist on a similar consensual connection for the judiciary would, however, impair its independence and thus destroy its capacity to discharge its constitutional function within our political system.

For these reasons it seems impossible to ground the historical critique either on the Constitution or on consent theory, and thus it, like the instrumental critique, fails to give dispute resolution a normative priority. There is one further strategy to be considered, the one I called axiomatic. It postulates one formal attribute of the social process as a morally necessary attribute, on the basis of which the structural and dispute resolution modes are to be evaluated. As it turns out, that attribute—individual participation, which is present in dispute resolution but absent in the structural mode—also implicates consent theory and shares many of its difficulties. The axiomatic approach places adjudication on a moral plane with two other activities exalted by consent theory, voting and bargaining, and then tries to construct an ideal form of adjudication that preserves this connection with consensual activity, now in a highly individualized form. It still fails to explain why consent is the touchstone of legitimacy for all institutions.

The most sustained effort to build a case for dispute resolution on the basis of moral axioms is Lon Fuller's essay, "The Forms and Limits of Adjudication."[45] This essay was written in the late 1950s, shortly before the heyday of structural reform. It was published in 1978, shortly after Professor Fuller's death, but it was not updated to account, either as a descriptive or normative matter, for the intervening twenty years, the civil rights era.[46] It is as though the period never occurred—an erasure of a significant part of the history of procedure. The essay is nevertheless important for our purposes, for it seems largely motivated by a desire to establish the limits of adjudication, and the one limit Fuller, in fact, develops is clearly at war with the notion of structural reform. Borrowing an idea of Michael Polanyi's, which was, interestingly enough, also introduced in the 1950s,[47] Fuller insists that courts cannot perform "polycentric" tasks.

Fuller does not give any single, straightforward definition of polycentrism. It seems to refer to a type of dispute or problem that is many-centered, much like, he says, a spider web. The resolution of a polycentric dispute would necessarily have broad and never-ending repercussions. Fuller finds these disputes inappropriate for adjudication. He explains why through an analysis of a series of examples. One example, appearing near the end of the essay, seems, remarkably enough, to address the problem of structural reform:

The suggestion that polycentric problems are often solved by a kind of "managerial intuition" should not be taken to imply that it is an invariable characteristic of polycentric problems that they resist rational solution. There are rational principles for building bridges of structural steel. But there is no rational principle which states, for example, that the angle between girder A and girder B must always be 45 degrees. This depends on the bridge as a whole. One cannot construct a bridge by conducting successive separate arguments concerning the proper angle for every pair of intersecting girders. One must deal with the whole structure.[48]

The reader is left to wonder why adjudication must proceed on the basis Fuller suggests—angle by angle. Certainly that is not required by rationality; reason, even the judge's reason, is not binary but can encompass whole structures. The explanation for the insistence that courts proceed angle by angle has less to do with a theory of rationality than with the simple fact of the enormous number of people affected by whole structures—by the construction of the bridge. Because of the number it is simply impossible, Fuller explains, to have everyone affected participate in the lawsuit in a meaningful way.[49]

At the core, then, of Fuller's conception of the limits of adjudication and of his objection to courts resolving polycentric problems is an individual's right to participate in a proceeding that might adversely affect that individual. This right might be preserved in a representative suit that accords with the traditional law of agency, with a true consensual bond between representative (agent) and principal. However, it should be recognized that this right, taken in its highly individualistic cast, is denied and indeed seriously compromised by the kind of representation lying at the heart of a structural suit—the representation of interests by spokespersons for groups and offices rather than identifiable individuals.[50] Just imagine the kind of representation implicit in the famed Arkansas prison litigation, in which the court's conclusion—for example, that the trusty system at Cummins Farm was a form of cruel and unusual punishment—must necessarily affect a never-ending spiral of persons, officers, and interests: inmates, guards, administrators, legislators, taxpayers, indeed all the citizens of the state—present and future.[51] The reconstruction of a prison, or, for that matter, the reconstruction of a school system, welfare agency, hospital, or any bureaucracy, is as polycentric as the construction of a bridge. All require the court to deal with whole structures. The judge must be certain that the full range of interests is vigorously represented, but he or she need not reject the constitutional claim nor deny an effective remedy because each and every individual affected will not or cannot meaningfully participate in the suit.

My conception of adjudication starts from the top—the office of the judge—and works down. I place adjudication on a moral plane with legislative and executive actions. I start with the conception of state power embodied in the judge, treat courts as a coordinate source of government power, and see the form of adjudication shaped by function and social setting. Fuller rejects such an approach. He starts from the bottom and works up. Fuller begins with the individual, rather than the judge. He places adjudication on a moral plane with elections and contracts; he analyzes these two social processes in terms of how the individual participates in each, through voting and bargaining; and then he seeks to distinguish adjudication from these social processes. The distinguishing feature of adjudication, naturally enough, is also cast in individualistic terms, more precisely, in terms of how the individual participates in that process as opposed to elections and contracts—through proof and reasoned arguments. He then treats this right of the individual to participate in the proceeding—the moral equivalent of the right to vote and the right to bargain—as the master idea of adjudication. For Fuller, it explains and justifies certain formal features of adjudication, for example, party structure and the passivity of the judge. It also sets limits on adjudication. The right of individual participation is violated only at a distinct moral risk: the process is deemed not a form of adjudication or, at best, is deemed a mixed or hybrid form of adjudication, which, Fuller claims, is parasitic on the ideal.

At various points Fuller speaks as though he is being merely descriptive. What distinguishes adjudication from other social processes, he says, is the "institutional commitment" of adjudication to a particular mode of individual participation. On a purely descriptive level there is not much to his claim. It is not supported by a presentation of the evidence, and it is contradicted by a great deal of the reality or experience we would consider to be adjudication. Moreover, a purely descriptive account could never yield the normative judgments implicit in his conclusion as to what might constitute "parasitic" adjudication. Fuller's essay should be recognized for what it is: a postulation that the standard for judging the legitimacy of a process that purports to be adjudication is the affected individual's right to participate. I use the term *postulation*, for, although much of the essay rightly celebrates the role of reason in human affairs, and sees the important connection between reason and adjudication, there is no explanation of why reason requires the kind of individual participation Fuller insists on. In structural reform reason enters the process, not through the arguments of each and every individual affected but through the arguments of the spokespersons for all the interests represented and through the decision of the judge. Reason is used to give meaning to our constitutional values.

How might an axiom such as Fuller's, proclaiming the sacredness of the individual right of participation, be judged? I realize that it may not be appropriate to demand justification of an axiom, for it is offered as a starting point, that is, as a proposition you cannot look behind. Yet there must be more that can be said about it. Acceptance of an axiom must turn on something more than a momentary flash of intuition. In my judgment, the axiom can be assessed in terms of its consequences and its underlying social vision. An axiom might at first glance seem attractive enough, but its appeal may decline radically once its full implications are understood.

In assessing the consequences of the individual participation axiom, it should first be understood that the issue is not whether there should be social processes that can further the participatory right—whether dispute resolution should exist—but whether a form of adjudication that violates that right—structural reform—is legitimate (or permissible). Fuller treats the participation axiom as a necessary condition of legitimacy, and that is the source of the problem. As a necessary condition, the axiom would render structural reform illegitimate, true enough, but, more important, it would render illegitimate almost all adjudication—both that of the common law and the constitutional variety—in which the courts were creating public norms. It would reduce courts to the function of norm enforcement and would reduce adjudication to a high-class (but subsidized) form of arbitration. It is no mere happenstance that Fuller spent a great deal of his professional life as an arbitrator; throughout the essay he refers to the judge as an "arbiter."

The creation of virtually all public norms is a polycentric process. It affects as many people as structural reform, and equally impairs the capacity of each of the affected individuals to participate in the process. More often than not, a myriad of possible rules or solutions could be formulated in each case. Consider the fellow-servant rule, the stop-look-and-listen doctrine, strict liability, the consideration requirement, the rules respecting offer and acceptance, the norms of the Marshall Court regarding the Commerce Clause, those of the Warren Court regarding free speech, racial equality, civil and criminal procedure. The list could go on and on. It would probably include all judge-made law, and the doctrine of precedent itself. The list surely includes many decisions that might be regarded as mistaken or wrong, but that is not the issue. The issue is whether all these acts of norm creation represent a misuse of the judicial power or an incorrect appropriation of the concept of adjudication. This is a conclusion that most of us—perhaps even all of us—would reject, and yet it is a conclusion that would seem to follow from Fuller's axiom.

This axiom would be only a formal triumph of individualism. The axiom seems to celebrate the individual, but honoring it would leave the individual at the mercy of large aggregations of power. Deprived both of the opportunity to use the courts to protect themselves and of the full use of these centers of government power that stand apart from the state bureaucracies, individuals would be thrown back to those social processes that are supposed to respect their participatory rights—dispute resolution, voting, and bargaining. Each of these processes has important roles to play in our social life, but it is hard to believe that any of them enhance the real or effective—as opposed to the formal—power of those individuals who are abused by the large-scale organizations of the modern state, such the school system, the hospital, the welfare department, or, even worse, the prison.

In truth, the individual participation axiom is rooted in a world that no longer exists. It is rooted in a horizontal world, one in which people related to one another on individual terms and on terms of approximate equality. It is rooted in a world that viewed the law of contracts as "The Law"— not so incidentally, Fuller's substantive field of law. Our world, however, is a vertical one; the market has been replaced by the hierarchy, the individual entrepreneur by the bureau.[52] In this social setting, what is needed to protect the individual is the establishment of power centers equal in strength and in resources to the dominant social actors; what is needed is countervailing power. A conception of adjudication that strictly honors the right of each affected individual to participate in the process seems to proclaim the importance of the individual; but, in fact, it leaves the individual without the institutional support necessary to realize his or her true self. Indeed, the individual participation axiom would do little more than throw down an impassable bar—the fear of polycentrism—to the one social process that has emerged with promise for preserving our constitutional values and the ideal of individualism in the face of the modern bureaucratic state: structural reform.[53]

The Problem of Remedy

Dispute resolution, either as a statement of form or function, does not represent the ideal for adjudication. Therefore the departures from dispute resolution required by structural reform do not, in and of themselves, deprive structural reform of its legitimacy. The function of adjudication is to give meaning to public values, not merely to resolve disputes. Structural reform is faithful to that function and adapts the traditional form of the lawsuit to the changing social reality—the dominance of our social life by bureaucratic organizations. A question of legitimacy might still persist, however, because, wholly apart from any comparisons with the dispute resolution model, the entitlement of courts to speak the law—to give meaning to our constitutional values—is limited. It is limited, as I suggested at the outset, by the judge's willingness and ability to adhere to a process that typifies the judicial branch and constitutes the foundation of its competence—dialogue and independence. Structural reform does not pose any distinct threats to the dialogic quality of this process: the obligation of the judge to confront grievances he or she would otherwise prefer to ignore, to listen to the broadest possible range of persons and interests, to assume individual responsibility for the decision, and to justify the decision in terms of the norms of the constitutional system. The transformation of party structure inherent in the structural suit stretches the notion of a dialogue, but to fault the structural suit on that ground is to exaggerate a metaphor, to think that it refers to a conversation between two. The term *dialogue* is simply meant to suggest a rationalistic or communicative process in which the judge listens and speaks back. That process is no less possible in the multiparty context, though the visual imagery shifts from a triad to an array. It just requires a little skill and imagination.

Admittedly, the capacity or even the willingness of judges to engage in this communicative process, to listen to all grievances and to painstakingly justify their decisions, is far from secure. Like any art, it always seems in peril. But the principal threats to this capacity—impatience, self-righteousness, judicial burnout—have nothing to do with structural reform; or, to put the same point somewhat differently, these threats to the integrity of the judicial process can be fought in ways that leave the structural suit untouched as a distinctive mode of constitutional litigation. Some of the critics of structural reform also voice the recurrent gripe that judges are overworked.[54] Though overwork may well threaten the integrity of the communicative process that lies at the core of adjudication, it is far from clear why the remedy should lie in the elimination of the structural suit. Each one is complex and difficult, but at the same time it may engage the judge in his or her most worthy and important function. A more sensible response to the claim of overwork may be to divert to other institutions the simpler, less complex cases (individual citizen versus individual policeman, inmate versus guard); they may represent a considerable burden taken as an aggregate. It may also be necessary to increase the social resources committed to the judicial branch. We cannot expect any agency of government to discharge its function adequately when it is forced to operate on a commitment of resources that reflect the needs of an earlier age. It would, of course, be a sad irony, and would seriously jeopardize judicial legitimacy, were these resources used to convert each judge into a mini-bureaucracy. The dialogue that so far has typified the judicial branch, and that underlies its claim of special competency, envisions individual responsibility for the decision and its justification. The judge must be the one who listens and speaks back.

Though these matters cannot easily be dismissed, my concern is not with the dialogic quality of the competency-giving process but rather with the threat the remedy poses to the ideal of independence. The remedy expresses the judge's desire to give a meaning to a constitutional value that is more tangible, more full-blooded, than a mere declaration of what is right. This desire to be efficacious is manifest in all forms of adjudication and creates similar dilemmas for the judge, but in structural reform it takes on a special urgency and largely gives this form of constitutional litigation its special cast. The desire to be efficacious leads the judge to attempt the remarkable feat of reconstructing a state bureaucracy, say, transforming a dual school system into a unitary one, and that ambition, in turn, forces the judge to compromise his or her independence and to enter the world of politics.

The New Formalism

To understand the roots of the dilemma it is necessary to understand the complicated relationship between rights and remedies. To do that we must first free ourselves from the hold of what has become known as the tailoring principle—the insistence that the remedy must fit the violation.

At first it seemed that the tailoring principle was of unquestionable validity; indeed, it might be tautological. The problem seemed not to be the principle itself but the definition of the violation—the Court had defined the violation too narrowly. It is now clear that the problem is deeper and that the tailoring principle fundamentally misleads. It does, in fact, tend to support an artificial conception of violation—one that looks back and sees discrete incidents as the object of the remedy—but it also errs in an even more basic way. It suggests that the relationship between remedy and violation is deductive or formal, and thereby gives us an impoverished notion of remedy.

Deduction, strictly speaking, is never possible in the law, as the authors of the tailoring principle might well concede. There are, however, certain features of the tailoring principle, particularly the concept of "fit," which suggest that the connection between violation and remedy has a highly formalistic, almost deductive quality, with the violation serving as the premise, and the remedy the conclusion: (a) The violation is viewed as the exclusive source of the remedy; (b) each specific provision of the remedy is explicable in terms of the violation; (c) it is assumed that a unique remedy exists, in the same way that there is a single conclusion to a syllogism; and (d) the remedy, also like the conclusion, is thought to follow from the violation with a high degree of certainty. In the structural context these formalistic qualities—exclusivity, a fully determined specificity, uniqueness, and certainty—are never present. The structural remedy is decidedly instrumental.

The object of the structural remedy is not to eliminate a violation in the sense the tailoring principle implies but rather to remove the threat the organization poses to the constitutional values. The concept of violation can be used to describe the object of the remedy only if it is understood in a prospective, dynamic, and systemic sense. It must also be understood that there are many ways to eliminate the alleged threat. Consider a well-known case in which the police had engaged in a massive manhunt in the black neighborhoods of Baltimore.[55] They conducted searches of many homes without probable cause and did so in a manner and at a time that the court concluded was wholly unjustified. This misconduct was part of a larger pattern of abuses by the police, and the court perceived an urgent need to protect Fourth Amendment values regarding the security and privacy of the home. It also became apparent that this might be done in at least three different ways: (a) a decree against the police officers, either at the operative or supervisory level, prohibiting them from engaging in conduct that violates the Fourth Amendment; (b) a decree requiring the chief of police to establish an internal disciplinary agency that would sanction individual police officers who engaged in such misconduct; or (c) a decree establishing (subject to some minor exceptions such as one for hot pursuits) that searches for suspects be conducted only with a search warrant, not because the Fourth Amendment requires it but as a means of checking the abuses that occurred in this city. When confronted with a threat to Fourth Amendment values, a court must choose between these alternatives (and maybe even others), and the tailoring principle distorts the remedial process by masking this basic fact. It obscures the need for a choice and the fact that the remedial phase of a structural suit is largely devoted to making that choice.

The tailoring principle also obscures the basis on which that choice will be made, for it suggests that the violation will be the exclusive source of the remedy. It implies that the shape of the remedy is exclusively a function of the definition of the violation. Granted, the overriding mission of the structural decree is to remove the threat the organization poses to constitutional values, but there are additional or subsidiary considerations—largely embraced within the traditional concept of "equitable discretion"—that play a critical role in the remedial process. They inform and guide the choice to be made between the many possible remedies, and then shape the alternative chosen. One set of subsidiary considerations might be considered normative, because they express values other than the one that occasioned the intervention. For example, a school decree might be predicated on a desire to eliminate a threat to racial equality, but other values—such as respect for state autonomy, evenhandedness, or a minimization of coercion—should be considered. Another set of subsidiary considerations concern efficacy. They reflect the court's best judgment on how to remove the threat to the constitutional value most effectively.

These subsidiary considerations have, as we saw earlier, an important bearing on some facets of the party structure, such as the divergence between victims and beneficiaries of the decree, and the identity of the office or agency that bears the burden of the remedy. They also give the structural decree a tentative and hesitant character. The familiar pattern is for the judge to try—sometimes in different cases and sometimes at different times in the same case—the whole range of remedial alternatives. The judge must search for the "best" remedy, but since this judgment must incorporate such open-ended considerations as effectiveness and fairness, and since the threat and constitutional value that occasions the intervention can never be defined with great precision, the particular choice of remedy can never be defended with any certitude. It must always be open to revision, even without the strong showing traditionally required for modification of a decree, namely, that the first choice is causing grievous hardship.[56] A revision is justified if the remedy is not working effectively or is unnecessarily burdensome.

These subsidiary considerations also explain the specifics usually found in a structural injunction. The specifics range from the date and content of the reports that must be submitted to the court on performance to the duties of the various institutional operatives. For some, these specifics are baffling. They wonder how can it be that the Constitution requires a report on September 15, or showers at 110°F, or a thirty-day limitation on confinement in an isolation cell?[57] The bafflement, it seems to me, results from a failure to recognize the instrumental character of the remedy, and the importance of considerations of efficacy and fairness in shaping that instrument. They incorrectly assume, as the tailoring principle permits, that the violation—viewed as a reciprocal of a constitutional right—is the exclusive source of each and every term of the remedy. The tailoring principle implies that the remedy fits the violation in the same way that a suit of clothing fits the body, with each nuance of the suit being traced to a twist in the body.

Specificity is not a fixed rule; there may be some distinct advantages to ambiguity as a technique of control. But when specificity is present, it can usually be traced to considerations of efficacy and sometimes to general considerations of fairness (such as in the case of notice requirements). These subsidiary considerations block the attribution of these specifics back into the Constitution. Although the rights to which such subsidiary considerations give rise might be thought of as instrumental or remedial rights rather than constitutional rights proper, it is equally important to recognize that these instrumental or remedial rights are created by courts in discharge of their constitutional function. The Constitution does not say anything about reports, showers, or isolation cells; much less does it say anything about the date reports are due, the temperature of showers, or the maximum number of days that can be spent in an isolation cell. But it does say something about equality and avoidance of cruelty, and a court trying to give meaning to those values may find it both necessary and appropriate—as a way of bringing the organization within the bounds of the Constitution—to issue directives on these matters. The court may also find it necessary and appropriate to be quite specific in these directives, either as a way of minimizing the risk of evasion or as a way of helping the bureaucratic officers know what is expected of them.

The Dilemmas of Instrumentalism

The formalism of the tailoring principle fails to capture the true nature of the remedial process required for structural reform (and maybe for other types of relief as well). It is a pretense that must be abandoned. The structural remedy must be seen in instrumental terms. First, the remedy exists for and is determined by the finite purpose of protecting the constitutional value threatened; second, the remedy actually chosen is one among many ways of achieving that purpose; and, third, the remedy incorporates considerations that might not be rooted in any direct and obvious way in the constitutional value that occasions the intervention. The remedy is shaped in part—in critical part—by considerations of fairness and strategy.

As an instrumental activity, structural reform will have its share of failures in the sense that the threat to the constitutional value may persist, because so much is required to eliminate the threat and so little is known about organizational behavior. Failure is always possible with any instrumental activity; and, as a mode of thought, the appeal of instrumentalism (as opposed to formalism) derives largely from the fact that it recognizes the possibility of failure. What is worrisome about the instrumentalism implicit in structural reform is not the risk of failure itself but the fact that a court is undertaking the reform. Even a success might raise questions of legitimacy, because the legitimacy of the institution turns on criteria that are independent of the result. Legitimacy is largely a point about institutional integrity.

Some might see the instrumentalism inherent in the remedial process as inconsistent with the dictates of formal justice, the requirement of treating similarly those who are similarly situated. It might even be thought to be at odds with the idea of a single, nationwide Constitution. The subsidiary considerations that give so much specific content to the remedy might, for example, require a freedom-of-choice desegregation plan in one community, whereas, in another, a geographic assignment plan would be best. Similar differences may emerge in the reorganization of the prisons, hospitals, or welfare agencies in various communities. Such a varying remedial pattern has, in fact, emerged, but it does not seem to me to be objectionable. There may well be differences between the various communities that justify the different treatment. Neither formal justice nor the ideal of a single, nationwide Constitution requires that *all* communities be treated identically but only that *similar* communities be treated alike.[58] For me, the real problem arises not from the varying remedial pattern but from an absence of a conceptual connection between the processes that give courts their special competency and instrumental judgments.

The rightful place of courts in our political system turns on the existence of public values and on the promise of those institutions—because they are independent and because they must engage in a special dialogue —to articulate and elaborate the true meaning of those values. The task of discovering the meaning of constitutional values such as equality, liberty, due process, or property is, however, quite different from choosing or fashioning the most effective strategy for actualizing those values or for eliminating the threat a state bureaucracy poses to those values.[59] As noted before, the judge has no special claim of competency on instrumental judgments, on means-end rationality, either in the bureaucratic context or elsewhere. The judge may be no worse than others, and now and then may even be better, but there is no general or systematic reason for believing he or she will be better. There is no likely connection between the core processes of adjudication, those that give the judge the special claim to competence, and the instrumental judgments necessarily entailed in fashioning the remedy. Sometimes the best strategy is laid in silence and by someone highly sensitive to the preferences of the body politic.[60] Why, then, do we entrust the remedial task to the judge?

Rights and remedies are but two phases of the single social process of trying to give meaning to our public values. Rights operate in the realm of abstraction, remedies in the world of practical reality. A right is a particularized and authoritative declaration of meaning. It can exist without a remedy; indeed, the right to racial equality can exist even if the court gives no relief (other than the mere declaration). The right would then exist as a standard for criticism or for evaluating present social practices. A remedy, on the other hand, is an effort of the court to give meaning to a public value in practice. A remedy is more specific, more concrete, and more coercive than the mere declaration of right; it constitutes the actualization of the right.

If the purpose of the remedy is to actualize the declared right, then the remedy might be understood as subordinate to the right. However, we must recognize that the meaning of a public value is a function—a product or a consequence—of both declaration and actualization. Rights and remedies jointly constitute the meaning of the public value. The right that is declared may be one of racial equality; but if the court adopts a freedom-of-choice plan as the mode of desegregation, then the right that is actualized is the right to choose schools free of racial distinction (subject to all the other restraints inherent in any process that relies on individual choice). A constitutional value such as equality derives its meaning from both spheres, declaration and actualization, and it is this tight connection between meaning and remedy, not just tradition,[61] that requires a unity of functions. It requires that the decision about remedy be vested in the judge, who is the agency assigned the task of giving meaning to the value through declaration. A division of functions or a delegation of the task of actualization to another agency necessarily creates the risk that the remedy might distort the right and leave us with something less than the true meaning of the constitutional value. Both sources of meaning must be entrusted to the same agency in order to preserve the integrity of the meaning-giving enterprise itself.

If the judge's function is to give meaning to our public values, and the remedy must be understood as an integral part of that process, then we can understand—and indeed appreciate—the judge's involvement in reforming the state bureaucracy. It is a necessary incident of the judiciary's broader social function. This is not, however, the end of the matter. Even though the meaning-giving process may require a unity of functions, the risk is always present that the performance of one function may interfere with the other. This, in fact, occurs in the structural context and constitutes its core dilemma. It is not that actualization and declaration are analytically incompatible but, rather, that they are very often in tension. Actualization of the structural variety creates a network of relationships and an outlook—a dynamic—that threatens the judge's independence and the integrity of the judicial enterprise as a whole.

To some extent this threat is tied to a peculiar characteristic of the structural remedy—it places the judge in an architectural relationship with the newly reconstituted state bureaucracy. A judge deeply involved in the reconstruction of a school system or prison is likely to lose much of his or her distance from the organization. The judge is likely to identify with the organization being reconstructed, and this process of identification is likely to deepen as the enterprise of organizational reform moves through several cycles of supplemental relief, drawn out over a number of years. There is, however, a deeper and more pervasive threat to judicial independence, one that turns not on the peculiar reconstructive character of the structural remedy but on the judge's very desire to give a remedy, any remedy—that is, the judge's desire to be efficacious.

Judges are not all-powerful. They can decree some results but not all. Some results depend on forces beyond their control. Judges can issue orders, and perhaps threaten the addressees of these orders—the officers within the hierarchy—with contempt. But the success of the actualization process depends on many other forces, less formal, less identifiable, and perhaps even less reachable. The desegregation of a school system is, for example, vulnerable to "white flight," that is, the capacity of white parents to withdraw from the public school system altogether; the reforms of a police system may depend on the cooperation of the police union; the reform of a total institution depends on preserving the intricate fabric of personal relationship between keepers and inmates; and the reform of the welfare bureaucracy—maybe of all state bureaucracies—may well depend on increased appropriations and increased revenues. In each of these instances, the judge may be able to devise strategies for inducing these forces into supporting the structural reform—judges are among the shrewdest persons I have known. But the issue is not shrewdness or the capacity of judges to devise strategies for dealing with these limiting forces; rather, the issue is the very need to devise these strategies and what the perception of this need does to their sense of independence. Judges realize that practical success vitally depends on the preferences or the will of the body politic.

This perception of dependence has obvious and important implications for the remedy: Judges are not likely to decree more than they think they have the power to accomplish. The remedy will be limited, and, even more important, it will be viewed in adaptive terms.[62] Judges will seek to anticipate the response of others, and though they may try to transcend the limits imposed by that response, they are likely to accept the reality of those limits and compromise what the law might require in order to obtain as much relief as possible. They will bargain against the people's preferences. The remedy is, as we saw, a vitally important part of the meaning of the public value, and even if the remedy were all that were affected or compromised, there would be reason to be concerned. But the truth is that the stakes are likely to be higher—the distortion will be felt in the realm of rights, too. Just as it is reasonable to assume that judges wish to be efficacious, it is also reasonable to assume that they are not anxious to proclaim or even reveal their impotence. They will strive to lessen the gap between declaration and actualization, and thus they will tailor the right to fit the remedy.

Some measures might seem capable of preserving the judge's independence, and thus of minimizing the threat to the judicial enterprise. In the early years, recourse was made to a rule of strict passivity in the remedial phase: The judge's role was simply to decide whether the existing arrangements were constitutional. If they were not, it was entirely the defendant's responsibility to propose steps that would remedy the situation. The judge was not to choose the remedy, nor even to assume responsibility for implementing it, but was to leave the remedial burden entirely on the defendant. If the defendant failed to discharge that responsibility, recourse could be made to the contempt power.

This rule left the judiciary in the awkward position of choosing between a heavy and frequent use of criminal contempt power or an endless series of declarations of what was unacceptable. It soon became clear— particularly through the New Orleans school crisis of the early 1960s[63]— that neither alternative would produce results or effectively desegregate the schools; as a consequence, the courts abandoned this posture of strict passivity. They began to participate actively in the fashioning of remedies. They made clear their expectations as to what would be acceptable and sometimes even fashioned the remedy itself. In either instance, strategic considerations entered the judicial process. What the judges required was, in part, shaped by what was obtainable: It was better to have something —maybe a grade a year, maybe freedom of choice—rather than nothing at all.

At this point one might be tempted to turn back in despair, renounce the adjudicative enterprise altogether, or escape to the formalism represented by the tailoring principle. These alternatives must be resisted at all costs. They deny an important social function, the meaning-giving enterprise implicit in constitutionalism itself, or, in the case of the tailoring principle, they distort the nature of an important facet of this enterprise. Alternatively, we could confine the judiciary to the declarations of rights and insist that judges abandon their desire to be efficacious. That would resolve the core dilemma, and yet it would require a detachment or an indifference to this world that seems to me neither a virtue nor a mode of behavior within the reach of most American judges. We should not view the desire to be efficacious as an assertion of will but rather as a willingness of the judge to assume responsibility for practical reality and its consonance with the Constitution.

The 1960s were an extraordinary period in the history of the judiciary in America, and, among its many lessons, that era suggests the possibility of still another alternative: to live with the dilemma. Judges might be seen as forever straddling two worlds, the world of the ideal and the world of the practical, the world of the public value and the world of subjective preference, the world of the Constitution and the world of politics. Judges derive their legitimacy from only one but necessarily find themselves in the other. Among all the agencies of government, the judiciary is in the best position to discover the true meaning of our constitutional values; at the same time, however, those who experience its power are deeply constrained, indeed sometimes even compromised, by their desire—the wholly admirable desire—to give that meaning a reality.

2

The Social and Political Foundations of Adjudication

In the late 1970s and early 1980s the legal profession became strongly divided on structural litigation. The Supreme Court had already made its hostility apparent, but many of the lower federal courts and some sections of the academy looked at it more sympathetically. In June 1980 a major conference on the subject was held at Bryn Mawr College, organized by Professor Joanna Weinberg. I decided to use the occasion to sharpen the contrast between the two models of adjudication—dispute resolution and structural reform—that I presented in chapter 1 of this volume, "The Forms of Justice." In that essay I linked the dispute resolution model to a familiar narrative about the origins of courts. In my Bryn Mawr paper I developed this narrative further and used it to identify with greater clarity the premises that gave the dispute resolution model its appeal and accounted for the resurgence it was experiencing. I was able to see the connection between the new popularity of the dispute resolution model and the growing disdain for government power in all its forms—a development that would reach a zenith during the 1980s and the presidency of Ronald Reagan.

The Bryn Mawr conference was interdisciplinary. Many social scientists who had studied institutional litigation were present. The conference also included a number of lawyers and judges who had been actively involved in structural cases. The most prominent was Judge Jack Weinstein, who had presided over the Coney Island school desegregation case. His presentation at the conference caused something of a stir, for he announced that he was having misgivings about the capacity, and maybe even the legitimacy, of the judiciary to effectuate structural reform. Most of the attendees, myself included (see chapter 1), looked upon what the Judge had earlier sought to accomplish in the Coney Island case with admiration, and we felt disheartened by what he now had to say. The increasingly prevalent attacks on judicial activism seemed to us to have been internalized by Judge Weinstein and turned into a form of self-doubt. All conference papers were later published in the 1982 issue of *Law and Human Behavior* (volume 6).

Shortly after the Bryn Mawr conference, I had occasion to give a slightly altered version of the essay I present here to a conference sponsored by the American Enterprise Institute. The sympathies of the persons attending that conference were entirely different from those of the participants at Bryn Mawr, which helped me to further test my defense of the structural model. The American Enterprise Institute had been at the forefront of the broad assault on government power (including power exercised by the judiciary) that had its roots in the 1970s and achieved its greatest prominence in the Reagan era. That version of the essay, now under the title "Two Models of Adjudication," was published in 1983, along with the other seminar papers, in a volume edited by Robert A. Goldwin and William A. Schambra entitled *How Does the Constitution Secure Rights?*.

ADJUDICATION is the process by which the values embodied in an authoritative legal text, such as the Constitution, are given concrete meaning and expression. In my judgment this has always been the function of adjudication, clearly embraced and legitimated by Article III of the Constitution and continuous with the role of courts under the common law, but in the civil rights era a new form of adjudication emerged.

This new form of adjudication is largely defined by two characteristics. The first is the awareness that the basic threat to our constitutional values is posed not by individuals but by the operations of large-scale organizations, the bureaucracies of the modern state. Second, this new mode of litigation reflects the realization that, unless the organizations that threaten these values are restructured, these threats to constitutional values cannot and will not be eliminated. For this reconstructive endeavor, the traditional universe of legal remedies, that is, the damage judgment or the criminal prosecution, are inadequate. The injunction is the favored remedy. It is not used, however, as a device for stopping some discrete act, as it might have been in other times, but instead is used as the formal medium through which the judge directs the reconstruction of a bureaucratic organization.

This new mode of litigation, which I call "structural reform," represents an important advance in the understanding of modern society and the role of adjudication. The bureaucratic character of the modern state and the public dimensions of the judicial power are properly acknowledged. It is also important to recognize, however, that this new mode of litigation raises a number of problems. One problem is that of instrumentalism. Simply stated, the question presented is how to do the job of structural reform, and how to do it well. A second problem, and the primary subject of my concern, is the question of legitimacy: Is structural reform an appropriate task for the judiciary?

The instrumental issues are of enormous importance and difficulty, and must be given their due, but I believe the question of legitimacy is primary. I say this in part because I believe the dictates of legitimacy impose limitations on the means courts can use to achieve their objectives. A blind commitment to remedial efficacy, an exclusive concern with the instrumental questions, may well call into question the legitimacy of the entire judicial enterprise. I am also moved by historical circumstance to address the issues of legitimacy first.

Structural reform emerged as a distinctive form of constitutional litigation largely in response to the dictates of *Brown v. Board of Education* and the problems of school desegregation in the early 1960s. In the late 1960s and early 1970s the scope of structural reform was broadened to include the police, prisons, mental hospitals, institutions for the mentally retarded, prosecutorial agencies, public housing, and public employment. Its scope became as broad as the modern state itself. History took a different turn in the late 1970s, however, and structural reform came under attack; ever since, its legitimacy has been subject to deep and disturbing challenges. The challenges I speak of are not confined to structural reform, or to any particular mode of adjudication, but extend to the 1960s in general and the conception of state power implied by those times.

Two Models of Adjudication

The distinctive features of structural reform can best be understood by contrasting it with a model of adjudication that has long dominated the literature and our thinking, and is often used as the standard for judging the legitimacy of all forms of adjudication. This model is called dispute resolution and, as explained in "The Forms of Justice" (chapter 1), is associated with a story of two people in the state of nature who each claim a single piece of property. They discuss the problem, reach an impasse, and then turn to a third party, the stranger, to resolve their dispute. Courts are viewed as the institutionalization of this stranger, and adjudication the process through which the judicial power is exercised. Though this story is used not as an argument for the primacy of dispute resolution but only as an illustration, it does reflect several premises on which that model depends. Structural reform challenges those premises.

First, dispute resolution reflects a sociologically impoverished universe, one that does not account for social groups and bureaucratic institutions. There is no room in the story for the sociological entities so familiar to contemporary litigation. Social groups, like inmates of a prison or patients in a hospital, have no place in the story. Nor is there recognition of the existence of groups that transcend institutions, like racial minorities or the handicapped groups whose social identity and reality are as secure in our society as the individual in the state of nature. Furthermore, there is no room in the story for the public school system, the prison, the mental hospital, or the housing authority. The world is composed exclusively of individuals.

The party structure of the dispute resolution lawsuit reflects this individualistic bias; one neighbor is pitted against another while the judge stands between them as a passive umpire. The structural lawsuit, on the other hand, defies this triadic form. Not two but a multiplicity of parties are involved, and the groups or organizations recognized as parties are likely to be internally divided on the issues being adjudicated. The antagonism is not binary. Instead, in a structural lawsuit, we find an array of competing interests and perspectives organized around a number of issues and a single decisional agency, the judge.

Dispute resolution also implies a unity of functions in party structure; the plaintiff is simultaneously the victim, the beneficiary of the remedy, and the spokesperson. Similarly the individual defendant functions as the wrongdoer, as the one who bears the expense and trouble of the remedy, and also as the spokesperson for his or her interests. The structural lawsuit entails a fragmentation of these roles largely because sociological entities are introduced. Typically we find spokespersons, such as the special master and litigating amicus, who are neither victims nor beneficiaries, but who represent important interests and perspectives of groups that are victims or alternatively purported to be beneficiaries of the court action. Looking at the matter from the defendant's side, it should also be noted that structural reform involves a shift away from the concept of a wrongdoer, understood in any individualistic sense; the function of the lawsuit is not to punish or judge the conduct of some individuals but to eliminate threats to constitutional values posed by any agent, including the modern bureaucracy. The court is thus able to think in wholly prospective terms and to place the burden of the remedy on an institution that could not rightly be considered a wrongdoer, even in a metaphoric sense, but is the one most capable of safeguarding the values in question.

In addition to altering the party structure, the introduction of sociological entities in the structural suit changes and complicates the nature of the remedial process. In contrast to the dispute resolution situation, in which an individual is both victim and spokesperson as well as the beneficiary of a court decree, the remedial task is much more complex when the victim or beneficiary is a social group. At the very least the judge will have to determine whether the victim and beneficiary groups should be coextensive, and will also have to develop criteria for including and excluding individuals within those groups. Similarly, if the defendant is not an individual who is seeking his or her neighbor's land but is a bureaucratic organization that, by virtue of its very structure, poses a threat to constitutional values, then a remedy like the issuance of a prohibition aimed at some discrete act is unresponsive to the nature of the threat. The remedial task requires the restructuring of the organization, a complex and difficult undertaking wholly alien to the dispute resolution model and one that requires a measure of activity on the judge's part that is inconsistent with the picture of the judge as a passive umpire.

Second, dispute resolution privatizes values. In the hypothetical state of nature, where the dispute resolution story transpires, there are no public values or goals, only the private desires of individuals, in this instance, the desire for property. We postulate that the judge/stranger settles a property dispute between neighbors, but the story does not even reveal how the judge resolves the dispute, only that it is resolved. According to this scheme, the judge could even settle the dispute by flipping a coin. The public value served by the judiciary need only be the minimal one of avoiding violence through the use of a settlement mechanism. The judge may resolve the dispute according to any set of rules that would, in the future, minimize disputes or maximize the satisfaction of private ends.

Structural litigation does not begin with indifference toward or ignorance of public values. Rather, structural litigation proceeds within the framework of a constitution; and the Constitution that stands vindicated by *Brown v. Board of Education* is one that does far more than simply establish a form of government. It identifies a set of values such as equality, liberty, no cruel and unusual punishment, due process, security of the person, and freedom of speech. These values transcend the private ends implied by the dispute resolution model, and they inform and limit the function of our government. They stand as the core of our public morality and serve as the substantive foundations of structural litigation. The social function of contemporary litigation is not to resolve disputes but rather to give concrete meaning to that morality within the context of the bureaucratic state.

A third supposition of the dispute resolution story, reflecting either its individualism or its indifference to public values, is that, without the intervention of courts or other government agencies, society is in a state of natural harmony. As suggested by the concept of a dispute itself, the story assumes that the subject of adjudication is an abnormal event that disrupts an otherwise satisfactory world. It also suggests that the function of adjudication is to restore the status quo. Structural litigation, on the other hand, denies that assumption and reflects doubt as to whether the status quo is, in fact, just. It is premised on skepticism about the existing distribution of power and privilege in American society. It fails to consider that perhaps neither of the neighbors should be entitled to the property.

This skepticism helps to explain why the requirements for initiating a structural lawsuit were lowered. In a structural case, pleading requirements became simplified, standing more permissive, and mootness objections less decisive. These developments reflected a growing distrust of that premise of the dispute resolution story that posits a harmonious and just status quo; the need for judicial intervention was no longer regarded as an aberration.

Doubts about the justice of the status quo are also reflected in the special nature of the remedial process. The goal of dispute resolution is to set things back to normal; the remedy is short and discrete, since it simply undertakes to reestablish the world that existed before the dispute. But this is clearly not a valid conception of the structural remedy, for the goal of this mode of litigation was to create a new status quo, one that would be more nearly in accord with our constitutional ideals. The restructuring of a prison or school system cannot be understood as an attempt to return to a world that existed prior to some dispute; it represents an attempt to construct a new social reality. The remedy may have to last almost as long as the social reality it attempts to create.

Finally, the dispute resolution model institutionally isolates the judiciary. The courts are not depicted as an integral part of a government. The quarreling neighbors ask the stranger—any stranger—to resolve their dispute. This mythical account of the process by which courts are created implies that courts can be understood apart from the larger system of government. It also suggests that the legitimacy of courts is derived from the consent of the citizenry in an institution-specific sense. The neighbors agree to take the dispute to the court and to abide by its outcome. In modern society, the connection to consent in the institution-specific sense is preserved but in more subtle forms. Lon Fuller, for example, tried to found the legitimacy of adjudication on the right of participation in the process, a highly individualized form of consent.[1] Others, such as John Ely, reflecting the *Carolene Products* tradition, attempted to found legitimacy on the ability of courts to represent the disenfranchised, as a means of perfecting the political process whereby American society consents to its government.[2]

In my view, courts should not be viewed in isolation but as a coordinate source of governmental power, and as an integral part of the larger political system. Democracy does, in fact, commit us to consent as the foundation of legitimacy, but that consent is not one that is granted separately to individual institutions. Democratic consent extends to the system of governance as a whole. The legitimacy of each institution within the system does not depend on the consent of the people who are subjected to it, either in the individualized or collective sense, but rather on the competence of an institution to discharge a social function within that system. In America the legitimacy of the courts, and the power they exercise in structural reform or, for that matter, in any type of constitutional litigation, is founded on the unique competence of the judiciary to perform their distinctive social function, which is, as I have already suggested, to give concrete meaning and application to the public values embodied in the Constitution.

It is not at all necessary, when speaking of this competence, to ascribe to judges the wisdom of philosopher kings. The capacity of judges to give meaning to public values turns not on some personal moral expertise, of which they have none, but on the process that limits their exercise of power. One feature of that process is the dialogue judges must conduct;

they must listen to all grievances, hear a wide range of interests, speak back and also assume individual responsibility for what they say. The judge must also remain independent of the desires or preferences of both the body politic and the particular contestants before the bench.

The judiciary's competence and thus its legitimacy depends on adherence to these two qualities of process—dialogue and independence—not on the willingness of the people to consent to particular outcomes or on the people's capacity to appoint or remove the individuals who hold the public office. The people's consent is required to legitimate the political system, of which the judiciary is an integral part, and the capacity of the people to respond to judicial decisions, say, through constitutional amendments, preserves the consensual character of the system as a whole. A tighter, more particularized dependence on the popular consent will deprive the judiciary of its independence and thus of its competence to speak the law.

The Sources of Resistance

The dispute resolution model is at odds with the social and political reality of modern society, and yet it rebounded from relative invisibility in the 1960s to enjoy a renewed popularity ever since the mid-1970s. This resurgence cannot be attributed to the rather banal poetry of the dispute resolution story, nor even to some nostalgic longing it may evoke for an oversimplified world. The resurgence is, I believe, a result of the internal contradictions engendered by structural reform and of the emergence of a vision of social life that privatizes all ends.

At the heart of structural reform is the conception of the judiciary as a coordinate source of government power that derives its legitimacy from a distinctive process. The judge's authority to give constitutional values their meaning stems from the judge's independence and willingness to engage in a special dialogue over that meaning. Judges engaged in structural reform invoke the interpretive authority that all judges traditionally possess and that is derived from the process through which they exercise power. At the same time, the distinctive remedial dimension of structural reform impairs the capacity of the judiciary to adhere to the dictates of the process that is the source of its legitimacy, and, as a consequence, questions arise as to the appropriateness of that task for the judiciary.

One obvious threat to the integrity of the judicial process, which had been minimized in "The Forms of Justice" (chapter 1) but which has become of increasing concern to me, is the bureaucratization of the judiciary (see chapter 4). There seems to be an increasing tendency, particularly pronounced in the structural context, for judges to surround themselves with a series of adjunct institutions—special masters, hearing officers, more law clerks—which begin to comprise a new bureaucracy now under judicial auspices. Donald Horowitz has suggested that this phenomenon is tied to a sociological law which predicts that the judiciary will mirror the essential character of the institutions it seeks to regulate or control.[3] I, on the other hand, suspect that the bureaucratization of the judiciary may have less grandiose, but more tractable, causes: overwork, the need for specialized knowledge, or a desire of judges to insulate themselves from public criticism and scrutiny. These causes can be overcome, and must be, because the bureaucratization of the judicial power, over time, will destroy the distinctive character of the dialogue that has long been central to the judicial function: It will be difficult to believe that a judge is truly listening or responding to the grievances or is assuming individual responsibility for the response.

Structural reform also presents a threat to judicial independence. This arises in part because of the special relationship between the judge and the newly reconstructed institution. Structural litigation involves the judiciary in the reconstruction of an ongoing institution, and, since judges serve as both architects and structural engineers on these projects, they are likely to lose their detachment from the institution. The reconstructed institution will be seen as largely a judicial creation. As a result, the judge may well view challenges to the newly reconstructed institution as challenges to his or her authority.

The threat to independence also arises because the remedial ambitions of structural reform make political maneuvering inevitable. Judges are not all-powerful, and, given the complex and far-reaching aspirations of the structural remedy and the dependence of that remedy on the cooperation of endless numbers of individuals and agencies, the danger is ever present that judges will compromise both remedies and rights in order to achieve remedial objectives; in other words, they may temper their idealism by what is realistic. They will become adaptive. Life tenure may continue to provide nominal independence, but the simple human desire to be efficacious may effectively jeopardize that independence.

These dynamics place strains on the idea of structural reform, yet I would insist that they do not render that model of adjudication either incoherent or beyond the reach of judicial power. Zeal is a personal quality that must be tempered but not surrendered. Though the limits of the judicial office must be recognized, it would be a mistake to renounce the remedial ambitions implied by the idea of structural reform, for they stem from a true perception of the nature of social reality and the entirely admirable commitment of the judiciary to make that reality comport with the values embodied in the Constitution.

Overzealous judges are not the only threat to the legitimacy of structural reform. A more basic and more pervasive threat arises from sources external to the judicial process, including one that extends to politics in general. Since, as I have suggested, the courts should be viewed as a coordinate source of government power, it would not be at all surprising to find the judiciary subject to the forces that are affecting governmental power in general. In fact, this has occurred. The resurgence of the dispute resolution model was not an isolated phenomenon but occurred within a larger political context characterized by a renewed interest in market economics and theories of laissez-faire and, more generally, by a reaffirmation of the theory of the social contract. At the heart of each phenomenon was a renewed belief in the private character of all ends.

I believe it is significant that the story of two neighbors fighting over land takes place in the state of nature, because it was in the state of nature where the social contract was formed. We can also see that social contract theory shares the premises of dispute resolution—it, too, lacks a sociology, ends are private, power is legitimated through individualized consent, and, at least according to John Locke's version of the social contract, natural harmony generally prevails. The concept of government enshrined by social contract theory and preeminent through much of the nineteenth century—the so-called night-watchman state[4]—is the analog to the minimalist conception of judicial power implied by the dispute resolution model. The chief end of the state is security: to develop those conditions that will allow private individuals to engage in commerce and to satisfy their own needs.

Twentieth-century America, particularly in the decades following the New Deal and World War II, saw the emergence of an entirely different kind of state; the state had become an active participant in our social life, supplying essential services and otherwise structuring the very terms of our existence. In order to legitimate that conception of state power, we had to develop a theory of consent that is radically different from the individualistic, unanimous consent exalted by the social contract tradition. We also had to develop a conception of social life that is sufficiently rich and purposive to render intelligible the pervasive and almost continuous interventions of a state committed to improving the welfare of its citizenry. That was largely the accomplishment of the civil rights era.

The emergence and legitimization of the activist state in the 1960s parallels the emergence and legitimization of this new form of litigation that I have called structural reform. Indeed, one can go further, as my colleague Bruce Ackerman has urged in conversation, and identify a common theoretical foundation for the two conceptions of governmental power. Just as the dispute resolution model shares the assumptions of social contract theory and the night-watchman state, structural reform and the modern activist state share a common political theory. Both take account of sociological realities, reflect skepticism as to the justness of the status quo, and represent an affirmative use of governmental power. Both are grounded on a belief in the existence and importance of public values and recognition of the need to translate those values into social reality through the use of governmental power. Equality was the centerpiece of the litigation of the 1960s, as it was for the legislative and executive action of that era, but equality only had a representative significance; it stood for an entire way of looking at social life. It emphasized what I have called public values—those values that define a society and give it its identity and inner coherence. Rights were seen as the concrete embodiment of these values and, as such, were an expression of our communality rather than our individuality.

Ever since the 1970s we have felt increasing doubts about the existence of public values—all is individual interests or at best individual morality—and the dispute resolution model of adjudication, like the night-watchman state, accommodates those doubts. Both afford an easy haven for all those who would deny or minimize the role of public values in our social life and the need for governmental power to realize those values. The problem is that if we retreat, if we accept the privatization of all ends or deny the government the power to realize the values that may fairly be deemed public, we will impoverish our social existence and undermine important institutional arrangements. The judiciary would be without the means to protect against the threats posed by the bureaucracies of the modern state, and the Constitution would be debased. The Constitution would be seen not as the embodiment of a public morality but simply as an instrument of political organization—distributing power and prescribing the procedures by which that power is to be exercised. Such a development must be resisted and can be, but to do so we must first rediscover the meaning and value of our public life.

3

The Right Degree of Independence

By the mid-1980s I had begun to lecture abroad. I had no expertise whatsoever in matters international, but the rest of the world was becoming increasingly curious about the purely domestic aspects of the American legal system. For many, that system represented an object to admire, and possibly emulate. A number of the essays in this book, including this chapter, were written in response to this perceived need. It deals with one of the most salutary features of the American experience, the independence of the judiciary.

In June 1985 I was invited to Argentina, along with a small group of lawyers and philosophers, to consult with the administration of President Raúl Alfonsín on the trials in process of the junta that had ruled Argentina from 1976 to 1983. (The circumstances of this trip, and its significance for my professional career, is described in more detail in "The Death of a Public Intellectual," originally published at 104 *Yale Law Journal* 1107 [1995].) As a result of that trip, I became increasingly involved in Latin America, particularly Argentina and Chile, and became fascinated with the transition from dictatorship to democracy in which those countries were engaged. In the case of Argentina, the transition began in 1983; in Chile, it began in 1989.

In each of the transitions a question arose as to the independence of the judiciary. Earlier many of the judges had served the dictatorship, and the new democratic governments had to decide whether those judges could continue to serve. Would their removal be consistent with the ideal of judicial independence? In 1991 Professor Irwin Stotzky convened a conference on this subject at the University of Miami. This chapter originated as a paper for that conference and is included in the volume edited by Professor Stotzky, *The Role of the Judiciary in the Transition to*

Democracy in Latin America (1993). Later I revised that essay to take account of the impeachment of a justice in Chile who had interfered with proceedings that sought to hold the military accountable for human rights abuses. That version of the paper was published in the 1993 issue of the *University of Miami Inter-American Law Review* (volume 25, page 57).

Soon after the appearance of these essays, I was invited to write the article on judicial independence for the *Encyclopedia of the American Constitution* (Supplement II, 1999). The present chapter was originally that article. Gone are all the references to Latin America and the special problems the change in regimes posed. Yet the essential point remains: We in the United States have reason to be proud of the degree of independence our judiciary has achieved—indeed, it is one of the pillars of judicial authority—but we should not assume that the judiciary's separation from politics is absolute.

LONG recognized as one of the hallmarks of American constitutionalism, judicial independence takes several different forms. Each type is essential to good judging, but none is absolute. One form of independence—party detachment—concerns the relationship between the judge and the parties before the court, and is rooted in the aspiration to impartiality. It requires that the judge is not related to these parties or under their control or influence in any way. Such a requirement guards against gross threats to impartiality, such as bribery and close kinship ties between judges and litigants. Often, however, less blatant violations, such as cultural ties and ideological sympathy, cannot realistically be prevented; judicial independence with respect to litigating parties is therefore an ideal that can only be achieved imperfectly.

A second form of judicial independence—individual autonomy—concerns the relationship between individual judges and other members of the judiciary. It demands that the judge be unconstrained by collegial and institutional pressures when deciding questions of fact and law. According to this rule, judicial decisions are matters of individual conscience and responsibility.

This aspect of judicial independence has its roots in broad cultural norms, largely of an individualist character, and is reinforced by the American practice of recruiting judges after they have had successful careers in practice or in politics. It is also reinforced by, and reflected in, the practice of judges signing their rulings and opinions. Requiring judges to assume individual responsibility for legal decisions fosters judicial accountability.

Like party detachment, individual autonomy is an ideal that is only partially realized. All judges are expected to adhere to the prior decisions of other judges through the doctrine of stare decisis. Lower court judges are even more constrained: They are subject to appellate review and even bureaucratic control. For example, the Judicial Councils Reform Act of 1980 allows groups of federal circuit judges to bypass ordinary appellate procedures and form committees to investigate and impose sanctions on individual district court judges.

A third form of judicial independence—political insularity—is perhaps the most complex. It requires the judiciary to be independent from popularly controlled governmental institutions, in particular, the executive and legislative branches. This form of independence overlaps with party detachment whenever one of the political branches is itself a party before the court, but it is a distinct requirement that encompasses a variety of other circumstances as well. Even when the parties before the court are purely private, the judge is expected to remain free from the influence or control of the political branches of government.

Political insularity is essential for the pursuit of justice, which I understand as an objective ideal that stands apart from popular sentiment. Courts are supposed to do what is right, not what is popular. Such a definition of mission—defended at length in "The Forms of Justice" (chapter 1) and again in "Objectivity and Interpretation" (chapter 9)—gives life to the separation of powers doctrine and enables the judiciary to act as a countervailing force within the political system, and to check abuses of power by the legislature and the executive. With that purpose in mind, the Constitution provides federal judges with life tenure and protection against diminution of pay. In addition, because the federal judiciary is the authoritative interpreter of the Constitution, only an amendment can override a constitutional interpretation. Constitutional amendment is a cumbersome process, requiring special majorities in each house of Congress and approval by three-fourths of the states.

Despite its importance, political insularity poses a certain dilemma for democratic theory: The more insulated the judiciary is from the popularly controlled governmental institutions, the more it is able to interfere with their policies and thereby frustrate the popular will. Accordingly, the demand for political insularity, perhaps even more so than party detachment and individual autonomy, is qualified. Some state judges are elected. Even the federal judiciary, long considered one of the most independent of all judicial systems in the world, is best understood not as a fully insulated branch of government but as one facet of an interdependent political system.

One of the primary constraints on the federal judiciary's political independence is the appointment process. In some countries, the judiciary is given authority to select its own members as a way of enhancing its political insularity. In the United States, the power to appoint federal judges is vested in the president, and this arrangement necessarily introduces an element of political control over the judiciary's composition. Presidents naturally will try to select judges whose conception of justice approximates their own and who are likely to further the policies of their administrations. Although the president is constrained by public expectations as to the qualifications of nominees, even the most insistent demand for excellence still allows the president wide latitude. The need to obtain Senate approval also qualifies the prerogatives of the president, yet this hardly depoliticizes the judicial appointment process, as the Senate is a political agency driven by its own agenda.

Even after a judge takes the oath of office, the president's control over the promotion process may serve as a continuing source of influence. Those who desire a higher position in the judicial hierarchy or perhaps another government post altogether may avoid decisions that would put them in disfavor with the president or pose an obstacle to the confirmation process. In addition, every judge is likely to feel a special debt toward the president who is responsible for his or her appointment. This sense of gratitude may produce a judicial bias in favor of the administration, though this risk is likely to wane over time as the judge comes to confront the policies of a president with whom he or she has no prior relationship. On a number of occasions, most notably involving Felix Frankfurter and Franklin Roosevelt, sitting Justices have acted as informal advisers to presidents, compromising their insularity most egregiously.[1]

Another important source of political influence over the federal judiciary is the impeachment process. Article II of the Constitution provides for the impeachment of all civil officers for "Treason, Bribery or other high Crimes and Misdemeanors." This is a remarkably high standard, but Article III uses more general language, stating that judges "shall hold their Offices during good Behavior." Indeed, in the nineteenth century, Congress invoked its impeachment power simply because it disapproved of certain judicial decisions. In fact, none of these particular proceedings resulted in the removal of the judge, and a general understanding has evolved that a judge may only be impeached for violation of the most elemental duties of office, for example, chronic drunkenness, corruption, or conviction of a crime. Still, the threat of impeachment, often voiced by ideologues without hope of ultimate success, may have an inhibiting influence on judges' behavior.[2]

Aside from the political elements introduced by the appointment and impeachment processes, and by the judge's own desire for higher office, economic imperatives may also compromise a judge's independence, even one who belongs to the highly esteemed federal bench. Although the Constitution provides a guarantee against pay diminution, it is now settled law in the United States that Congress is not obliged to raise federal judicial salaries to keep pace with inflation.[3] Judges seeking to protect the real value of their compensation might therefore tailor their actions so as not to offend the political branches. A judge's attachment to certain incidental benefits of office, such as secretaries, law clerks, and chauffeurs, can produce a similar effect, for these, too, are within the control of Congress and the president. In these matters, the political branches cannot target individual judges but must establish rules applicable to all federal judges, or at least to specific categories (e.g., the Supreme Court, the lower courts). This blunts the usefulness of this method of control as a sanction, unless, of course, the situation has so deteriorated as to justify a blanket assault.

A more precise form of control may come through the exercise of Congress's lawmaking power. Although a judicial decision interpreting the Constitution may only be overridden by a constitutional amendment, Congress may reverse a statutory interpretation with a simple legislative enactment. This power has been exercised countless times, though it is subject to a rule that denies Congress the power to prescribe or alter the rule of decision in a case already pending.

Congress may also intervene by limiting the jurisdiction of the federal courts and thereby remitting the claimants to state courts or to other federal agencies (for example, administrative agencies, bankruptcy judges, or magistrates, none of whom are as insulated from the political branches as Article III judges). As with efforts to prescribe the rule of decision, congressional power to withdraw jurisdiction may be limited by a rule that denies it this power in pending cases. Jurisdiction-stripping measures have also been resisted on the theory that a federal right necessarily implies a federal remedy.

In more recent years Congress has occasionally sought to exercise control over the adjudication of constitutional claims by placing limitation on judicial remedies as opposed to stripping the federal courts of jurisdiction over those claims. With school segregation, for example, Congress has limited the conditions under which busing may be ordered.[4] Congress recently employed a similar strategy to curb federal court litigation aimed at reforming prison conditions.[5]

The political branches can also influence the course of decision through their control over the number of judgeships. Although the Constitution establishes the Supreme Court, it does not prescribe the number of Justices, nor does it set down any rule as to the number of lower-court judges. Since the power of appointment lies with the president, subject of course to confirmation by the Senate, Congress may endow a president, whose policies or stance toward the judiciary it supports, with new judgeships to fill. Conversely, Congress may try to freeze or shrink the number of judgeships available to a president with whom they disagree on these matters.

In the nineteenth century Congress occasionally manipulated the number of justices on the Supreme Court as a way of influencing the course of judicial decisions. However, since President Franklin Roosevelt's unsuccessful attempt to pack the Court in the 1930s—a scheme that envisioned adding a new justice for every one who had turned seventy as a way of undermining decisions striking down his New Deal programs—an informal norm has emerged in the United States that disfavors such manipulation.[6] Yet there are many reasons, including population growth and caseload volume, for altering the size of the judiciary, and Congress may appeal to any or all of them to mask manipulative motivations. Furthermore, because maintenance of the status quo is less likely to be perceived as a manipulative act, Congress may exert pressure on federal judges by failing to increase their number in response to increases in their workload. These exercises in legislative control are even more feasible for the lower federal courts, because no general norms have evolved as to the number of lower-court judges (whereas the popular imagination seems to have fixed on the number nine for the Supreme Court), and the lower courts are rarely subject to widespread public attention.

Finally, the judiciary is dependent on the other branches to enforce its decrees. President Jackson is said to have responded to a Supreme Court decision on a treaty dispute between Georgia and the Cherokee Indians in rather sharp terms: "John Marshall has made his decision, now let him enforce it."[7] In the modern period the president has been more cooperative and, in fact, called out the troops during the civil rights era to enforce judicial decrees. Although the judiciary welcomed such measures, these actions also underscored the judiciary's dependency and inability to enforce policies when other branches strongly and persistently oppose them. Judges possess the contempt power, but contempt orders are not self-enforcing and may themselves require the assistance of the other branches.

Thus the much-celebrated independence of the judiciary, even the federal judiciary, is in many ways limited. Federal judges enjoy a substantial amount of independence with respect to litigating parties and other members of the judiciary, but this independence is far from absolute. It is also true that federal judges are insulated from the political branches of government because they have life tenure, are assured that their pay cannot be diminished by legislative fiat, and, thanks to an evolving public understanding, cannot be removed simply because of disagreement with their decisions. Yet they are by no means fully independent of the political branches. The Constitution grants the executive and the legislature the power to make appointments, to decide whether salaries should be adjusted for inflation, and to define the judiciary's jurisdiction and structure, and because the courts often need the political branches to implement their decisions, these branches are able to exercise significant influence over the judiciary. Judges are independent, but not too independent, as is indeed appropriate in a democracy.

4

The Bureaucratization of
the Judiciary

Benjamin Cardozo's *The Nature of the Judicial Process* stands as a classic statement of the dilemmas facing a judge. It was first published in 1921. Some sixty years later, Judge Gilbert Merritt of the United States Court of Appeals for the Sixth Circuit thought that it might be a good idea to revisit Cardozo's work and use it to measure the changes to the judiciary that had occurred in recent decades. Merritt was the program chairman of the Sixth Circuit Judicial Conference that was to be held in Asheville, North Carolina, in July 1982, and he invited me to participate in a panel organized around this theme. I was intrigued by Judge Merritt's idea and immediately accepted the invitation. This chapter was first prepared for that occasion and was later published in a 1983 issue of the *Yale Law Journal* (volume 92, page 1442).

My work on the structural injunction exposed me to the vast sociological literature on bureaucracy. In "The Forms of Justice" (chapter 1), and again in "The Social and Political Foundation of Adjudication" (chapter 2), I had argued that in contemporary society the principal threat to constitutional values was posed not by the individual government official but by the bureaucratic organizations that constitute the modern state. I also maintained that in order to provide an effective remedy, the judge had to use his or her injunctive powers to reform the structure of the state bureaucracy.

At the Bryn Mawr conference described in the prologue of chapter 2, Professor Donald Horowitz of Duke University, a critic of structural reform and the author of the well-known book *Courts and Social Policy* (1977), discussed in chapter 1, linked the increasing bureaucratization of the judiciary with the judicial engagement with state bureaucracies. According to Horowitz, the judiciary was merely taking on the character of the institutions it sought to reform. My inclination, however, is to treat the bureaucratization of both the judiciary and the other branches of government as a natural, almost inevitable, response to the increasing size and complexity of American society.

In this chapter I give further content to this claim: I explain how the judiciary was transformed over the course of the twentieth century and examine the threat such a change poses to the judiciary's authority. I also suggest a number of reforms of the judiciary system that might lessen the threat posed by bureaucratization. Judge Merritt has his own views about these issues, as elaborated in his essay, *Owen Fiss on Paradise Lost: The Judicial Bureaucracy in the Administrative State*, published in the *Yale Law Journal* (volume 92, page 1469).

THE history of the twentieth century is largely the history of increasing bureaucratization. Almost every phase of American life has come to be dominated by large-scale, complex organizations—the corporation, the labor union, the university, the public hospital, and even our national political agencies. The national executive does not simply consist of the president and a small group of trusted advisers but, instead, is composed of a vast, sprawling conglomerate of administrative agencies, which are staffed by millions of employees. We have come to accept this and often refer to the executive branch as "The Bureaucracy," but a similar development has occurred within the legislature. In addition to 535 senators and representatives, Congress now consists of almost 25,000 employees, approximately 200 committees and subcommittees, and a good number of internal agencies (like the General Accounting Office and the Congressional Budget Office). Against this background an account of the judiciary that, like Benjamin Cardozo's, focuses exclusively on the agony of a lonely, isolated judge seems somewhat dated. Today the judiciary must be seen as a large-scale, complex organization, responding to the growing size and complexity of American society.

Although the bureaucratization of the judiciary parallels similar developments in the other branches of government, it raises a unique challenge to the institution's legitimacy. The legislative and executive branches derive their legitimacy from their responsiveness to popular will, and bureaucratization acts as a screen that impairs the responsiveness of officials within these branches. With the judiciary, however, the impact of bureaucratization is felt in another domain altogether: Bureaucratization tends to corrode the individualistic processes that are the source of judicial legitimacy.

The foundation of judicial power is process. Judges are entrusted with power because of their special competence to interpret public values embodied in authoritative texts, and this competence is derived from the process that has long characterized the judiciary and that limits the exercise of its power. One aspect of that process is independence. Judicial independence is not threatened by bureaucratization, and, indeed, today the independence of the judiciary from the political branches might depend on its capacity to develop the organizational resources usually associated with a bureaucracy. But a second aspect of the legitimating process of the judiciary is threatened. I am referring to the obligation of judges to engage in a special dialogue—to listen to all grievances, hear from all the interests affected, and give reasons for their decisions. Signing his or her name to a judgment or opinion assures the parties that the judge has thoroughly participated in that process and assumes individual responsibility for the decision. We accept the judicial power on these terms. Yet bureaucratization raises the specter that the judge's signature is but a sham and that the judge is exercising power without genuinely engaging in the dialogue from which his or her authority flows.

The Judicial Bureaucracy

Not all organizational relationships are bureaucratic. The allocation of power to both state and federal courts creates a complex set of organizational relationships among the judges of the two political systems, but I regard these relationships more as coordinate than bureaucratic.[1] Similarly, I do not regard as bureaucratic the organizational relationships that arise from the fact that appellate courts today generally act through groups of judges. Interactions between the members of each group may create relationships that threaten the integrity of the judicial process because compromises must be made to secure a majority, but these relationships are more collegial or committee-like than bureaucratic.[2] For me, the feature that distinguishes bureaucracy from these other organizational relationships is hierarchy: The bureaucratic relationship is vertical rather than horizontal.

Bureaucracy is a term often used with pejorative connotations because of the pathologies or dysfunctions connected with complex organizations, but I use it descriptively. I will use the term *bureaucracy* to refer to a complex organization with three features: (1) a multitude of actors; (2) a division of functions or responsibilities between them; and (3) reliance on a hierarchy as the central device to coordinate their activities. In stressing the hierarchical element, I do not claim that hierarchy is the only coordinating device, for in bureaucracies of professionals, like the judiciary, hierarchy is often supplemented by a common culture—a set of shared norms and ideals. But this qualification does not destroy the central importance of hierarchy to the organization and the usefulness of the concept in analyzing a series of organizational relationships that characterize the modern judiciary.

I focus on the federal judiciary because it is often thought to be the fullest embodiment of the judicial ideal and also because it is considered the least bureaucratic of all our judicial systems. In this system, three hierarchical relationships can be identified: judge-judge, judge-staff, and what I shall call judge-subjudge. Of all the hierarchical relationships, the first— that between judges on different levels of the judicial system—is the weakest, and, as is often true in bureaucratic organizations, those at the bottom of the hierarchy have considerably more power than the organizational chart indicates.[3] There is a gap between formal power and real power. This gap stems in part from the fact that the Supreme Court lacks the time, resources, and information needed to supervise the lower courts effectively. The Supreme Court fully considers fewer than one hundred cases a year, whereas the federal courts of appeals dispose of more than fifty thousand cases a year. Nor can the courts of appeals fill the supervisory void left by the Supreme Court. They are not organized to exercise managerial duties. Each court of appeals consists of a multitude of judges, who do not speak with one voice, and the control of each court is confined to a geographical region of the country and does not extend to the entire nation, as federal law must.

The hierarchy among judges is further weakened by the absence of any sanctioning system.[4] In the judicial hierarchy, unlike the practice in most bureaucracies, those higher up have no authority over the appointment, removal, promotion, or pay of those below. Sometimes the especially obedient are rewarded by compliments in appellate opinions; sometimes the especially recalcitrant are publicly reprimanded; and sometimes judges high in the hierarchy will be consulted when a judge below seeks to move up. For the most part, however, the hierarchical control over judges is exercised through review of the work product of those below. Granted, the conscientious do not take such review lightly, but it must be seen as a rather weak and indirect instrument of control. Since 1980 Congress has provided the judicial councils of the circuits power to investigate complaints against lower judges, but the sanctions stop short of removal.[5] The applicable statute surrounds the judge accused of misbehavior with elaborate procedural protections, nearly equivalent to those available in a criminal prosecution, and specifically provides that a complaint may be dismissed if it relates to the merits of a decision. In many respects, the statute stands as a symbol of the weakness of the controls of one judge over another.

The second hierarchical relationship is that between a judge and his or her staff. Some of that staff—for example, the clerk of the court, the bailiff, and the judge's secretary—generally do not participate in the decisional process, and, for the purposes of examining how bureaucratization affects the integrity of that process, they can be safely ignored. Law clerks, however, cannot be ignored.[6] One must begin an analysis of their role by making a distinction between two types of law clerks: elbow clerks, who are chosen by and work under the direct supervision of a particular judge, and a position sometimes known as a staff attorney. Staff attorneys are not assigned to any particular judge but belong to what has become known as the central legal staff.[7]

The role of staff in the decisional process is not publicly or formally defined and, in any event, varies from judge to judge and from court to court. Elbow clerks may write memoranda recommending how cases should be decided (referred to as bench memoranda), discuss cases with the judge, research issues that are not fully briefed, and draft opinions. Staff attorneys might do the same, but their primary function is to screen cases for appellate courts. A staff attorney usually prepares a memorandum for a panel of judges recommending whether a case should be disposed of summarily through issuance of a judgment order, rather than being fully argued and decided with a full opinion.

The third hierarchical relationship in the federal system is that between judges and certain auxiliary personnel such as magistrate judges, bankruptcy judges, and special masters, all of whom I call subjudges. Subjudges participate in the decisional process but fall somewhere between law clerks and judges in terms of their power. In contrast to law clerks, subjudges are formally and publicly entrusted with some measure of decisional power, and yet are distinguished from judges because of special restrictions on their power. The scope of their jurisdiction is especially limited (e.g., bankruptcy, pretrial discovery, habeas corpus petitions, or the trial of petty crimes). Their decisions are subject to review by a judge under more stringent standards than when one judge is reviewing the work of another judge. Subjudges serve for limited terms and are subject to the hierarchical controls—appointment and dismissal—that are not exercised by one judge over another. As a consequence, the hierarchy between judges and subjudges, like that between judge and staff, is stronger than the hierarchy among judges.

Putting together these three hierarchical relationships—judge-judge, judge-staff, and judge-subjudge—one can discern the familiar bureaucratic structure: a pyramid. The federal judicial system consists of three tiers of courts—the Supreme Court, the courts of appeals, and the district courts. Within each of these tiers is a shadow consisting of the law clerks or staff. The bottom tier has a second shadow, consisting of the subjudges, who are primarily used and supervised by the district judges. As a purely formal matter, this bureaucratic structure is not new. Almost every element of it can be traced back to 1900, when Congress created the circuit courts of appeals and transformed the federal judicial system from a two-tiered to a three-tiered system. What is new, and what has provoked the bureaucratization debate of recent years, is not the formal structure itself but rather its internal density—the proliferation of participants within the structure.

In 1900 there were just over one hundred federal judges—nine Supreme Court Justices, twenty-four circuit judges, and seventy-seven district judges. Today there are more than one thousand. In 1900 there were only nine stenographic clerks—one for each Justice.[8] The modern law clerk can be seen to have evolved from that position, but today the role of the clerk has become more important in the decisional process and the number of law clerks has greatly increased. Some judges have two, others three, and some four. The total number of elbow clerks today remains unclear, but there are probably close to two thousand. The staff attorneys probably number into the hundreds. It seems likely that their number will grow now that the position has been institutionalized and the need for screening cases has become more important.

Within recent years as their use increased, a great deal of attention has focused on special masters.[9] This is probably owing to the hotly contested and protracted nature of the cases they are involved in (e.g., school desegregation or prison reform) rather than their number; in fact, their closest historical counterparts—the receivers of the railroad reorganizations at the turn of the century—were fairly numerous.[10] Attention has also focused on the subjudges used in the bankruptcy system, who, for most of the twentieth century, had been known as referees but today are called judges, even though they do not enjoy the full protection of Article III of the Constitution.

It seems to me, however, that the most significant subjudges are neither the special masters nor the bankruptcy judges but the magistrates. They are not specialists but, in background and work, generalists much like the federal district judges. Magistrates handle matters as varied as habeas petitions and social security claims; they manage pretrial discovery, adjudicate petty crimes, and, with the consent of the parties, can try all matter of civil cases. The present scheme contemplates almost six hundred magistrates, which makes them almost as numerous as district judges. The commissioners, whom the magistrates succeeded, were also quite numerous (in 1900 they numbered over eleven hundred), but this statistic obscures important distinctions. The contemporary magistrate is a lawyer and charged with more significant decisional responsibility than were the commissioners; and the magistrates' role will probably increase as Congress entrusts them with more responsibility and as the Supreme Court continues to remove the constitutional objections to this legislative program.[11] It is likely that, in time, the elaboration of the magistrate system will create a permanent corps of subjudges—magistrates are more formally called magistrate judges—and that the second shadow on the bottom level of the pyramid will become a fourth, but somewhat irregular, tier of the federal system.

The Pathologies of Bureaucracy

With the growth of American society, it seems inevitable that the number of judges will increase. Nothing would be more absurd than to assume that the number of judges in 1900 would be sufficient to do justice in 2000. The claims of injustice have grown. Moreover, the social reality that must be analyzed today, and possibly reformed, by a judiciary determined to do justice is infinitely more complex, as are the sources of decision (e.g., precedents, statutes, and law review articles). It thus seems inevitable, and probably desirable, for the judiciary to turn to staff and other auxiliary personnel for help in discharging its duties. The number of personnel who participate in any judicial decision will therefore multiply, as will the total number of judges. Hierarchical relationships will then be created to coordinate the work of all these people and the judicial system will become bureaucratized.

To coordinate the work of all the judges, hierarchy is required by the sheer numbers involved and by certain political and legal imperatives—the need for uniform national norms and for consistent application of these norms. The professional culture that judges share will facilitate coordination, and may indeed be necessary to support and temper the hierarchical relationships, but this common culture is not itself sufficient. Hierarchy is also necessary. On the other hand, the hierarchical relationships between each judge and his or her staff and between judge and subjudge are not attributable to size. Staff and subjudges are distributed to individual judges and to courts throughout the nation, and thus the number of persons whose work must be coordinated is quite limited. The work of a judge and his or her staff could conceivably proceed on a collegial or non-hierarchical basis. But there is a need for hierarchy between a judge and his or her staff, and also between the subjudges and the judge to whom they are assigned. It arises not from size but from inequalities inherent in the constitutional distribution of power: The power to adjudicate is given to judges, not to their staff or to subjudges.

Thus the issue is not whether we have a bureaucracy, for bureaucratization, as I have defined the term, seems inevitable and perhaps desirable. The bureaucratization of the judiciary, like the bureaucratization of the world, cannot be avoided. The issue is a narrower one, namely, whether bureaucratic organizations produce pathologies or dysfunctions that threaten the foundations of the judicial process. If they do, and if we can identify those pathologies, then we may be able to devise institutional arrangements that might contain, or at least alleviate, the seemingly inescapable dangers to the judicial process that such a development presents.

The Weberian Model

There is a strong tradition in sociology, associated with the work of Max Weber, that identifies bureaucracy with rule-governed behavior: A Weberian bureaucrat is an official governed by a rule that prohibits the official from taking individual circumstances into account.[12] According to this tradition, the bureaucratic pathology is excessively rigid behavior, which, in turn, stems from the obligation of the bureaucrat to adhere to the general rules that define the powers and duties of his office.

I question the validity of the Weberian emphasis on rules in any bureaucracy because it ignores the fact that general rules are only one type of hierarchical control.[13] In any event, it seems that the Weberian emphasis has little import for the judicial bureaucracy. Rigidity is not one of the judiciary's sins. Weber himself sensed this point. He did identify the bureaucratic mentality—thinking according to rules—with the legal mentality, and thus often described bureaucratic authority as a rational-legal authority; but he specifically acknowledged that the legal method of England and America (as opposed to that of the Continent) was not bureaucratic. Weber described Anglo-American adjudication as "empirical justice": "Formal judgments are rendered, though not by subsumption under rational concepts, but by drawing on 'analogies' and by depending upon and interpreting concrete 'precedents.'"[14] Weber wrote these words in the early part of the twentieth century, but none of the developments in the intervening years has made his observation less apt.

One part of the judicial bureaucracy does seem to fit the Weberian model—the office of the clerk of the court. The clerk has general rules governing such matters as when briefs should be filed and on what size paper, and presumably the clerk enforces these rules with some regularity. Such behavior no doubt angers many litigators, but there is no evidence (other than the occasional anecdote) suggesting it is excessive. In any case, those complaining about the bureaucratization of the judiciary are rarely concerned with the behavior of the clerks of the court. Instead, the charge of bureaucratization is leveled at those who decide cases (the judges) and at those who participate in the decisional process (law clerks and subjudges). With respect to the non-judicial officers, the Weberian emphasis on rigidity seems wholly inapposite.

At the start, it must be remembered that general rules play an important and wholly legitimate role in any legal system. Adherence to rules is required by the very idea of the rule of law and by the maxim that insists on a "government of laws and not of men." The charge must therefore be that the decisional process manifests excessive rule-bound behavior or excessive rigidity. No one has a standard for determining when adherence to general rules is excessive, but there are several reasons for believing that this condition does not now exist in the judicial bureaucracy and that it will not arise in the immediate future. There is all the difference in the world between the Prussian civil service and the American federal judiciary, even in its present form.

The smaller the number of subordinates for each supervising official, the less the need to rely on general rules as a mechanism of controlling subordinates; and with respect to the judge-staff and judge-subjudge relationships, this number is relatively small. Recent years have seen a proliferation of staff, but the span of control for each supervising official (the judge) has nevertheless remained limited. Indeed, it is minuscule compared to that found in the bureaucratic organizations at the center of Weber's analysis. With respect to elbow clerks, a judge must supervise the work of four people, at most, or, in the case of the Chief Justice, five. The same narrow span of control characterizes the relation between judge and subjudge. Special masters are usually appointed for a particular case, and the judge is not likely to use more than one. The total number of magistrates is significant, and likely to grow, but they are distributed throughout the United States, according to judicial districts, and thus the span of control is also limited. Even in the busiest district, the Southern District of New York, twenty-eight active district judges supervise fifteen magistrates. (The total number of district judges, which includes judges on senior status, is forty-six.) When the span of control is so narrow, judges are likely to avoid general rules and to stress particularized methods of control, such as individual review of the official's work product.

The span of control in the judge-judge relationship has increased in recent years, to the point where only nine justices supervise roughly two hundred and fifty circuit judges, who, in turn, supervise almost one thousand, including both active and senior judges. This has resulted in increased reliance on general rules, as is evidenced by the proliferation of uniform procedural rules (e.g., Federal Rules of Civil Procedure, Federal Rules of Criminal Procedure, Federal Rules of Appellate Procedure, and Federal Rules of Evidence). There are, however, three factors that operate to offset the drive toward rigidity that might otherwise arise from the increased use of general rules. One is the ideological commitment to "empirical justice," which shapes the content of the general rules and leaves them rather open-ended. Another is the role of lawyers, who are given considerable power to shape and control judicial proceedings and constitute the group from which judges are selected. Lawyers are usually commissioned by a specific situation and are devoted to it, and they are likely to carry their perspective onto the bench. A third factor is the relative autonomy of the judges on the lower tiers of the pyramid. Although lower judges, as a formal matter, are bound by general rules, the hierarchy among judges is, in fact, so weak that they can often deviate from general rules with little fear of censure. Admittedly, judges exert stronger control over staff and subjudges than they do over other judges, but, as I pointed out earlier, the narrow span of control in these other relationships reduces the need for general rules. It is also true that judges are unlikely to expect their subordinates (staff and subjudges) to behave bureaucratically in the sense that Weber used the term. Judges are likely to structure their expectations in terms of their own self-image, and that consists of a complicated blend of the specific and the general.

Hannah Arendt's Model

For these reasons I believe that the Weberian model does not fit the American judiciary. Excessive rigidity is not the danger. Given the hold of Max Weber on the sociological imagination and even on everyday usage (where the descriptive usage collapses into the accusatory, and bureaucratic dysfunction is often thought of as rigidity), one might be tempted to dismiss the charge of bureaucratization altogether. But that would be a mistake. There is another intellectual tradition concerned with bureaucratization that has great relevance for the judiciary. It consists of the work of Hannah Arendt, who identifies the pathology of bureaucratization in terms of its impact on the moral character of those who act within the bureaucratic structure. For Arendt, bureaucracy is not so much Weber's Rule by Rules as it is Rule by Nobody. The Arendtian pathology can arise even when the scale of bureaucracy is small and hierarchy is weak. Indeed, as we will see, weak hierarchy often exacerbates the corrosive effect of organizational complexity on individual responsibility.

Arendt's most sustained analysis of bureaucracy appears in her account of Adolf Eichmann, though it appears there only indirectly, largely for the reader to infer from her historical narrative.[15] Her method is to tell a story, in this instance about an operative within the Nazi organization charged with the task of transporting Jews as part of a deportation program and later as part of the Final Solution. In Eichmann, Arendt sees the "banality of evil." By this Arendt does not mean that Eichmann was crass or ordinary, in the way that an uneducated or unsophisticated person might be (though Eichmann was that, too), but rather that he was not motivated by some special hatred toward Jews. He was not demonic but thoughtless. He did not fully consider (through the "soundless dialogue . . . between me and myself"[16] which, for Arendt, constitutes thinking) what he was doing.

As she put it, in what I regard as the crucial sentence of the book, "He merely . . . never realized what he was doing."[17]

There is, of course, a question (of no concern to me here) as to the accuracy of this characterization of Eichmann. There is the further and more important question as to the explanation of this thoughtlessness—not what made Eichmann the person he was, which may be discovered in the details of his biography (of little interest to Arendt), but how a person could exercise the power Eichmann did and yet not realize what he was doing. It is here that bureaucracy emerges as a social structure that makes possible, facilitates, and perhaps even causes the thoughtless use of public power. This can occur in two ways. First, through the fragmentation and compartmentalization of tasks, bureaucracy insulates those acting within it from critical educational experiences. Giving orders that result in transporting Jews to a camp in which they might be killed is far different from arresting individuals, tearing them away from their homes, bringing them to a camp, and clubbing them to death. The bureaucrat does not have to see or in any direct way experience the full scope of the organization's activities. Second, bureaucracy tends to diffuse responsibility. No single individual or group of identifiable individuals bears the full responsibility for the action of the organization. The organization's action is the synthetic product of the action of individuals within the organization (many of whom are not identifiable) and the complicated network of relationships among these individuals, the structure of the organization, which combines and refracts individual actions.

The fragmentation and compartmentalization of tasks that Arendt describes in the Nazi organization is, in fact, present in the American judiciary, and can insulate judges from those critical intellectual experiences that should inform their judgments. To illustrate this danger, consider the use of the magistrate system to rule on motions, for example, to suppress confessions on the ground that they were coerced. Under this system, it is the magistrate who first hears the evidence and applies the law. The magistrate announces a recommended decision and then transmits the decision to the judge, who can decide to hold a full hearing on the motion and listen to the grievance in all its particularity, make a decision, and then justify that decision. The magistrate's inquiry may be viewed as a supplementary procedure that enables the judge to understand the issues better. The issues will be tried twice. There is a great risk, however, that the judge will not use the magistrate in this way but instead will act on the basis of the written transcript and thus delegate the power to decide by merely "rubber stamping" the magistrate's decision. When this happens, the judge does not genuinely consider what the privilege against self-incrimination means, either in the particular case or in general.

The magistrate may well have considered the issue fully, but this is small consolation. When the delegation occurs, the judge has lost the opportunity for the intellectual and moral education that comes from listening, deciding, and justifying a decision; and, after all, it is the judge and not the magistrate who is entrusted with the judicial power of the United States. There is also the danger that the uncertain division of decisional power—an ambiguity in the hierarchical relationship between judge and magistrate—will skew the magistrate's own decisions. A magistrate never fully knows whether he or she is responsible for actually deciding the coerced confession issue or for making a recommendation that will in time be fully scrutinized by a judge.

A case involves a fragmentation of human experience because it represents an artificial and necessarily truncated presentation of a specialized concern. Contemporary injunctive litigation of the structural variety has vastly expanded the parameters of what has been considered a case, all to the good, but limits still exist. I complain of the bureaucratization of the judiciary not because it introduces limits where none exist but because it accentuates or aggravates the fragmentation of human experience that is otherwise endemic to adjudication and the idea of a case. In the example I discussed, one issue—the coerced confession claim—was taken out of the case and given to the magistrate to resolve while the judge played an ill-defined background role. The use of the magistrate insulates the judge from the presentation of the facts and the law on that particular issue, thus accentuating the incompleteness of perspective, and relieving the judge of some of the obligation to explain and justify.

The bureaucratic insularity I have spoken about in the context of the magistrate does not arise from the proliferation of judges, because that pathology requires a fragmentation of the judicial task—giving to someone else part of the job of judging—and neither the duties of a judge nor the parameters of a case is affected by the number of judges. Even with the multiplication of judges, each judge remains assigned to a case, and thus an increase in the total number of judges does not give rise to bureaucratic insularity. On the other hand, bureaucratic insularity is not confined to the magistrate system or to my particular illustration. It arises with other sub-judges as well, for example, a special master charged with the task of formulating and implementing a school desegregation decree. It also arises with law clerks. They have a role, as Judge Harry Edwards insists, in the judicial process, just as much as secretaries do.[18] They can help judges in many of their endeavors; they can assist in research and, through argument and criticism, force judges to reexamine their premises. To the extent, however, that critical components of the judicial process—I am not referring to the typing—are separated and delegated to others, so that the person who hears a case is neither the one who studies the issues nor the one who decides the case nor the one who explains or justifies the result, then the task of judging is fragmented, the judge remains insulated from various components of the process, and the same thoughtlessness that Arendt found in Eichmann may emerge in judicial guise.

Of course, the consequences of judicial thoughtlessness are unlikely ever to be as great or as horrible as those attributable to Eichmann's action—it is hard to believe anything could. On the other hand, in the judicial context, thoughtlessness is not just a personal failing nor one that might be evaluated in terms of the consequences it produces. It represents, instead, a failure of legitimacy. Thoughtlessness refers to the degeneration of the intellectual process through which judges come to know the law and achieve their moral authority. Judges who exercise power without fully engaging in the dialogue that is the source of their authority—who leave it to others to listen to a grievance or to explain a decision—are like biologists who offer opinions they have not tested by the scientific method. They may have hit on the right result, but there is no reason for us to believe that they are right or even that they are likely to be so. They have no claim to our respect. As Chief Justice Charles Evans Hughes insisted, "The one who decides must hear."[19]

Bureaucratization, as Arendt suggests by her account of Eichmann, not only produces a dangerous insularity but also dilutes an individual's sense of responsibility. To the extent that the work of the organization is divided among many people, and is shaped by the organizational structure, the individual need not accept full responsibility for the decisions or actions of the organization. With any organization this would be a loss, because no system of accountability, political or otherwise, will be wholly effective. We always must rely on an individual's sense of responsibility. With the judiciary the loss would be even greater. This, in part, is because of the political independence of the judiciary and the fact that a judge's willingness to assume responsibility for his or her decisions constitutes the primary check on the judicial power. Even more important, a sense of individual responsibility is necessary to animate and motivate the special dialogue that is the source of judicial authority: It supplies the judge's reason for listening and explaining. Responsibility is the essential predicate for thoughtfulness.

The proliferation of staff and subjudges and the delegation of power to them weaken the judge's individual sense of responsibility. The judge acts on the assumption that the decision is the product of "many hands,"[20] and of the complicated network of relationships that exists among the individuals in the organization. The decision is not wholly his or her own. The relatively strong hierarchical relationship between the judge and subordinates ensures that the judge assumes some responsibility for their work—judges must answer for their staff—but this hierarchical relationship does not wholly compensate for the diffusion of responsibility that otherwise occurs.

For one thing, elements of weakness in the hierarchy remain, and they attenuate responsibility. The hierarchy is strongest between judge and elbow clerk, and it can fairly be said that a judge is responsible for his or her clerks; on the other hand, the judge does not individually select or supervise the staff attorneys. It is the chief judge or some committee of judges that selects them, and, as implied by the term *central legal staff*, they serve no particular judge but the court as a whole. Similar distinctions could also be made between different kinds of subjudges. Special masters are chosen by the individual judge and work under the judge's direct supervision. Magistrates, however, are chosen by a majority vote of the judges of the district court and are supervised by no individual judge. In the case of staff attorneys and magistrates the individual judge has only a weak duty of supervision, and thus he or she feels less responsibility for their work.

Moreover, the duty of supervision, even when it is very strong, is not a sufficient substitute for a primary duty like the duty to decide. This can be seen by assuming, first, that a judge delegates power to a special master to devise and implement a school desegregation plan and, second, that the special master fails in the discharge of his duty, so that the desegregation plan is a disaster, from either a constitutional or pragmatic perspective. The judge bears some responsibility for this disaster; she could be said to have breached her duty of supervision by placing an inadequate person in charge or by not looking over the shoulder of the special master with sufficient care. But these breaches of the duty of supervision seem to be of a different and lesser order than would be attributed to the judge had she formulated and implemented the faulty desegregation plan herself. The special master clearly bears some burden for failing to discharge the duty to decide (the primary duty), but he is not the official entrusted with the judicial power of the United States and he can deflect some responsibility for his failure onto the judge who appointed him, assigned him his task, and supposedly looked over his shoulder. In short, the breach of the two duties arising from the division of responsibility within a bureaucratic organization—a delegated duty to decide subject to supervision and the duty to supervise—does not equal the breach of a single individual responsibility within an individualistic framework. One-half plus one-half does not equal one, especially when the connector—the plus, the hierarchy—is weak or ill-defined.

Although I have focused on the relationship between judge and sub-judge in order to explain why the duty of supervision does not wholly compensate for the diffusion of responsibility that occurs when the duty of judging is divided and various components are delegated, I believe that a similar analysis applies to the relationship between judge and staff. No matter how strong the hierarchical relationship, whenever judges use staff to discharge judicial duties they diffuse responsibility. A weak hierarchy only aggravates the problem. The analysis of the diffusion-of-responsibility issue in the context of the judge-judge relationship, however, is more complicated because responsibility among judges is supposed to be shared: No single judge is free to shape the law as he or she believes is right. Individual judges are properly constrained by the interpretations of other judges. They need not accept full responsibility for their decisions in the way that they must when we consider their interaction with their staff and subjudges. Responsibility is shared with other judges. This is the necessary implication of stare decisis, for it entails a sharing of responsibility over time, and it also arises from the hierarchical relationships that exist between judges on different tiers of the pyramid. Lower-court judges must follow orders from higher judges and can rightly shift some measure of responsibility to those who issued the orders. Some district judges may believe, for example, that the Constitution prohibits de facto as well as de jure segregation, but they are obliged by prevailing Supreme Court doctrine to reject claims attacking de facto segregation alone. Such deference is justified by the various normative and institutional considerations that justify the hierarchical relationship among judges: equal treatment under the law, the aspiration for a uniform national law, and the role of the Supreme Court in our constitutional scheme.

In the modern world, judging necessarily entails a sharing of the power and responsibility of decision. The judicial power is exercised through a multitude of judges. We can acknowledge this fact and still be concerned about the endless increase in the number of judges because it splinters the judicial power and tends to reduce the power and responsibility of each individual judge for the law. Admittedly we do not want judges to project their personal predilections; we want them to act as officials, disciplined by the norms of their office and profession. Yet we insist that each judge—as an individual and as an official—accept full responsibility for his or her decisions by signing the opinion. The proliferation of judges lessens the significance of that act for the individual judge and creates the need for complex organizational structures (e.g., informational systems) that inevitably come to shape the course of the law. Responsibility is shared with the multitude of other judges and with the impersonal forces and inanimate mechanisms that so pervade complex organizations. The Rule of Nobody triumphs.

In a bureaucratic world, individual responsibility may give way to corporate responsibility: We may not be able to hold an individual executive responsible for the action of the organization, but we can hold the corporation responsible.[21] We may not be able to hold an individual judge responsible for an outcome, but it might be thought that we can hold the judiciary—as a corporate entity—responsible. We can blame mistakes on the judiciary as a whole, and individual judges would share in that responsibility in some proportion to their role in the organization. Experience teaches, however, that corporate responsibility is a weak substitute for individual responsibility. Once individual responsibility is diffused or blurred to the degree Arendt described, an organization can embark on, or drift into, a course of action that seems to have few limits. In the case of the judicial bureaucracy, this danger is particularly acute because the principle of judicial independence, amply protected by the Constitution, leaves the people served by the organization with very few means indeed for holding the corporate entity accountable. The public can do little more than reverse a particular decision or two, perhaps through a constitutional amendment or by revising a statute perceived to have been interpreted incorrectly or by restricting the jurisdiction of the organization. Such action might be intended as a repudiation of the organization's decision, but it scarcely constitutes a vigorous system of accountability and, in any event, paradoxically places the public in the position of reducing the workload of the organization while continuing to supply it with the same amount of resources.

The Remedies

Joseph Vining, in his article *Justice, Bureaucracy, and Legal Method*, ends his analysis of the bureaucratization of the judiciary with a romantic glance backward. He invites us to rediscover the methods, largely those of an individualistic character, that make law authoritative. He urges us to give more attention to the underpinnings of law and, on only a slightly more constructive note, pleads that we look "anew at the connections and distinctions between lawyers and the practitioners of other disciplines—all disciplines, not just the social sciences."[22] He believes that the bureaucratization of the judiciary can be reversed. I am less sanguine and, precisely because I share so many of his aspirations, feel obliged to speak more specifically about the issue of remedy.

In *Bureaucratic Justice: An Early Warning*, Wade McCree is more specific, but his proposal—to ease the caseload of the courts[23]—rests on questionable premises. First, the growing caseload has not been the only cause of bureaucratization. The need for more staff, for example, stems not only from the increasing caseload but also from the increasing volume and complexity of the information to be processed in contemporary litigation. Second, increasing caseload is itself the result of broader developments that are not within our power to reverse. The growing caseload of the federal judiciary is not a function of the excessive generality of legislation or of excessive judicial innovation but stems from the growing size and complexity of American society. The caseload of the federal judiciary would be enormous today even if jurisdiction were cut back to what might be regarded as an irreducible "central core," for example, to claims arising under federal statutes and the Constitution.[24]

Questions of caseload should not, of course, be ignored; the burden on the system should be reduced wherever possible. But it should also be understood that we will never deal adequately with the problem of bureaucratization and the threats bureaucratization poses to the integrity of the judicial process if caseload is viewed as the exclusive, or even the primary, remedial target and other dimensions of the problem are ignored. I suggest that we view the issue of bureaucratization from another perspective altogether—one that is defined by two premises. The first denies that adjudication is a discrete aberrational process, an intervention by the state needed now and then to settle a dispute that disrupts a just and harmonious society. Adjudication should be seen, instead, like the interventions of the executive and legislative branches, as an exercise of collective power needed on an almost continuous basis to assure that social life conforms to the public values embodied in the Constitution and other authoritative legal texts. The need for judicial intervention will always be great; the caseload of the judiciary will constantly grow; and the claims presented will make enormous informational demands on the judges. Second, bureaucratization should not be seen as an isolated phenomenon occurring only in the judiciary. It is present in all forms of public authority, precisely because bureaucratization is tied to the increasing size and complexity of American society. Indeed, an increase in the organizational capacity of the judiciary (e.g., more judges and staff) may be preferable to the alternatives—constricting jurisdiction, thereby leaving claims of justice unanswered, or instituting mass-production techniques like rulings from the bench and summary dispositions, which is an even greater threat to the legitimacy of the judicial power.[25]

Once the bureaucratization of the judiciary is understood as inevitable, and to some extent desirable, the organizational needs of the judiciary can be dealt with more explicitly. The managerial and adjudicatory functions of judges could be separated, as Judge Alvin Rubin has suggested, and new managerial structures, like a circuit executive, could be created to deal directly and explicitly with organizational needs.[26] Such an arrangement would reflect the fact that the special processes—dialogue and political independence—that have traditionally limited the exercise of the judicial power have no special role to play in resolving managerial questions. These processes may give judges a special competence to explicate public values, but they do not help in managing a complex organization and, in that domain, may in fact prove counterproductive.

Even more important, separating the legal and managerial duties of the judge's job will strengthen that fragile institution of judicial accountability—public criticism. Judges will remain responsible for both their legal and managerial judgments, but, once separated, each type of judgment will have to stand on its own. Each will have to meet a separate and distinct set of criteria. When these judgments are blended together in some indeterminate proportions, however—as they might have been in the *Reynolds v. Sims*[27] one person, one vote formula or in many of the doctrines the Burger and Rehnquist Courts fashioned to establish control over the lower courts[28]—those seeking to evaluate a judicial decision never know whether the proper standard is managerial or legal. They only know that the managerial is becoming increasingly important. The problem is the constantly moving target. Criticism will always be slightly inapposite and the prospect of an abuse of the judicial power that much more real.

Recognizing bureaucratization as an inevitable and, to some degree, desirable feature of the modern judiciary will also enable us to deal more effectively with the two bureaucratic dysfunctions—insulation from critical educational experiences and diffusion of responsibility—that threaten the moral foundations of the judicial power. It will lead to a remedial strategy that focuses on organizational design. The issue is not whether we can eliminate bureaucratization altogether but whether we can contain the dysfunctions or pathologies of bureaucratization, and certain organizational changes may help in that regard. These changes will not, to be sure, dismantle the judicial bureaucracy. That is not our purpose nor is it even possible. They may, however, curb the dysfunctions and thereby preserve the integrity of the judicial process.

In order to expose judges firsthand to the underlying facts of a case and to ensure that judges are responsible for their decisions, an effort should be made to reduce the frequency with which judges appoint special masters. They have been appointed most frequently in cases seeking the structural reform of large-scale organizations, such as schools, prisons, or institutions for the mentally retarded, because of the special need those cases create in terms of social knowledge and representational structure. These cases are critical to a proper discharge of the judicial function, and special masters can help to meet their special needs. But these needs can be met through alternative organizational forms, such as expert witnesses or amici, which do not involve a fragmentation and delegation of the judicial task and thus do not create the bureaucratic dysfunctions that arise from the use of special masters. The judge should therefore be pressed to explore alternative means of meeting the special needs of structural litigation before appointing a special master.[29] In fact, appointing a special master should be an option of last resort.[30]

When it is the judge who creates a subjudge like a special master, there is particular reason to be wary, because the judge has incentives to do it for the wrong reasons, for example, to be shielded from responsibility or relieved of the drudgery that sometimes comes from total immersion in the details of a complex case. Thus judicially created subjudges should be especially disfavored. But there are also reasons to be wary when the legislature creates subjudges, as it did with the magistrates.[31] The legislative creation of subjudges burdens judges with the duties of appointing, supervising, and deciding to retain the subjudges, thereby adding to their managerial tasks. It also brings into being a group of officials who tend to insulate judges from critical educational experiences and diffuse their responsibility. On this score, there is no difference between magistrates and special masters. This is not to deny the need that might have led Congress to the magistrate system in 1968—the rising caseload—but only to suggest that there are good and important reasons for exploring alternative organizational forms for meeting these same needs.

One alternative is simply to create more district and circuit judgeships. In contrast to the proliferation of subjudges, increasing the number of judges does not create the bureaucratic pathology linked to the fragmentation and compartmentalization of task. It does not insulate the judge from critical educational experiences. An increase in the total number of judges does not make any single judge more insulated. I admit that it may dilute judicial responsibility, because any increase in the number of judges will weaken each judge's sense of individual responsibility and will create the need for new organizational structures to minimize the risk of inconsistent and unequal adjudication. But responsibility will be diffused—perhaps to an even greater degree—when subjudges are used to meet the need for more personnel. Subjudges multiply the number of decision makers and create the need for coordinating structures, and thus pose the additional dangers associated with bureaucratic insularity.

Subjudges might be cheaper than an increase in the number of judges, and some might view them as less threatening to the elite status of the federal judge. I, however, doubt that the savings would be decisive and that the special status of the federal judiciary in any important sense depends on the number of judges in the system. Rather, it depends on their role in the political and social system. Justice Rehnquist, arguing the contrary, imagined an increase in the number of the district judges in Kentucky from nine to forty-one by the year 2027, and then asked: "Could anyone seriously maintain that the judicial 'coin' would not [be] somewhat debased by this great increase in its numbers?"[32] I could (depending on what he meant by "somewhat"). But even if I am wrong, and these relatively small changes in number are decisive, the fact is that the "coin" might have to be "debased" in order to avoid the bureaucratic pathologies—and maybe even constitutional objections—associated with meeting the contemporary need for adjudicatory personnel through the use of subjudges.

A second alternative to the use of subjudges is for Congress to create specialized tribunals that would stand outside the bureaucratic pyramid of the general federal system. The tax court and the court of military appeals are examples of what I have in mind. We may, as a result, end up with two or more smaller bureaucracies in the place of one mammoth bureaucracy, and lines of review would have to be created to the Supreme Court. In terms of the integrity of the judicial process, however, more but smaller bureaucracies would be a gain. The larger the bureaucracy, the greater would be the diffusion of responsibility.

Establishing specialized courts also raises questions about the value of a general, non-specialized perspective on legal issues. There is an undeniable freshness and richness to the judgments of a non-specialist. There is also less chance of capture by a special interest group. I would not, therefore, establish a separate, specialized tribunal to deal with school desegregation, to mention one example, but rather would confine this strategy to areas where there is less value to the generalist's insight and less danger of capture. Tax and bankruptcy are perfect examples; admiralty may be another; so may patents. The standard should be, to borrow Justice White's phrase, "extreme specialization."[33]

We should realize, moreover, that we are considering the prospect of creating specialized tribunals under two very special assumptions—first, that we are unwilling to deal with the increased caseload by the creation of new judges of general jurisdiction; and, second, that we are comparing the specialized tribunal with the alternative of creating more subjudges, whose jurisdiction also tends to be specialized. Under these assumptions, the task is not to choose between the generalist and the specialist but how to organize specialists. Subjudges are specialists with considerable power (though perhaps a little less than a specialized tribunal would have). They would, in contrast to the specialized judges, also compound the managerial duties of the general judge, insulate those who decide from those who hear, and diffuse responsibility for decisions.

A remedial strategy that emphasizes alternative organizational forms also has implications for the use of staff. I start with the proposition that staff is indispensable to assist the judge in modern litigation—as indispensable as it is for the modern trial lawyer to be helped by a staff of young associates and paraprofessionals. It is possible, however, to organize the judicial staff in a way that minimizes bureaucratic pathologies. In the case of elbow clerks, who work under the immediate and direct supervision of a particular judge, the judge can institute the optimum organizational arrangement. She simply should keep the clerk at her elbow: She should not delegate any critical component of the decisional process to the clerk, and she should maintain strong supervision over the work that the clerk is allowed to do. The judge will thereby avoid insulating herself from critical educational experiences and minimize the diffusion of responsibility that inevitably comes from the proliferation of staff. The judge should know that she will be held fully responsible for the work, style, and errors of her elbow clerks, and she should organize her staff accordingly.

With respect to the staff attorney, however, we must consider a more radical, more formal change—abolishing the position altogether. This proposal stems from my belief that staff attorneys pose too great a risk of diffusing responsibility precisely because they are responsible to no particular judge but only to the court in general. Staff attorneys usually work under the loose supervision of several judges, but their work is never imputed to any particular judge. They remain faceless, as does much of their work. Indeed, accompanying the advent of the staff attorney is the proliferation of anonymous edicts—the "judgment order" and the "per curiam"—which, oddly enough, are sometimes used to dispose of difficult and far-reaching questions.[34] The use of staff attorneys to screen so-called meritless cases not only produces an anonymous form of justice, but it also tends to insulate judges from the ebb and flow of the law and the full impact of the grievances presented. Judges may need more staff in order to work through their increasing caseload and to help in more complex cases, but their staff should be organized in a way that reinforces rather than diminishes the judge's sense of responsibility, and that increases rather than reduces her participation in the dialogue which is the source of judicial authority.

These suggestions—curbing the use of special masters and other subjudges such as magistrates, strengthening the supervision of elbow clerks, and eliminating staff attorneys altogether—are not meant to be exhaustive. They are meant only to indicate the range of alternatives within a remedial strategy that seeks to end the obsession with caseload and to invite attention to issues of organizational form. They are intended only to render that remedial strategy credible; the list of particular suggestions can and must be continued. I must admit, however, that even when that list is continued, we will be left with a judiciary that is bureaucratized—a highly complex organization that is characterized by a number of hierarchical relationships and that tends to insulate judges from critical educational experiences and to diffuse responsibility. This seems to me to be part of the modern predicament. The world changes—we move from a society of individuals to a society of organizations—yet we must live and work with forms of authority that presuppose a world that no longer exists and that is beyond our power to recall.

The response to this predicament should not be resignation or despair. It would be a mistake to conclude from this analysis that we should renounce the judicial power, for we have no other way of protecting our public values and checking the political branches of the activist state. There are, instead, two other responses that seem most encouraging. One is to reexamine our individualistic ideals and the forms of authority they give rise to; maybe, as Bruce Ackerman suggested at a carefree luncheon, when I was about to begin this paper, bureaucracies can engage in dialogue. The other and, to my mind, more realistic alternative is to search for those small incremental changes in institutional design that may enable us to realize more fully our individualistic ideals within a world of a wholly different character.

5

Against Settlement

Starting in the mid-1970s Chief Justice Burger periodically called on the bar to seek alternatives to adjudication. He viewed adjudication as nothing more than a method to resolve disputes. He thought that more efficient ways could be found to achieve the same purpose. Given the assault on adjudication then afoot in the Supreme Court, Chief Justice Burger's calls were not at all surprising.

What caused a stir was the report issued in the spring of 1983 by Derek Bok, once a law professor, then the president of Harvard University. Supporting the turn away from adjudication, Bok called on law schools to train their students "in the gentler arts of reconciliation and accommodation." Either because of the prominence of Harvard and his position within the university or because Bok had been identified with liberal or progressive causes, most of which, like affirmative action, were anathema to the Chief Justice, the media treated Bok's report as front page news.

Today the Alternative Dispute Resolution (ADR) Movement, as it came to be known, is fully entrenched. It started to gather steam during the late 1970s and early 1980s. In fact, Bok's report, which was part of the process through which it gained institutional support, was issued contemporaneously with the decision of the Association of American Law Schools to establish a new section of its organization that would be devoted to ADR. The initial meeting of the section was to be held in January 1984, as a joint session with the Civil Procedure section. Professor Stephen Burbank of the University of Pennsylvania, then chair of the Civil Procedure section, asked me, along with Leo Levin of Pennsylvania and Marc Galanter of Wisconsin, to participate in a panel discussion celebrating the inauguration of the new ADR section. The result was "Against Settlement," which first appeared in the May 1984 issue of the *Yale Law Journal* (volume 93, page 1073) and is presented here. A companion piece, focusing on consent decrees, entitled "Justice Chicago Style," appeared in the 1987 *University of Chicago Legal Forum* on page 1.

Many responses to "Against Settlement" have appeared. The one published in the 1985 *Yale Law Journal* (volume 94, page 1660), by Andrew McThenia and Thomas Shaffer, entitled "For Reconciliation," introduced a religious dimension. Emphasizing reconciliation as opposed to settlement, Professors McThenia and Shaffer seemed moved by a conception of social organization that takes the insular religious community as its model. As they wrote, "Justice is what we discover—you and I, Socrates said—when we walk together, listen together, and even love one another, in our curiosity about what justice is and where justice comes from" (ibid., 1665).

I responded to Professors McThenia and Shaffer in "Out of Eden" (*Yale Law Journal* 94 [1985]: 1669). In that essay I explained why it was inappropriate to model law and the legal system of modern America on insular religious communities, which are defined by their cohesiveness and the shared experiences of their members. In voicing this criticism, I also made reference to Robert Cover, who, in his rightly famous foreword to the 1983 *Harvard Law Review*, "Nomos and Narrative," also modeled law on the basis of insular religious communities, such as the Mennonites or ancient Hebrews. In that regard, he seemed to be making the same error as McThenia and Shaffer.

Robert Cover depicted law as evolving from the norms of tightly knit communities, and saw the function of the judge as choosing among these norms, killing off some but not others—in his terms, judges are *jurispathetic*, not *jurisgenerative*. During his college days Cover was active in the Civil Rights Movement, and traveled to Albany, Georgia, to protest the Jim Crow regime that governed in that community. Yet I felt that his view of law and, in particular, his declaration in "Nomos and Narrative" that "judges are people of violence" did great disservice to the federal judges who had risked so much to make *Brown* a living reality.

Robert Cover was a very close friend and important colleague. From the days I first joined the Yale faculty in 1974 until his death in 1987, we worked closely on a casebook on procedure. Cover and I often disagreed, but the almost endless conversation with him profoundly shaped my understanding of the law (see *Yale*

Law Journal 96 [1987]: 1717). On his death, Judith Resnik and I went through his papers and found the handwritten beginning of a response to "Out of Eden" and, more broadly, to the views I advanced in "Against Settlement," and the principles on which it rested. His note included this passage:

> I am insistent that the apparent capacity of the courts to fashion a life of shared meaning is always seriously compromised and often destroyed by the violence which is the implicit or explicit threat against those who do not share the judge's understanding. I, like Owen, celebrate the achievements of federal courts in destroying apartheid in America. Like Owen, I favor federal courts taking a lead in reforming institutions when the other officials fail. But it is Fiss not Cover who is the romantic here. It is Fiss who supposes that these achievements emerge out of a shared community of interpretation that is national in character. I support those efforts because I believe them right and justified, because I am sufficiently committed to them to join with others in imposing our will on those who disagree. At times the federal courts have been our allies in those commitments. There is every reason to believe that such a convergence of interests was temporary and accidental; that it is already changing and will soon be a romantic memory of the sublime sixties.

I N a 1983 report to the Harvard Overseers, Derek Bok called for a new direction in legal education.[1] He decried "the familiar tilt in the law curriculum toward preparing students for legal combat," and asked instead that law schools train their students "for the gentler arts of reconciliation and accommodation."[2] He sought to turn our attention from the courts to "new voluntary mechanisms"[3] for resolving disputes. In doing so, Bok echoed themes that have long been associated with Chief Justice Burger[4] and that have become a rallying point for the organized bar as well as the source of a new movement in the law, known as ADR (Alternative Dispute Resolution).

The movement promises to reduce the amount of litigation that is initiated, and, accordingly, the bulk of its proposals are devoted to negotiation and mediation prior to suit. But the interest in the so-called gentler arts has not been confined to these areas alone. It extends to ongoing litigation as well, and the advocates of ADR have sought new ways to facilitate and perhaps even pressure parties into settling pending cases. New procedural rules have been instituted to serve this end. Rule 16 of the Federal Rules of Civil Procedure was amended in 1983 to strengthen the hand of the trial judge in brokering settlements: The "facilitation of settlement" became an explicit purpose of pre-trial conferences, and the judge was invited, if that is the proper word, to take action regarding "settlement or the use of extra-judicial procedures to resolve the dispute."[5]

The advocates of ADR are led to support such rules and, more generally, to exalt the ADR idea of settlement, because they view adjudication as a process to resolve disputes. They act as though courts arose to resolve quarrels between neighbors who had reached an impasse and turned to a stranger for help. According to the now familiar narrative, courts are seen as an institutionalization of the stranger, and adjudication is viewed as the process by which the stranger exercises power. The very fact that the neighbors have turned to someone else to resolve their dispute signifies a breakdown in their social relations; the advocates of ADR acknowledge this, but, nonetheless, they hope that the neighbors will be able to reach agreement before the stranger renders judgment. Settlement is that agreement. It is a truce more than a true reconciliation, but it seems preferable to judgment because it rests on the consent of both parties and avoids the cost of a lengthy trial.

In my view, however, this account of adjudication and the case for settlement rest on questionable premises. I do not believe that settlement as a generic practice is preferable to judgment or should be institutionalized on a wholesale and indiscriminate basis. It should be treated instead as a highly problematic technique for streamlining dockets. Settlement, for me, is the civil analogue of plea bargaining: In both, consent is often coerced; the bargain may be struck by someone without authority; the absence of a trial and judgment renders subsequent judicial involvement troublesome; and, although dockets are trimmed, justice may not be done. Like plea bargaining, settlement is a capitulation to the conditions of mass society and should neither be encouraged nor praised.

The Imbalance of Power

By viewing the lawsuit as a quarrel between two neighbors, the dispute resolution story that underlies ADR implicitly asks us to assume a rough

equality between the contending parties. It treats settlement as the anticipation of the outcome of trial and assumes that the terms of settlement are
simply a product of the parties' predictions of that outcome.[6] In truth,
however, settlement is also a function of the resources available to each
party to finance the litigation, and those resources are frequently distributed unequally. Many lawsuits do not involve a property dispute between
two neighbors but, rather, may concern a struggle between a member of a
racial minority and a municipal police department over alleged brutality
or a claim by a worker against a large corporation over work-related injuries. In these cases the distribution of financial resources, or the ability of
one party to pass along its costs, will invariably infect the bargaining process. Settlement in such cases will be at odds with a conception of justice
that seeks to make the wealth of the parties irrelevant.

The disparities in resources between the parties can influence the settlement in three ways. First, the poorer parties may be less able to amass and
analyze the information needed to predict the outcome of the litigation,
and thus be disadvantaged in the bargaining process. Second, they may
need the damages they seek immediately and thus be induced to settle as a
way of accelerating payment, even though they realize they would get less
now than they might if they awaited judgment. All plaintiffs want their
damages immediately, but rich defendants may exploit indigent plaintiffs
whose need is so great that the defendants can force them to accept a sum
that is less than the present value of the anticipated judgment. Third,
poorer parties might be forced to settle because they do not have the resources to finance the litigation, to cover either their own projected expenses, such as their lawyers' time, or the expenses their opponent can
impose through the manipulation of procedural mechanisms such as discovery. It might seem that plaintiffs would benefit by a settlement because
it would allow them to avoid the costs of litigation, but this is not so. Defendants can anticipate plaintiffs' costs were the case to be tried fully, and
then decrease their offer by that amount. Indigent plaintiffs are victims of
the costs of litigation even if they settle.

There are exceptions. Seemingly rich defendants may sometimes be
subject to financial pressures that make them as anxious to settle as indigent plaintiffs. But I doubt that these circumstances occur with great frequency. I also doubt that institutional arrangements such as contingent
fees or the provision of legal services to the poor will, in fact, equalize resources between contending parties. The contingent fee does not equalize
resources; it only makes indigent plaintiffs vulnerable to the willingness of

the private bar to invest in their cases. In effect, the ability to exploit the plaintiffs' lack of resources has been transferred from rich defendants to lawyers, who insist upon a hefty slice of plaintiffs' recovery as their fee. These lawyers, moreover, will only work for contingent fees in certain kinds of cases, such as personal-injury suits, and the contingent fee is of no avail when the defendant is the disadvantaged party. Government subsidies for legal services have a broader potential, but in the civil domain the battle for these subsidies has been hard-fought, and what has been obtained is increasingly limited, especially when it comes to cases that seek systemic reform of government practices.

Of course, imbalances of power can distort judgment as well: Resources influence the quality of presentation, which, in turn, has an important bearing on who wins and the terms of victory. We count, however, on the guiding presence of the judge, who can employ a number of measures to lessen the impact of distributional inequalities. The judge can, for example, supplement the parties' presentations by asking questions, calling witnesses, and inviting other persons and institutions to participate as amici.[7] These measures are likely to make only a small contribution toward moderating the influence of distributional inequalities, but they should not be ignored for that reason. Not even these small steps are possible with settlement. There is, moreover, a critical difference between settlement, which is based on bargaining and accepts inequalities of wealth as an integral and legitimate component of the process, and judgment, which knowingly struggles against those inequalities. Judgment aspires to autonomy from distributional inequalities, and it gathers much of its appeal from that aspiration.

The Absence of Authoritative Consent

The argument for settlement presupposes that the contestants are individuals. These individuals speak for themselves and therefore should be bound by the rules they generate. In many situations, however, individuals are ensnared in contractual relationships that impair their autonomy. Lawyers or insurance companies might, for example, agree to settlements that are in their own interests but are not in the best interests of their clients, and to which their clients would not agree if the choice were still theirs.[8] But a deeper and more intractable problem arises from the fact that many parties are not individuals but rather organizations or groups.

We do not know who is entitled to speak for these entities and to give the consent that so much of the appeal of settlement depends on.

Some organizations, such as corporations or unions, have formal procedures for identifying the persons who are authorized to speak for them. But these procedures are imperfect: They are designed to facilitate transactions between the organization and outsiders, rather than to insure that the members of the organization in fact agree with a particular decision. Nor do they eliminate conflicts of interests. The chief executive officer of a corporation may settle a suit to prevent embarrassing disclosures about leaders' managerial policies, but such disclosures might well be in the interest of the shareholders. The leaders of the union may agree to a settlement as a way of preserving their power within the organization; for that very reason, they may not risk the dangers entailed in consulting the rank and file or in subjecting the settlement to ratification by the membership. Moreover, the representational procedures found in corporations, unions, or other private organizations are not universal. Much contemporary litigation, especially in the federal courts, involves government agencies,[9] and the procedures in those organizations for generating authoritative consent are far cruder than those in the corporate context. We are left to wonder, for example, whether the attorney general should be able to bind all state officials, some of whom are elected and thus have an independent mandate from the people, or even whether the incumbent attorney general should be able to bind his or her successor.

These problems become even more pronounced when we turn from organizations and consider the fact that much contemporary litigation involves even more nebulous social entities, namely, groups. Some of these groups, such as ethnic or racial minorities, inmates of prisons, or residents of institutions for mentally retarded people, may have an identity or existence that transcends the lawsuit, but they do not have any formal organizational structure and therefore lack any procedures for generating authoritative consent. The absence of such a procedure is even more pronounced in cases involving a group of consumers—for example, passengers on some particular airline during a specific period of time—which is constructed solely in order to create funds large enough to make it financially attractive for lawyers to handle the case.

The class action rule of the federal courts requires that such groups have a representative; this representative purports to speak on behalf of the group but receives his or her power by the most questionable of all elective procedures—self-appointment or, if we are dealing with a defendant class, appointment by an adversary. The rules contemplate notice to the members of the group about the pendency of the action and the claims of the representative, but it is difficult to believe that notice could reach all members of the group or that it could cure the defects in the procedures by which the representative is appointed. The forces that discourage most members of the group from stepping forward to initiate suits will also discourage them from responding to whatever notice may reach them.

Going to judgment does not altogether eliminate the risk of unauthorized action, any more than it eliminates the distortions arising from disparities in resources. The case presented by the representative of a group or an organization admittedly will influence the outcome of the suit, and that outcome will bind those who might also be bound by a settlement. On the other hand, judgment does not ask as much from the so-called representatives. There is a conceptual and normative distance between what the representatives do and say, and what the court eventually decides, because the judge tests those statements and actions against independent procedural and substantive standards. The authority of judgment arises from the law, not from the statements or actions of the putative representatives, and thus we allow judgment to bind persons not directly involved in the litigation even when we are reluctant to have settlement do so.

The procedures that have been devised for policing the settlement process when groups or organizations are involved have not eliminated the difficulties of generating authoritative consent. Some of these procedures provide a substantive standard for the approval of the settlement and do not even consider the issue of consent. A case in point is the Tunney Act. The Act establishes procedures for giving outsiders notice of a proposed settlement in a government antitrust suit and requires the judge to decide whether a settlement proposed by the Department of Justice is in "the public interest."[10] This statute implicitly acknowledges the difficulty of determining who is entitled to speak for the United States in some authoritative fashion and yet provides the judge with virtually no guidance in making this determination or in deciding whether to approve the settlement. The public-interest standard, in fact, seems to invite the consideration of such nonjudicial factors as popular sentiment and the efficient allocation of prosecutorial resources.[11]

Other policing mechanisms, such as the rule governing class actions, make no effort to articulate a substantive standard for approving settlements but, instead, entrust the whole matter to the judge.[12] In such cases the judge's approval theoretically should turn on whether the group consents, but determining whether such consent exists is often impossible, since true consent consists of nothing less than the expressed unanimity of all the members of a group, which might number in the hundreds of thousands and be scattered across the United States. The judge's approval, instead, turns on how close or far the proposed settlement is from what he or she imagines would be the judgment obtained after suit. The basis for approving a settlement, contrary to what the dispute resolution story suggests, is therefore not consent but rather the settlement's approximation to judgment. This might appear to remove my objection to settlement, except that the judgment being used as a measure of the settlement is very odd indeed: It has never in fact been entered, but only imagined. It has been constructed without benefit of a full trial and at a time when the judge can no longer count on the thorough presentation promised by the adversary system. The contending parties have struck a bargain, and they have every interest in defending the settlement and convincing the judge that it is in accord with the law.

Lack of Foundation for Judicial Supervision

The dispute resolution story trivializes the remedial dimensions of lawsuits and mistakenly assumes judgment to be the end of the process. It supposes that the judge's duty is to declare which neighbor is right and which is wrong, and that this declaration will end the judge's involvement (save in that most exceptional situation where it is also necessary for the judge to issue a writ directing the sheriff to execute the declaration). Under these assumptions, settlement appears as an almost perfect substitute for judgment, for it, too, can declare the parties' rights. As explained in *The Forms of Justice* (chapter 1), however, judgment is often not the end of a lawsuit but only the beginning. The involvement of the court may continue almost indefinitely. In such cases settlement cannot provide an adequate basis for that necessary continuing involvement, and thus it is no substitute for judgment.

The parties may sometimes be locked in combat with one another and view the lawsuit as only one phase in a long continuing struggle. The entry of judgment will then not end the struggle but rather change its terms and the balance of power. One of the parties will invariably return to the court and again ask for its assistance, not so much because conditions have changed but because the conditions that preceded the lawsuit have unfortunately not changed. This often occurs in domestic-relations cases, where the divorce decree represents only the opening salvo in an endless series of skirmishes over custody and support.[13]

The structural reform cases that play such a prominent role on the federal docket provide another occasion for continuing judicial involvement. In these cases courts seek to safeguard public values by restructuring large-scale bureaucratic organizations. The task is enormous, and our knowledge of how to restructure ongoing bureaucratic organizations is limited. As a consequence, courts must oversee and manage the remedial process for a long time—maybe forever. This, I fear, is true of most school desegregation cases, some of which have been pending for thirty years or more. It is also true of antitrust cases that seek divestiture or reorganization of an industry.

The drive for settlement knows no bounds and can result in a consent decree even in the kinds of cases I have just mentioned, that is, even when a court finds itself embroiled in a continuing struggle between the parties or must reform a bureaucratic organization. The parties may be ignorant of the difficulties ahead or optimistic about the future, or they may simply believe that they can get more favorable terms through a bargained-for agreement. Soon, however, the inevitable happens: One party returns to court and asks the judge to modify the decree, either to make it more effective or less stringent. But the judge is at a loss: There is no basis for assessing the request. The judge cannot, to use Cardozo's somewhat melodramatic formula, easily decide whether the "dangers, once substantial, have become attenuated to a shadow,"[14] because, by definition, there were never any findings about the dangers.

The allure of settlement largely derives from the fact that it avoids the need for a trial. Settlement must thus occur before the trial is complete and the judge has entered findings of fact and conclusions of law. As a consequence, a judge, who is confronted with a request for modification of a consent decree and is faithful to the Cardozo standard, would have to retrospectively reconstruct the situation that existed at the time the decree was entered and decide whether conditions today had sufficiently changed to warrant a modification in that decree. In the Meat Packers litigation, for example, where a consent decree governed the industry for almost half a century, the judge confronted with a request for modification in 1960 had to reconstruct the "dangers" that had existed at the time of the entry of the decree in 1920 in order to determine whether the danger had, in fact, become a "shadow."[15] Such an inquiry borders on the absurd and is likely to dissipate whatever savings in judicial resources the initial settlement may have produced.[16]

Settlement also impedes vigorous enforcement, which sometimes requires use of the contempt power. As a formal matter, contempt is available to punish violations of a consent decree. But courts hesitate to use that power to enforce decrees that rest solely on consent, especially when enforcement is aimed at high public officials, as became evident in the Willowbrook deinstitutionalization case[17] and the Chicago desegregation case.[18] Courts do not see a mere bargain between the parties as a sufficient foundation for the exercise of their coercive powers.

Sometimes the agreement between the parties extends beyond the terms of the decree and includes stipulated "findings of fact" and "conclusions of law," but even then an adequate foundation for a strong use of the judicial power is lacking. Given the underlying purpose of settlement— to avoid trial—the so-called findings and conclusions are necessarily the products of a bargain between the parties rather than of a trial and an independent judicial judgment. Of course, a plaintiff is free to drop a lawsuit altogether (provided that the interests of certain other persons are not compromised), and a defendant can offer something in return, but that bargained-for arrangement more closely resembles a contract than an injunction. It raises a question, which has already been answered whenever an injunction is issued, namely, whether the judicial power should be used to enforce it. Even assuming that the consent is freely given and authoritative, the bargain is at best contractual and does not contain the kind of enforcement commitment already embodied in a decree that is the product of a trial and the judgment of a court.

Justice Rather Than Peace

The dispute resolution story makes settlement appear as a perfect substitute for judgment, as we just saw, by trivializing the remedial dimensions of a lawsuit and also by reducing the social function of the lawsuit to one of resolving private disputes. In that story, settlement appears to achieve exactly the same purpose as judgment—peace between the parties—but at considerably less expense to society. The two quarreling neighbors turn to a court in order to resolve their dispute, and society makes courts available because it wants to aid in the achievement of their private ends or to secure the peace.

In my view, however, the purpose of adjudication should be understood in broader terms. Adjudication uses public resources, and it employs not strangers chosen by the parties but public officials chosen by a process in which the public participates. These officials, like members of the legislative and executive branches, possess a power that has been defined and conferred by public law, not by private agreement. Their job is not to maximize the ends of private parties nor simply to secure the peace but to explicate and give force to the values embodied in authoritative texts such as the Constitution and statutes: Their job is to interpret those values and to bring reality into accord with them. This duty is not discharged when the parties settle.

In our political system, courts are reactive institutions. They do not search out interpretive occasions but, instead, wait for others to bring matters to their attention. They also largely rely on others to investigate and present the law and facts. A settlement will thereby deprive a court of the occasion, and perhaps even the ability, to render an interpretation. A court cannot proceed (or cannot proceed very far) in the face of a settlement. To be against settlement is not to urge that parties be "forced" to litigate, since that would interfere with their autonomy and distort the adjudicative process.

To be against settlement is only to suggest that when the parties settle society gets less than what appears, and at a price it does not know it is paying. Although the parties will be inclined to make the court believe that their bargain is justice, they might well settle while leaving justice undone. The settlement of a school suit might secure the peace but not racial equality. Although the parties are prepared to live under the terms they bargained for, and although such peaceful coexistence may be a necessary precondition of justice[19] and itself a state of affairs to be valued, it is not justice itself. To settle for something means to accept less than some ideal.

I recognize that judges often announce settlements not with a sense of frustration or disappointment, as my account of adjudication might suggest, but with a sigh of relief. But this sigh should be seen for precisely what it is. It is not a recognition that a job is done, nor is it an acknowledgment that a job need not be done because justice has been secured. Rather, it may express another sentiment altogether, namely, that one more case has been "moved along," which is true whether or not justice has been done. Or the sigh might be based on the fact that the agony of judgment has been avoided.

Sometimes, of course, there is a value to avoidance. This value is not just for the judge, who is thereby relieved of the need to make or enforce a hard decision, but also for society, which sometimes thrives by masking its basic contradictions. But will settlement result in avoidance when it is most appropriate? Other familiar avoidance devices, such as certiorari,[20] at least promise a devotion to public ends. Settlement is controlled by the litigants, and is subject to their private motivations and all the vagaries of the bargaining process. There are also dangers to avoidance, and these may well outweigh any imagined benefits. Partisans of ADR—Chief Justice Burger or even President Bok—may begin with a certain satisfaction with the status quo. But when one sees injustices that cry out for correction—as Congress did when it endorsed the concept of the private attorney general and as the Court of another era did when it sought to enhance access to the courts—the value of avoidance diminishes and the agony of judgment becomes a necessity. Someone has to confront the betrayal of our deepest ideals and be prepared to turn the world upside down to bring those ideals to fruition.

The Real Divide

One can readily imagine a simple response to all this by way of confession and avoidance: We are not talking about *those* lawsuits. Advocates of ADR might insist that my account of adjudication, in contrast to the one implied by the dispute resolution story, focuses on a rather narrow category of lawsuits. They could argue that, while settlement may have only the most limited appeal with respect to those cases, I have not spoken to the "typical" case. My response is twofold.

First, even in purely quantitative terms, I doubt that the number of cases I am referring to is trivial. My universe includes those cases in which there are significant distributional inequalities; those in which it is difficult to generate authoritative consent because organizations or social groups are parties or because the power to settle is vested in autonomous agents; those in which the court must continue to supervise the parties after judgment; and those in which justice needs to be done (or to put it more modestly, where there is a genuine social need for an authoritative interpretation of law). I imagine that the number of cases that satisfy one of these four criteria is considerable; in contrast to the kind of case portrayed in the dispute resolution story, such cases probably dominate the docket of a modern court system.

Second, to be concerned only with the number of cases demands a certain kind of myopia, as though all cases are equal simply because the clerk of the court assigns each a single docket number. All cases are not equal. A desegregation case, for example, is not equal to the allegedly more typical suit involving a property dispute or an automobile accident. The desegregation suit consumes more resources, affects more people, and provokes far greater challenges to the judicial power. The ADR Movement must take a more qualitative perspective; it must speak to these more significant cases and demonstrate the propriety of settling them. Otherwise, the movement will soon be seen as an irrelevance, dealing with trivia rather than responding to the very conditions that give it its greatest sway and saliency.

Nor would sorting cases into "two tracks," one for settlement and another for judgment, avoid my objections. Settling automobile cases and leaving discrimination or antitrust cases for judgment might remove a large number of cases from the dockets, but the dockets will nevertheless remain burdened with the cases that consume the most judicial resources and represent the most controversial exercises of the judicial power. A two-track strategy would drain the argument for settlement of much of its appeal. I also doubt whether the two-track strategy can be sensibly implemented, simply because it is so difficult to formulate adequate criteria for prospectively sorting cases. The problems of settlement are not tied to the subject matter of the suit but, instead, stem from factors that are harder to identify, such as the wealth of the parties, the likely post-judgment history of the suit, and the need for an authoritative interpretation of law. It is, moreover, hard to see how these problems can be avoided. Many of the factors that lead a society to bring social relationships that otherwise seem wholly private (e.g., marriage) within the jurisdiction of a court, such as imbalances of power or the interests of third parties, are also likely to make settlement problematic. Settlement is a poor substitute for judgment; it is an even poorer substitute for the withdrawal of jurisdiction.

For these reasons, I remain highly skeptical of a two-track strategy and would resist it. But the more important point to note is that most ADR advocates make no effort to distinguish between different types of cases or to suggest that "the gentler arts of reconciliation and accommodation" might be particularly appropriate for one type of case but not for another. They lump all cases together. This suggests that what divides me from the partisans of ADR is not that we are concerned with different universes of cases, that Derek Bok, for example, focuses on boundary quarrels while I see only desegregation suits. I suspect, instead, that what divides us is much deeper and stems from our understanding of the purpose of the civil lawsuit and its place in society. It is a difference in outlook.

Someone like Bok sees adjudication in essentially private terms: The purpose of lawsuits and the civil courts is to resolve disputes, and the amount of litigation we encounter is evidence of the needlessly combative and quarrelsome character of Americans. Or, as Bok put it, using a more diplomatic idiom: "At bottom, ours is a society built on individualism, competition, and success."[21] I, on the other hand, see adjudication in more public terms: Civil litigation is an institutional arrangement for using state power to bring a recalcitrant reality closer to our chosen ideals. We turn to the courts because we need to, not because of some quirk in our personalities. We train our students in the tougher arts so that they may help secure all that the law promises, not because we want them to become gladiators or because we take a special pleasure in combat.

To conceive of the civil lawsuit in public terms as America does might be unique. I am willing to assume that no other country—including Japan, Bok's paragon[22]—has a case like *Brown v. Board of Education* in which the judicial power is used to eradicate a caste structure. I am willing to assume that no other country conceives of law and uses law in quite the way we do, or at least the way we once did. But this should be a source of pride rather than shame. What is unique is not the problem that we live short of our ideals but that we alone among the nations of the world seem willing to do something about it. Adjudication American-style is not a reflection of our combativeness but rather a tribute to our inventiveness and, perhaps even more, to our commitment to our chosen ideals.

6

The Allure of Individualism

The structural model emphasizes the representative character of all lawsuits—the participants speak not only for themselves but also for countless others. If all goes well, the cause of those represented will be advanced, but the risk is ever present that the representatives will fail and that those represented will suffer the consequences the representation provided. The underlying premise is that the action of the representative—good or bad—will be binding on individuals who do not formally participate in the lawsuit. Yet such a rule conflicts with the axiom, arguably resting on the most elemental notion of procedural fairness, that guarantees to each individual the right to participate in any judicial proceeding that will be binding on that individual.

This conflict between the suppositions of structural litigation and the right of participation came into sharp focus in the 1989 decision in *Martin v. Wilks*. In that case the Supreme Court reopened a judgment that had provided a measure of preferential treatment to blacks seeking promotion in the Birmingham Fire Department. The judgment in question was intended to remedy discriminatory procedures of the fire department and was reopened at the behest of white firefighters, who had not been allowed to participate in the lawsuit but whose interest was purportedly represented by the City of Birmingham. William Rehnquist, by then the Chief Justice, wrote the Supreme Court's opinion. In this chapter I focus on *Martin v. Wilks* and analyze the contested right of participation advanced by the white firefighters. The essay was first published in the July 1993 issue of the *Iowa Law Review* (volume 78, page 965).

From the very beginning *Martin v. Wilks* divided the civil rights community. Many criticized it, and certain provisions of the Civil Rights Act of 1991 sought to overturn the Court's ruling. Some civil rights lawyers were of another mind. They understood the practical implications of the decision for the structural injunction but were unprepared to compromise the right of participation or to trust the city to be an adequate representative for the white fire-fighters. An important statement of this position can be found in Samuel Issacharoff's essay "When Substance Mandates Procedure: *Martin v. Wilks* and the Rights of Vested Incumbents in Civil Rights Consent Decrees" published in the *Cornell Law Review* in 1992, starting at page 189. It was therefore not at all surprising that, when Peter Shane, then a professor of law at the University of Iowa, invited me to present a paper to the Remedies Section of the American Association of Law Schools, I chose to focus on *Martin v. Wilks*. The subject of the meeting, which was held in San Francisco in January 1993, was "Public Law Remedies in the Nineties: The Rehnquist Court's War on the Civil Rights Injunction."

I shared the podium with Professor Douglas Laycock of the University of Texas and Professor Susan Sturm, then of the University of Pennsylvania, now at Columbia University. Like Peter Shane, as well as a large number of persons in the audience (including Samuel Issacharoff), Laycock and Sturm were my former students and they paid their former teacher the highest compliment—they brilliantly and passionately disagreed with almost all I had to say. Laycock accused me of sacrificing due process for civil rights, and Sturm explained how essential full participation is for the efficacy of decrees. Their papers were published in the same issue of the *Iowa Law Review*.

CIVIL rights remedies take many forms, but none is as significant as the structural injunction. It is the formal medium through which the judiciary seeks to reorganize ongoing bureaucratic organizations so as to bring them into conformity with the Constitution. The structural injunction represents the most distinctive contribution of the civil rights era to our remedial jurisprudence, and though the structural injunction has been used in all manner of cases—housing, mental health, and prisons—its origins must never be forgotten. The structural injunction received its most authoritative formulation in school desegregation cases and achieved its legitimacy through those cases. To defend structural relief, reference will always be made to *Brown v. Board of Education* and the duty it imposed on the courts of the nation to transform dual school systems into constitutionally acceptable forms.

The fate of the structural injunction has also been tied to that of the Civil Rights Movement. The remedy grew in power and scope over a twenty-year period, beginning in 1954 and continuing until 1974. Ever since, it has been under attack. William Rehnquist has led the assault, first as an Associate Justice and later as Chief Justice. He sees the structural injunction as the epitome of Warren Court activism and appears determined to curb that remedy in all manner of ways. Now and then, a narrow majority of the Court has managed to defeat his purposes, but the formation of such coalitions has been the exception. The structural injunction has suffered many defeats over the last twenty-five years, and has been confined and enfeebled by a plethora of devices.

This essay addresses one such device, created by Rehnquist in *Martin v. Wilks*,[1] a 1989 case involving a structural decree seeking to end racial discrimination against blacks in the Birmingham Fire Department. A group of firefighters who were not parties to the initial proceeding in which the decree was entered claimed that the decree was invalid because it required unconstitutional actions by the city. These firefighters were white and complained specifically that the system of preferences for blacks created by the decree was a form of "reverse discrimination." In an opinion by Chief Justice Rehnquist, a narrow majority held that the white firefighters were entitled to a full hearing on the merits of their claim.

The Chief Justice based his ruling in terms of technical preclusion rules, more specifically, the notion that individuals cannot be bound by a previous adjudication in which they did not participate. However, the decision in *Martin v. Wilks* has far-reaching implications for all structural injunctions, rendering them vulnerable to collateral attack and thus interfering with the implementation process. The irony is that, whereas in other areas of the law, most notably in reviewing state criminal convictions,[2] Rehnquist and a number of other Justices have insisted on the need for finality and remedial efficacy, in the context of the structural injunction these very same values were thrown to the wind.

I believe that the doctrine announced in *Martin v. Wilks* will have great practical importance, for it placed all structural decrees under a cloud of uncertainty. But in choosing it as my subject, I do not mean to suggest that, of all the devices created by the Court in recent decades to cabin the structural injunction, the rule of *Martin v. Wilks* is the most efficacious. Rather, my choice of topic reflects another consideration altogether. I focus on *Martin v. Wilks* because it makes claim to a value—providing every citizen a day in court—that resonates with members of the legal profession, myself included, who are deeply attached to the structural injunction and the substantive values it seeks to further. *Martin v. Wilks* may not be the most important practical setback for the structural injunction, but it is the most defensible. It is a hard case, maybe the hardest; it has divided the civil rights community and even put friends of the structural injunction at odds with one another.[3]

At the heart of *Martin v. Wilks* is what I call the right of participation. It postulates that every person is entitled to a day in court and that no one can have his or her substantive rights determined by a court without having participated in the proceeding.[4] However, the formal basis or nature of the right of participation is not clear. At various points in his opinion, Chief Justice Rehnquist invoked the Federal Rules of Civil Procedure. Although Rehnquist seemed to acknowledge the undesirable consequences that will flow from his ruling—structural decrees will forever be open to relitigation—he insisted that he had no choice. He said that the result is required by the Rules and that he is bound by the Rules.

I take issue with both these assertions, but there is no need to engage the Chief Justice on this level, for if *Martin v. Wilks* rests on the Rules, it has subsequently been undermined by the Civil Rights Act of 1991.[5] That Act sought to alter the result in *Martin v. Wilks* and, in so doing, disputed Rehnquist's reading of the Rules and his claim that the Rules give rise to a right of participation. Congress should have the last word when it comes to construing the Rules, for they are promulgated pursuant to a congressional statute and obtain whatever authority they possess from that statute.

Some might let the matter rest with the Civil Rights Act but I cannot, because I fear that *Martin v. Wilks* is a due process, not a Rules, decision. Rehnquist quoted Justice Brandeis's opinion in *Chase National Bank v. Norwalk*[6] and, in so doing, suggested that the Rules codify a more fundamental principle of our jurisprudence. The Chief Justice also spoke of a deep historical tradition that guarantees to everyone a day in court.[7] I am not sure there is any such tradition, but, if there is, *Martin v. Wilks* would survive any attempt by Congress to alter those requirements.

Martin v. Wilks involved a decree entered on the basis of consent rather than a full adjudication, and my concern with the decision would be considerably diminished if it were so confined. This is not to diminish or over-look the role of consent decrees in structural litigation but only to recognize their specific limitations. As explained in "Against Settlement" (chapter 5), consent decrees are essentially contracts and obtain their authority from the consent of the parties as opposed to a judgment of a court of law.[8] As a contract, all affected parties must consent to it, for simple justice requires that a contract should not bind anyone who has not participated in its creation.

Considerations of remedial efficacy also dictate a generous measure of inclusiveness when it comes to consent decrees. The comparative efficacy of consent decrees is difficult to judge, because they are only a poor approximation of what would have been obtained after a full adjudication; like the outcome of any bargaining process, they turn on a myriad of strategic considerations that have little to do with justice. Nevertheless, the claimed efficacy of consent decrees stems from the entirely plausible hypothesis that people are more likely to do what they have agreed to do than what they are ordered to do. To capture this advantage, however, it is essential to obtain the consent of all the people who are needed to implement the decree or who otherwise will be affected by it, or at least to allow them to participate in its formulation.[9]

Thus, whether the concern is justice or a proper regard for remedial efficacy, I would be inclined to support the rule of *Martin v. Wilks* if it were confined to consent decrees. The white firefighters of Birmingham should not be precluded from challenging the constitutionality of action that the city was prepared to take pursuant to the consent decree, since they were in no sense parties to the agreement. *Martin v. Wilks* does not, however, turn on the negotiated character of the decree. It threatens to prevent any decree, even one fully litigated, from binding those who did not participate in the proceeding that led to its issuance. In *Martin v. Wilks* the Chief Justice declared that "a person cannot be deprived of his legal rights in a proceeding in which he is not a party,"[10] and this declaration was in no way limited to consent decrees nor made dependent on the fact that the decree in question was entered on the basis of a negotiation between the parties. *Martin v. Wilks* would come out exactly the same way, I venture to say, even if it had been fully litigated.

To test this hypothesis, and to explore more fully the consequences of such a rule, imagine a lawsuit in which there is a claim by black firefighters against a municipal fire department. There is a full trial on the merits, a judgment that the defendant fire department discriminated on the basis of race in initial hires and promotions, a hearing on the remedy, and then the issuance of a strong decree. Such a decree might require an aggressive recruitment program aimed at blacks; a prohibition against discrimination in the future; and, to compensate for past discrimination, a preferential treatment program intended to give blacks an advantage in both initial hires and promotions. To give the preferential program some bite, assume that the decree also contains goals and timetables.

Let us further assume that persons such as the white firefighters, who were not parties to the case but who will be adversely affected, subsequently attack the decree. They claim that the system of preferential treatment is a form of unjust discrimination and thus unconstitutional. In resolving this claim, the trial court might be constrained by considerations of stare decisis but not, according to *Martin v. Wilks*, by the tougher preclusion rules of res judicata and collateral estoppel. The trial court would have to give the white firefighters a full hearing on their claim even though, before entering the decree, the court had already concluded that such preferences were constitutional, indeed necessary, to correct for the past violations. Even if it is unlikely that the white firefighters will prevail on the merits, these new challengers could not be precluded from adjudicating the issue afresh since they did not participate in the initial proceedings. They did not have their day in court.

I take this to be the true import of *Martin v. Wilks*, and one can see at a moment's glance the unsettling consequences of such a rule. It exposes every decree to the risk of a subsequent challenge, actually to an almost endless series of such challenges. Ultimately the trial court may decide the subsequent challenge has no merit, and the precedential value of the earlier decision may help it to reach that conclusion, but the very need to adjudicate the merits of the challenge will postpone the implementation of the decree. That postponement will last as long as is needed to litigate the merits of the claim attacking the decree, and that period will be considerably extended because the trial court cannot invoke the stronger preclusion doctrines to dismiss the challenge.

At various points in his opinion, the Chief Justice tried to minimize the consequences of his ruling by claiming that finality could be achieved and the right of participation honored by joining all the would-be challengers as parties in the initial proceeding. Although this response might be adequate in some contexts, in the structural context it is not. Two features of the structural injunction make the kind of joinder Rehnquist envisioned a virtual impossibility.

One is the simple fact that structural injunctions affect countless people, indeed the entire public. Consider, for example, the number of people affected by the typical school desegregation decree: every child and family in the school district; teachers and administrators; residents and shopkeepers in the areas close to the schools; police and transportation officials who will have their schedules and workloads affected; and, of course, the taxpayers of the school district who will have to shoulder the financial burden of the busing plan. Fewer persons may have to be joined in an employment case like *Martin v. Wilks* to give effect to the right of participation, but not significantly so. The persons affected would include all the present workers, managerial personnel, new applicants, the owners of the firm, or, in the case of a government agency, the taxpayers, and the customers or those otherwise dependent on the service provided by the firm or agency.

Granted, there is an ambiguity in Rehnquist's conception of the universe of persons to be joined: At some points he speaks very broadly of all those "who could be adversely affected by a decree,"[11] but at other times he refers more restrictively to someone who will "be deprived of his legal rights."[12] The narrower reading would lessen the damage wrought by *Martin v. Wilks*, but that damage would still remain substantial, for the group of possible challengers to a structural decree—those who could advance a legal claim against its validity—is enormous. Is there any interest today that cannot be transformed into a legal claim? It is also important to bear in mind that *Martin v. Wilks* requires not that these interests be adequately represented, which might be manageable, but that each of the individuals adversely affected be joined in the initial proceeding. Joinder of that magnitude is simply not manageable. Indeed, it is hard to imagine what such a lawsuit might look like.

A second difficulty with Rehnquist's response that finality can be achieved through joinder, stems from the forward-looking aspects of structural decrees. Because structural injunctions seek to reorganize bureaucratic organizations, they will necessarily affect people who, at the moment of the initial suit, have no relationship whatsoever to the organization but who may be brought into contact with the organization at some later day, and only then be adversely affected by the decree. Reorganizing the Birmingham Fire Department will affect not only those who are working for the department today but those who one day may seek employment in the department—many of whom are not in the community at the moment or perhaps some who may not even have been born at the time of the suit. As a result, the joinder Rehnquist offers by way of consolation is not simply impractical but downright impossible. It requires the plaintiff to have knowledge about matters that cannot be known.

Of course, we might have to live with these consequences were the right of participation constitutionally grounded, but that is far from clear. I believe that the Constitution guarantees not a right of participation but rather what I will call a right of representation—not a day in court but the right to have one's interest adequately represented. The right of representation provides that no individual can be bound by adjudication unless his or her interest is adequately represented in the proceeding. This means that finality can be conferred on a structural decree if, but only if, all the interests are adequately represented in the proceeding. If any interest is not adequately represented, then the decree remains vulnerable to a new challenge. If, however, that interest was fully represented in the proceeding that led to the entry of the decree, then the court could summarily dismiss the new challenge on the ground that it was already adjudicated—even though the challenger had not participated in the initial suit.

The application of this rule to *Martin v. Wilks*—or, more specifically, my imagined recasting of it—is not entirely clear. If the city or any other party who fought the claim of liability and the entry of the decree adequately represented the interests of the white firefighters, then the white firefighters would be foreclosed from re-litigating the validity of the decree. On the other hand, none of the parties may have adequately represented his or her interests. Racial politics may make a city government led by blacks a most unreliable representative of the white firefighters. Or there may be good reason to doubt that an employer can ever be an adequate representative of the employees.[13] In that instance, then, the interest of the white firefighters would not have been adequately represented in the initial proceedings, and thus, even within my framework, the white firefighters would be entitled to a hearing on their claim, unconstrained by the tougher preclusion doctrines.

On the last hypothesis, namely, that the interests of the white firefighters were not adequately represented in the initial proceeding, the result I envision seems to be exactly the same as the one the Court reached in *Martin v. Wilks*: The claim tendered by the white firefighters against the validity of the decree must be fully litigated. There is, however, an important difference arising from the ground or basis of the decision. Whereas my result turns on the right of representation, Rehnquist invoked not that right but the right of participation. This difference is not only of theoretical significance but also has great practical consequences for structural decrees, since a far greater measure of finality would be achieved under the right of representation. The white firefighters' claim against the validity of the decree would have to be litigated only if they could show that their interest was not adequately represented. Under the rule of *Martin v. Wilks*, there is virtually no threshold requirement. The would-be challengers need only show that they were not parties in the initial proceeding.

In drawing this distinction between the participatory and representational rights, I have assumed that the inquiry into the adequacy of representation would take place in the subsequent proceeding. This might be deemed undesirable, however, because the inquiry into whether the would-be challenger's interests were adequately represented in the initial proceeding might itself interfere with the implementation process. Every hearing takes time and creates uncertainty. This delay in implementation could be avoided, however, by requiring, first, that all challenges to the adequacy of representation take place in the initial proceeding and, second, that failure to challenge the adequacy of representation at that stage would foreclose any subsequent attacks on the decree at all. Then the difference between the representational and participatory scheme would be even more dramatic. Implementation would have to begin at once, with no delay occasioned by a hearing on the merits of the claim against the decree or even on the adequacy of representation in the initial proceeding.

While such a rule would confer finality on the decree and avoid the burdens and delays of subsequent challenges, it creates new burdens for the initial proceeding. Cutting off the possibility of any subsequent proceeding would be strictly dependent on there having been full and ample notice of the initial proceeding, so that those who might one day claim that their interests were not adequately represented would have already had the opportunity to challenge the adequacy of the representation of their interests. In addition, a hearing would have to be held in the course of the initial proceeding on any such challenges to the adequacy of the existing representational structure, with two possible outcomes: displacing the putative initial representative with the new challenger or, more realistically, allowing the new challenger to intervene and then to share in the representational role.

Such inquiries into the adequacy of the representational structure in the initial proceeding and any efforts to correct that structure by allowing intervention might seem to confront courts with the same practical difficulties that I see in Rehnquist's scheme of mandatory joinder. Perhaps that is why the issue in *Martin v. Wilks* is often presented as a purely technical one (joinder vs. intervention), with no great practical differences turning on how it is resolved. I believe this is a mistake. Although the burden on courts working within the representational framework would be considerable, it is not nearly as oppressive as the one imposed by *Martin v. Wilks*.

In large part, this is because the representation I speak of is not a representation of individuals but one of interests. It is not that every person has a right to be represented in structural litigation but that every interest must be represented. If an individual's interest has been adequately represented, then he or she has no further claim against the decree. The right of representation is a collective, rather than an individual, right, because it belongs to a group of persons classed together by virtue of their shared interests.

The notice required in the initial proceeding must be adjusted accordingly. In one sense, the notice must be broad and comprehensive. It must give those whose interests are at stake a fair opportunity to contest the adequacy of the representation being provided for their interests. Also, the notice requirement must take account of the chance, rightfully underscored by Professor Susan Sturm,[14] that interests may change over time and may become realigned once the proceeding moves from the liability to the remedial stage. A second round of notice may thus be required at the remedial stage to take account of this contingency. On the other hand, there is no need to give each and every individual member of the group, whose interests are being represented, notice of the proceeding. It is sufficient that notice be given to a substantial number of persons within the group since, by definition, all members of the group have similar or comparable interests, and, in the absence of any special indication, one person is as likely as the next to protect his or her interest and that of the group. Given the nature of the representational right, what is required is collective, not individual, notice.

Similarly one need not be especially concerned with those individuals who have not yet arrived in the community or who have had no contact with the organization. They are an embarrassment to Rehnquist's scheme, for they cannot possibly be joined in the initial proceeding and thus could not be barred from challenging the validity of the decree once they appear on the scene. But they are not a special problem within the framework founded on the right of representation. Notice could not be given to them, but there is no need to, for presumably they would fall into one of the categories (e.g., job seekers, incumbent employees) who received notice and whose interests were represented in the initial proceeding.

Effective notice is likely to produce a number of applications for intervention, and, although that, too, will complicate the initial proceeding, I believe that this scheme is still better than Rehnquist's. Intervention, like joinder, is a mechanism for participation, but it differs from joinder in three important respects. First, the burden moves from the plaintiffs to the would-be challengers—assuming that there is adequate notice. Second, intervention requires a special showing. There is no need to allow intervention to everyone who might be adversely affected by the decree or has a legal claim against its validity; intervention, as a matter of right, is conditioned on a showing that the applicant's interest is not being adequately represented. Third, whereas the participation allowed under intervention is intended to serve a discrete purpose—to perfect the representational structure—the participation permitted under joinder is more ambiguous as to purpose and thus is more open-ended and less controllable. It is harder for a court to control the participation of a person allowed to join as a defendant than one who is allowed to intervene.

Admittedly, even if the right of intervention is specially conditioned and limited to perfecting the representational structure, it will have a significant impact on structural litigation. The interests at stake in such cases are manifold, and it is always difficult to know with certainty what those interests are and whether they are being adequately represented. The prudent judge, determined to achieve a measure of finality and to get on with the business of structural reform, is likely to err on the side of inclusiveness. As a result, the initial lawsuit is likely to become multi-centered or to involve so many different parties as to make it resemble a town meeting.[15] But that new construct still would fall far short of the phantasm produced by the kind of joinder required to give effect to Rehnquist's right of participation—putting the burden on the plaintiff to join each and every individual who might be adversely affected by the decree or who might have a claim against its validity.

In contrast to what Rehnquist offers in *Martin v. Wilks*, the scheme I propose, and one that is incorporated into and affirmed by the Civil Rights Act of 1991, makes structural litigation a real possibility. It does require, however, qualifying the commitment to the notion that every individual is entitled to a day in court before his or her right is adjudicated, and this compromise of individualistic values is no small matter. The right of participation appears to afford more respect or control to the individual than does the right of representation, and these days, when we have become skeptical of all kinds of state power, including that wielded by the judiciary, it seems more and more desirable to build a fortress around the individual. Ever since the 1970s much of the energy behind the drive for equal rights has come from the Feminist Movement, and the foundational decision in that movement—not so much *Brown* but *Roe v. Wade*[16]—has commonly been taken to affirm the value of individual autonomy. Relinquishing the right of participation and placing in its stead the right of representation might be thought—by all of us, not just Chief Justice Rehnquist—to betray this very same value.

Some forms of representation are fully consistent with individualistic values, for example, when a person appoints an agent and has full control over that agent. The kind of representation obtainable in the electoral context is also consistent with individualistic values,[17] though obviously the power of the individual voter depends on a number of factors, including the total size of the electorate, the party structure, and the distribution of resources. Compared to the ordinary agency relationship, the influence of the individual in electing a representative is likely to be minuscule. The kind of representation present in structural litigation, however, differs qualitatively from that found in the ordinary agency relationship or even in electoral representation. As I acknowledged before, it is a representation of interests. An individual can be bound by the action of someone purporting to be his or her representative even though that individual had no say whatsoever over the selection of that representative, indeed, might not have even known of the appointment or that he or she was being represented.

To some, interest representation may seem a strange form of representation, but in truth it can be found in many social settings, including the family, organized religion, and universities. A president of a university is often said to represent the faculty in important policy disputes with the trustees or students even though the faculty had no role whatsoever in choosing the president. The tie between the two is largely one of interest. Interest representation also plays a role in some forms of our political life outside the electoral context and has recently produced dramatic changes in world history. In some of the so-called roundtable negotiations of 1989 that resulted in the collapse of the communist regimes in Eastern Europe, the vast majority of ordinary citizens were represented by a small group of self-appointed representatives who claimed their authority on the basis of a shared interest.[18] As is often the case, the leaders of the so-called opposition spoke for and bound others, indeed entire populations, even though these leaders were not empowered by an election or in any meaningful sense chosen by the citizenry.

Even in the law, representation of interest is not confined to the structural injunction. It can be found in the law regarding common trusts and was sustained by Justice Robert Jackson in *Mullane v. Central Hanover Bank and Trust Co.*[19] as consistent with due process. In that case, New York relied on the representation of interests when it established the procedures to settle accounts and to foreclose the right to an accounting by the beneficiaries of common trusts. In a proceeding to be brought by the trustee, the interests of the beneficiaries were to be represented by a guardian appointed by the court, not by the beneficiaries. The judgment rendered would fully bind the beneficiaries and foreclose their right subsequently to obtain an accounting even though they did not participate in the initial proceeding.

The dispute in the *Mullane* case largely centered on the notice that was to be provided to the beneficiaries in the initial settlement proceeding. One part of Justice Jackson's decision was negative. The Court held that newspaper notice allowed by New York was not sufficient for purposes of due process. Letters would have to be sent. A second part of the decision was more affirmative in that it sought to ease the burden on the trustee. The Court held that the settlement proceeding could bind beneficiaries who never received notice (because their letter went astray) or who were never sent notice (because their interests or addresses were presently unknown).

The purpose of the rule disallowing newspaper notice and requiring more individualized notice is ambiguous. On the one hand, it might be thought to be protective of the right of participation. The notice advises individuals that the settlement proceeding constitutes their opportunity to challenge the way the common trust was handled—it is their day in court —and that failure of them to step forward constitutes a waiver or abandonment of that right. Alternatively, the rule requiring more individualized notice might be seen as a better mechanism than newspaper publication for insuring the adequacy of representation. Letters are sent to a large number of individual beneficiaries to alert them that their interests are being represented by a person appointed by the court and to invite them to speak up if they have any information indicating that the representation will not be adequate.

While taken by itself the requirement of more individualized notice is ambiguous, this ambiguity is resolved decisively in favor of the representational interpretation once account is taken of the more affirmative dimension of *Mullane*: the decision of the Court allowing individual beneficiaries who never received any notice whatsoever of the pendency of the settlement proceeding—because the letter went astray or their address was not at hand —to be bound by that proceeding. That result is easily understandable within the representational framework, for not every single member of a group need receive notice in order to provide a check on the adequacy of representation; it would be intolerable, however, if the foundational right were one of participation. There would be no basis at all for concluding that these individuals had their day in court or somehow relinquished it. They never even knew of the suit.[20]

In some scattered places, Justice Jackson used the rhetoric of participation to justify the ruling that due process required more than notice by publication. He spoke of a "right to be heard" and said that it would have "little reality or worth unless one is informed that the matter is pending and can choose for himself whether to appear or default, acquiesce or contest."[21] But this would not be the first time that Justice Jackson used language that exceeded his analytic point. As can be seen most clearly in his unwillingness to impose a requirement of actual notice, his fundamental concern was to render the common trust a viable financial instrument, and, for that purpose, he was prepared to compromise certain individualistic values and to allow what I have called a representation of interests. As he put it, getting to the core of his decision: "The individual interest does not stand alone but is identical with that of a class. . . . Therefore notice reasonably certain to reach most of those interested in objecting is likely to safeguard the interests of all, since any objection sustained would inure to the benefit of all."[22]

A similar use of the concept of interest representation can be found in the class action, so central to modern procedure, though only grudgingly acknowledged in a footnote by Chief Justice Rehnquist in *Martin v. Wilks*.[23] As explained more fully in the next chapter, the class action permits representation of interest in order to enhance private enforcement of public laws. In a plaintiff class action, the representative is self-appointed; in the defendant class action, the adversary appoints the representative. Notice is provided to the members of the class, but only as a way of checking on the adequacy of representation, not to protect the individual's right to participation.[24] One of the principal tasks of a court in a class action is to make certain that the interests of the members of the class are adequately represented, for the law provides that all members of the class will be fully bound by the judgment rendered.

In *Eisen v. Carlisle and Jacqueline*,[25] Justice Lewis Powell broke from

Mullane—not *Mullane*'s specific ruling about the insufficiency of newspaper notice but its underlying principle. *Eisen* involved a plaintiff class action seeking enforcement of the federal antitrust and securities laws against an odd-lot trader, and the district court had devised a notice scheme that seemed ample for the purpose of insuring the adequacy of representation: (1) publication in prominent newspapers; (2) individual notice to all members of the New York Stock Exchange, all commercial banks with large trust departments, and all large odd-lot investors, that is, those with ten or more transactions; and (3) individual notice to a number of small odd-lot investors who would be chosen at random.

Justice Powell disallowed the random notice to the small odd-lot investors and, in an extravagant expression of individualism foreshadowing *Martin v. Wilks*, insisted that every small odd-lot investor whose address was known—some 2.25 million—be sent individual letters. This escalated the costs of notice considerably and thus impaired the efficacy of the class action as a law enforcement device by requiring a greater front-end investment. Yet the damage wrought by *Eisen* to the class action was less significant than that inflicted by *Martin v. Wilks* on the structural injunction. *Eisen* was largely justified in terms of the requirements of the Federal Rules of Civil Procedure, not due process; in any event, it was limited to the special type of class actions involved ("(b)(3)") and presumably does not apply to the other types of class actions permitted by the Rules—those seeking injunctions or those justified on the ground of avoiding inconsistent adjudications or facilitating the distribution of a limited fund ("(b)(2)" and "(b)(1)").[26]

Despite the *Eisen* setback, *Mullane* and the very idea of the class action allows interest representation to achieve worthy pragmatic objectives. Similarly we should allow interest representation and tolerate a compromise of individualistic values in a case like *Martin v. Wilks* in order to make the structural injunction a viable remedy. The structural injunction is as worthy of our respect as the common trust or class action. We can all feel the attraction of individualism, but too rigid an insistence on individualistic values, or on an individualistic conception of representation as might be entailed in the ordinary agency relationship, would virtually destroy the structural decree. That would, in turn, deprive the black firefighters, or other persons whose rights have been denied, any viable remedy for the injustices they suffer.[27]

To be sure, the value of individual participation has an important role to play in the legal process, but we must also recognize that we accord that value different weight in different contexts. Where particular individuals have been singled out, as in the criminal law, or in administrative contexts where an individual's welfare payments are in jeopardy, the value of individual participation ranks very high, maybe even supreme. In those situations, participation is a value in its own right. It manifests a public commitment to the dignity and worth of the individual, as well as serving a more instrumental end by ensuring that the facts and issues are presented to the court in the sharpest possible terms. In structural litigation, however, no individual is singled out; the remedies are forward-looking and the practices of a bureaucratic organization are examined for the impact on the welfare of a social group. Accordingly the value of participation, understood in its individualist form, loses some of its force. We may value individual participation in structural litigation, but only to serve instrumental rather than dignitary ends: to insure that all interests are accounted for and that the strongest arguments are made on their behalf.

In "The Forms of Justice" (chapter 1) I indicated that structural injunction might be justified within an individualistic framework. It could be conceived as a countervailing power needed to protect individual rights. Although it might sacrifice some individual rights, we need to aggregate the losses and gains. The conception is that, on balance, individuals will come out ahead. Even with this assumption, I am doubtful that such a defense of the structural injunction is faithful to the kind of individualism that Chief Justice Rehnquist had in mind in *Martin v. Wilks* or that underlies the right of participation. That kind of individualism springs from a conception of individual autonomy that does not allow sacrifices of the rights of some individuals to advance the rights (much less the welfare) of other individuals. It is Kantian in nature and gives to each individual total control over his or her rights; it creates a certain kind of veto power for the individual. The structural injunction departs from that kind of individualism—it is, most emphatically, a collective instrument—but that does not doom it as a matter of due process.

Due process requires that procedures be fair, but fairness is a pragmatic ideal. It affords protection to the individual, but not in a way that would require the sacrifice of other important rights. As the reference to *Mullane* and our experience with the class action make clear, due process has never been reduced to the kind of individualism that informs Rehnquist's opinion in *Martin v. Wilks*. It does not give absolute control to each and every individual. It does not require a disregard for the social consequences of a procedural rule. It permits a rule—whether propounded by a court or by legislature, as in the case of the Civil Rights Act of 1991—that seeks an accommodation of both the procedural rights of the white firefighters and the substantive rights of the black firefighters.

In order to achieve some measure of finality and efficacy for the structural injunction, it may be necessary to adjust the procedural rights of the white firefighters or other would-be challengers. It may be necessary to forego the right of participation and to leave various individuals with no other assurance than that their interests will be adequately represented. But this adjustment of the procedural rights of would-be challengers rests on the most appealing of all premises—that doing so will more fully remedy the violation of the rights of others, including the right to be free from discrimination. This is not to sacrifice due process for the sake of civil rights but, rather, to free due process from the grips of an overly individualistic conception of due process and to acknowledge that the fairness of procedures turns, in part, on the social ends they serve. Due process does not write into law the ethical theories of Professor Immanuel Kant.

7

The Political Theory of the Class Action

The United States is responsible for many innovations in civil procedure but probably the most striking is the class action. It arose long before the civil rights era and has not been confined in any way to structural cases. Indeed, it received its most important use in damage actions seeking recovery for violations of antitrust statutes and of laws protecting consumers and the environment. Yet the federal rule governing class actions was enlarged in important ways in 1966, and the use of this procedural device achieved great prominence during the late 1960s and early 1970s.

The class action finds its most compelling use when recovery is sought for dispersed harm—where the defendant inflicts harm on a great number of people only slightly. In such a situation, the total amount of harm may be enormous, but it would not make economic sense for an individual to bring suit on his or her own since the potential recovery in such a case would be miniscule. The class action enables an individual to seek damages on behalf of the group of persons injured. The total amount recovered is distributed to the members of the class, but only after the attorneys representing the class collect their fee.

In essence, the class action is a device for funding a private attorney general—for making it financially feasible for private parties to seek full enforcement of public laws. It is not surprising, therefore, that the class action gained great currency during the civil rights era, when private attorneys generally received their greatest endorsement through the actions of groups such as the NAACP Legal Defense Fund. Nor is it surprising that the class action became a target of attack in ways described in this chapter during the period of retrenchment that began in the 1970s and that has lasted to this very day.

The class action devices provide endless fascination for lawyers abroad. They, too, feel the need for private attorneys general. In 1995 I was invited to lecture in Argentina at the inauguration of a masters in law program at one of the new private universities, and I chose the class action as my topic. The lecture was first published in Spanish in the inaugural issue of the *Revista Jurídica de Universidad de Palermo* (volume 1, page 5). The next year an English version was published in an issue of the 1996 *Washington and Lee Law Review* (volume 53, page 21) that was dedicated to one of its most distinguished graduates and a true hero of the civil rights era —Judge John Minor Wisdom of the United States Court of Appeals for the Fifth Circuit.

~ COURTS are not self-starting. Their proceedings must be initiated by some outside agency, and it is that agency, not the courts, that will conduct the factual investigation, devise the discovery program, select and examine witnesses, write the legal briefs, and monitor the implementation of the remedy. Who might play that role?

When the remedy for violation of a legal norm consists of jail or some other form of punishment and the judicial proceeding is considered a criminal one, the power of initiation in the United States is exclusively in the hands of an officer of the state, for example, the attorney general or district attorney. Victims of crimes cannot commence criminal proceedings, and over the years the Supreme Court has been reluctant to grant individual citizens any power to review or otherwise superintend the government's decision to commence a criminal prosecution.

The situation is entirely different in the civil context. There the purpose is not to punish for a past violation but to compensate for past injuries or to stop future violations, and the remedy sought is damages or an injunction rather than a fine or imprisonment. For such proceedings, the power of initiation has been allocated to two different agencies: public officers and private citizens. In my judgment, the class action can be understood best as a fusion of both these agencies.

Civil suits initiated by private citizens may serve their private purposes.

Imagine a price-fixing agreement among stockbrokers and a suit by one of the investors for an injunction to prevent price-fixing in the future or to recover damages for the harm inflicted. The suit may vindicate or protect the individual rights of the investor. A public purpose may, however, also be served by this very same suit in the sense that, if successful, it will bring the brokers' behavior into accord with antitrust law. An injunction against price-fixing in the future clearly would have that effect, but so would an award of damages to the investor. The damage award would force the stockbrokers to internalize the costs of their wrongdoing and, through the operation of ordinary principles of deterrence, discourage future violations by the defendants and other brokers.

In many instances, there is no need to disentangle the private and public purposes of a citizen-initiated lawsuit. The citizen furthers the public interest by pursuing private ends. However, there is a category of cases—of increasing importance in modern times—when the two purposes become distinct. This occurs when the harm to an individual citizen is not sufficient to give that citizen a good reason to bring a lawsuit, yet the aggregate harm to society is quite considerable. Once again, consider a price-fixing agreement. This time the agreement involves stockbrokers who handle small transactions. The damage inflicted on an individual investor may be seventy dollars, but the aggregate damage inflicted on all the investors—numbering in the millions—is sixty million dollars. In such an instance, the legal system could be relatively indifferent as to whether the seventy dollars is ever collected but not at all indifferent to the public ramifications of the defendants' action because of the enormous social loss incurred.

To some extent, suits brought by public officers can handle such situations. If the public interest is great and the private interest relatively trivial, then the attorney general should be able to sue the stockbrokers. Accordingly, we have a strong tradition, dating from the late nineteenth century, that authorizes government-initiated civil suits as an alternative to criminal prosecution in select areas.[1] Yet we have been reluctant to make such suits the only alternative for dealing with dispersed harm. We have tried to create room for private litigation.

In doing so, we may be reflecting the characteristic American distrust of government power and the desire to preserve a place for the ingenious and imaginative citizen. More concretely, the unwillingness to make the government-initiated lawsuit the only civil option in situations of dispersed harm may be rooted in misgivings with the official system of governance and the way public officials discharge their duties. The issue is accountability. The power vested in the attorney general is discretionary, and there are fears that discretion might be abused because of corruption or that the needs of certain sections of society—for example, the politically powerless—might be systematically slighted.

As a result of these dynamics, the idea of the private attorney general has emerged. The power of initiation is vested in the individual citizen, but the function of the suit is the same as one brought by the public attorney general, namely, to vindicate the public interest.

How is such a citizen-initiated lawsuit to be financed? The suit might be brought in the name of some individual citizen, but the work will be done by lawyers. Although the term *private attorney general* is usually applied to the plaintiffs, it is the lawyers who, in reality, fulfill that role, and they must be compensated for their time and effort. Indeed, going even further, the level of compensation must be high enough to make it worthwhile for the best and the brightest to undertake such ventures. Because we in the United States operate under a rule that does not award attorney's fees to the victor, there is no separate award for fees, and that means that the lawyer for the plaintiff must be paid out of the damages collected by the plaintiff from the defendant if the suit is successful. When the damage award is sixty million dollars, there is more than enough to go around; there would be an army of lawyers prepared to handle that case on a contingent fee basis. This is not the case when the award is seventy dollars.

Our response to this dilemma, like all things American, has been both varied and pragmatic. One approach has been to relax the American rule on attorney's fees when the named plaintiff is acting as a private attorney general. In such a case there can be a separate award of attorney's fees to compensate the lawyers who served in that role for their time and effort. In some jurisdictions, this change was wrought by the courts alone; at the federal level, it took the enactment of a statute.[2] Most of the federal fee-shifting statutes are asymmetrical; defendants receive attorney's fees only on a special showing, for example, that the litigation was brought in bad faith, whereas plaintiffs receive the fees for their attorneys simply on condition that they prevail.[3]

A second approach has been to create a separate corps of lawyers that might act as private attorneys general and then to pay them out of funds that come from the public itself, sometimes in the form of tax revenue but most often out of private donations. This has led to the emergence of an entire panoply of organizations—the NAACP, ACLU, Natural Resources Defense Council, Legal Services Corporation, Center for Law and Social

Policy, Equal Rights Associates—that provide lawyers to serve as private attorneys general.[4]

The third and perhaps most imaginative solution to the problem of funding the private attorney general is the class action. In essence, the class action allows the named plaintiff to collect not just the seventy dollars—the amount the plaintiff was injured—but rather the sixty million dollars—the damages due to all investors. Most of that award would be paid to the investors, but a hefty chunk—perhaps as much as six million dollars (10 percent) or even twenty million dollars (33.3 percent)—would go to the lawyers for the plaintiff. The lawyers would be paid from the common fund they create.

In short, the class action could be viewed as a device to fund the private attorney general. It permits the aggregation of the claims of a large number of persons who have similar or identical claims, none of which—standing alone—would justify the suit. The person who brings the suit is referred to as "the named plaintiff," and the others are referred to as "the unnamed members of the class." The named plaintiff acts on behalf of the unnamed members of the class, and to more fully understand the dilemmas created by the class action we must consider the impact the action of the named plaintiff will have on the rights of the class.

A victory by the named plaintiff will preclude any further action on their claims by the unnamed members of the class. This seems relatively straightforward. The unnamed members of the class will have no reason whatsoever to pursue their claims because, in theory, their claims have been paid or honored and, in any event, the most elementary fairness would require that result. The defendants should not have to pay twice.

But what should happen if, as indeed is possible, the named plaintiff loses the suit? The general rule is to bar the unnamed members of the class from any further action, but the reasons for that rule are far from clear. One notion, perhaps more appropriate to gambling than to litigation,[5] assumes that the risks of the defendant should be symmetrical. If the defendant loses, the loss is big; so if the defendant wins, the win also should be big. Alternatively the rule might be based on a fear of wearing down the defendant—after winning one case, the defendant might have to mount a second defense, then a third, and so forth. Admittedly, the size of the claim is too small to assume that one named plaintiff after another will bring suit on an individual basis, but there are no obvious reasons why the first person to bring a class action should be the only one able to do so.

Whatever its rationale, the rule preventing unnamed members of the class from bringing claims if the named plaintiff loses has become well entrenched and gives rise to the central normative tension in the class action: a conflict with the ideal of each person having his or her day in court. At a superficial level, this tension has been resolved by conceiving of the class action as a form of representative action because, to be precise, the legal system does not guarantee that every person will have a day in court but only that the interest of each person will be represented in court. As all acknowledge (see chapter 6), if I appoint an agent to represent my interest and that agent brings a lawsuit on my behalf and then loses, I will not be able to sue again.

The class action is, in fact, a representative lawsuit—as noted, the named plaintiff is bringing a suit on behalf of all the unnamed members of the class—but it employs a peculiar concept of representation: self-appointment. Contrary to the ordinary situation where I appoint someone as my agent, in the class action the named plaintiff appoints him- or herself as the representative of the class. Self-appointment is not unheard of in the world of politics and other social domains. Indeed, it is quite commonplace in political situations where there is a radical shift in regimes. The persons who gathered in Philadelphia in the summer of 1787 to draft the U.S. Constitution appointed themselves to represent the people. Those who gathered at the roundtable in Budapest in the summer of 1989 assumed their mandate in a similar fashion. Yet there is no denying that self-appointment is an anomalous form of representation, only justified, if at all, by the most exceptional circumstances. The use of it in the class action reveals the truly exceptional—perhaps even revolutionary—character of that procedural device.

At this juncture in the history of the class action, little attention is paid to the concept of self-appointment itself, however odd it initially may seem as a form of representation. Yet the normative tension it generates has not disappeared; the battles are simply being fought on other fronts, above all, over the requirements of notice. All agree that some notice must be provided to the unnamed members of the class concerning the pendency of the lawsuit and the decision of the plaintiff to appoint him- or herself as the representative of the class. But there is a sharp dispute— fueled by differing attitudes toward the social utility of the class action and the very notion of a private attorney general—over the form of notice as well as who must bear its cost.

One school of thought insists on what may be referred to as individualized notice: Each individual within the class must be informed of the plaintiff's decision to appoint him- or herself as the representative of the class. The individual who receives this notice then has the option of disavowing the purported representation, either by opting out of the class or by intervening and contesting the adequacy of the representation afforded by the plaintiff. Silence will be taken as acquiescence. Those who subscribe to this view nominally accept the concept of self-appointment but, in fact, seek to re-create the agency form of representation and the consensual tie it presupposes between the representative and the represented. The only concession to the social purposes served by the class action are, first, a temporal reordering—consent can come after the appointment—and, second, a willingness to treat silence or inaction as a form of consent.

Those who want to broaden the scope of the class action, and are thus more accepting of the notion of self-appointment, acknowledge the importance of notice but insist that it take a collective form: Only some, but not all, members of the class need be informed of the pendency of the suit. According to this school of thought, the purpose of the notice is not to construct a consensual link between the representative and the members of the class but rather to make certain that the powers of self-appointment are not abused. The notice informs a good portion of the class of what is about to transpire in their name and gives them the opportunity to complain to the court about the adequacy of the self-appointed representative. Notice is not a proxy for consent but an instrument for making certain that the named plaintiff will be a strong and effective advocate for the class.

This theoretical dispute over the two types of notice—individual versus collective—has important pragmatic implications simply because individual notice tends to be more expensive. *Eisen v. Carlisle and Jacquelin*, a landmark class action case discussed in the previous chapter, illustrates this dynamic. The case involved a price-fixing scheme among stockbrokers who handled odd-lots, that is, sales of stock in units less than one hundred. The class consisted of all odd-lot investors. Individual notice would have required a first-class mailing to some 2.25 million persons who purchased fewer than ten shares from the brokers over a certain period of time —the small fries. The cost of such a mailing was estimated at the time to be $225,000. In contrast, the cost of collective notice was estimated only to be slightly more than $20,000. It consisted of advertisements in major newspapers, a first-class mailing to those who were regular or large investors in the market, and then a first-class mailing to five thousand of the small investors, who were to be chosen at random from the group of 2.25 million.

The battles in *Eisen* were fought primarily over the type of notice—specifically whether random notice was acceptable—but a question was also raised as to who should pay for it. The costs of notice must be paid at the front end of the lawsuit, before any recovery. From the perspective of the plaintiff's lawyer, such expenditures could be viewed as an investment. The expected returns—the amount of the aggregate claim times the probability of winning—may be so large as to justify the expenditure. If not, however, the lawyer will not bring the lawsuit. To avoid this contingency, some have argued that the costs of notice could be reallocated and placed on the defendant.

In the *Eisen* case, the trial court in fact reallocated notice costs to the defendant, but the Supreme Court balked, insisting that the plaintiff must pay for the costs of his lawsuit. In justifying its ruling in these terms, the Court overlooked the public dimensions of the lawsuit—that the plaintiff was bringing the suit for the public, not just for himself. Even so, there may be other reasons to be wary of reallocating the costs of notice to the defendant.

For one thing, such a reallocation may work to the detriment of the unnamed members of the class. In the typical class action, the unnamed members of the class actually may be protected by the actions of the defendant; the defendant aims to unseat the plaintiff or add to the plaintiff's financial burden, and thus has reason to insist on a robust notice to the unnamed members of the class. Placing the costs of notice on the defendant, however, may make the defendant think twice about demanding such notice.

Second, such a reallocation will add to the burdens the defendant must shoulder in defending the action. The pressure on the defendant to capitulate would be intensified, and the defendant's right to a day in court may be compromised. The trial judge in *Eisen* was aware of this danger and, as a result, conditioned the reallocation of the costs of notice to the defendant on a finding that the probability was quite high that the defendant would lose. But such a finding can be made only after some judicial inquiry into the merits of the underlying claim. That itself would burden the defendant and put the court in the position of acting on the basis of an incomplete hearing—at best a summary of the evidence or a presentation of the highlights—because that inquiry must precede the certification of the class and the full trial on the merits.

Aside from leaving the costs on the plaintiff or reallocating them to the defendant, another alternative might be to have the government pay the costs of notice. The costs of notice then would be treated as one of the many expenses incurred by the state in maintaining a court system, comparable, for example, to the costs of the courthouse or the judge's salary. Such a financing scheme, however, would produce an odd result. It would give private citizens a power over the public purse much like the real attorney general, but without being accountable to the public for their expenditures.

To some extent, therefore, one can understand the difficulty of always reallocating the cost of notice from the named plaintiff to the defendant or government. Admittedly, leaving it on the shoulders of the named plaintiff has its problems because it makes the pursuit of the claim less attractive to the enterprising lawyer—he or she must put up the money at the front end of the lawsuit, and, in many cases, this may be a decisive impediment to bringing the suit at all. Yet the alternatives also have their drawbacks. On balance, it seems that the most sensible way out of this predicament would be to opt in favor of collective notice, because it allows us to be somewhat indifferent to the method of allocation since the sums are sufficiently small. Even if the burden is left on the plaintiff's shoulders, it is not likely to be decisive.

From this perspective, the *Eisen* decision seems especially unfortunate. The Supreme Court not only rejected the effort of the trial judge to reallocate the costs of notice, it also rejected the notion of random notice and insisted on the particularly costly form of individualized notice—first-class mailings to each and every member of the class whose name and address were known—all 2.25 million.

The Supreme Court rationalized this result in terms of the special wording of the class action rule then in force.[6] In my view the Court was not bound by this rule or, for that matter, any other of the federal procedural rules. The process by which the federal rules were promulgated resulted in rules that could not bind the Court in any meaningful sense.[7] The rules do not satisfy the case-or-controversy requirement of the Constitution nor any of the other requirements surrounding judicial decisions and thus cannot even be afforded the weight customarily accorded precedents. Nor might the rules be considered to have the binding force of a statute. Under Section 2072 of the Judicial Code, enacted in the 1930s, the class action rules took effect because Congress did not reject them within a specified period, but this reliance on inaction seems to abridge the most elementary requirement for the enactment of a statute—a vote by both houses of Congress and the signature of the president.

Moreover, it is not clear that the particular rule the Court invoked in *Eisen* was the relevant one. The result in Eisen turned on classifying or characterizing the class action in a certain way, and the Court never adequately explained why the class action should be classified in the way it chose. Put technically, the Court insisted that the suit be treated as a (b)(3) class action, thereby triggering the individualized notice requirements of Rule 23(c)(2). Yet no satisfactory explanation was given for the Court's unwillingness to treat the suit as one of the other types of class actions, which have less stringent notice requirements.

One alternative (provided by Rule 23(b)(2)) is geared to injunctive proceedings, as opposed to ones seeking money damages. In fact, in *Eisen* the plaintiff sought an injunction as well as damages, and thus the injunctive component could have been viewed as that type of class action. The Court dismissed this alternative on the theory that *Eisen* was not primarily a suit seeking injunctions.

Another provision that permitted collective notice, (23(b)(1)), authorized class actions when needed to avoid the risk of inconsistent adjudication that might arise if suit were brought individually. The Court refused to allow the *Eisen* suit to be brought under this provision, arguing that the risk of inconsistent adjudication through individual suit was virtually nonexistent because each individual investor had so little stake in the outcome (seventy dollars). As a purely practical matter, the Court may have a good point—no one would bring the suit on an individual basis—but then it is hard to understand from that perspective, given the small stake at issue, why the Court was so insistent on individual notice to every single investor.

This odd oscillation of the Court between a formal and a pragmatic perspective—one, when it decided on the need for individual notice, the other, when it came to classify the class action—suggests that perhaps larger considerations, largely of a political character, were at play and that these considerations, not the specific wording of the class action rule itself, accounted for the Court's decision. Certainly political factors, in the broadest sense, must account for the failure of Congress, the Judicial Conference of the United States, or, for that matter, the Court itself to revise the allegedly restrictive language of the particular procedure invoked. *Eisen* was handed down in 1974. In the year 2002 the Advisory Committee on the Civil Rules proposed a major overhaul of the class action rule, the first since 1966, and left untouched the restrictive language of the rule the *Eisen* Court had relied on.

The momentum behind the concept of the private attorney general and thus of the class action was at its strongest during the 1960s and the Warren Court era. In the 1970s and 1980s American politics and American law moved to the Right, and, in that climate, the class action became a frequent target of conservative forces. Indeed, the *Eisen* decision may be seen as one of the many victories of those forces: Individualized notice escalates the costs of notice and thus makes the class action less attractive as a purely financial matter. It dampens the enthusiasm of the private attorney general, who, after all, must shoulder those costs, at least at the front end, and thereby protects the status quo. Such an interpretation of the Court's decision is made all the more plausible once it is seen as part of a larger program to curtail the private attorney general, a program that gathered force during the 1970s and 1980s and included the refusal of the Supreme Court to modify the traditional American attorney's fees rule for public interest suits and also the repeated assaults by Republicans, in the White House and in Congress, to the government-funded legal service organizations.

Couched in purely political terms, this explanation for the turn in American law is perhaps, in the end, too facile. It does not wholly explain *Eisen* and ignores the deep theoretical—maybe even constitutional—question raised by the class action. Individualized notice is indeed very costly and a burden in the class action, but it also can be seen as an attempt to respond to the anomalous character of self-appointment as a mode of representation. The truly disquieting fact about the class action is that it creates a situation in which I may be represented in proceedings I know nothing about and by someone I do not know and had no role whatsoever in choosing. The social purposes served by the class action may well justify this odd form of representation, but it would be a mistake to ignore or deny its very oddity, and the fact that it runs counter to the individualistic values that so permeate our legal system. As explained in chapter 2, these values were given dramatic expression in America during the 1970s and 1980s, when we experienced a revival of orthodox capitalism and classical liberalism—the most individualistic of all ideologies—but this development might only be a matter of emphasis. The individualistic values that the class action calls into question are all pervasive features of our law, perhaps of all law. For better or for worse, they will always exert a restraining influence on the great temptation of social reformers to create collective instruments that might better serve to further their ends.

8

The Awkwardness of the
Criminal Law

Starting in 1976 Argentina was ruled by a military dictatorship, probably the most brutal in all its history. Then, in late 1982, owing to a series of fortuitous events, including a deteriorating economy and a defeat in their attempt to take control of the Malvinas, the dictators called for elections and a return to civilian rule. Raúl Alfonsín won the election and, true to his campaign promise, brought the dictators to justice. They were tried in Buenos Aires in 1985, and that trial ended in a judgment convicting five of the nine members of the junta who had ruled the country from 1976 to 1983. The details of this proceeding, and its significance in world history are described in Carlos Nino's 1996 book, *Radical Evil on Trial*, published by Yale University Press.

I first traveled to Argentina in the midst of the trial of the junta in 1985, and have returned almost every year since. On one trip I was invited to participate in a Criminal Justice and Human Rights conference held on April 12-13, 1987, at the Universidad de Buenos Aires. Most of the speakers, including the chief prosecutor, pointed to the criminal proceedings against the junta with pride and marveled at the capacity of the civilian government to hold the junta accountable without the aid of a conquering army. Although I greatly admired what the Alfonsín administration had achieved (see "Human Rights as Social Ideals," in *Human Rights in Political Transitions*, edited by Carla Hesse and Robert Post, Zone Books, 1999), I used the occasion to warn about excessive reliance on the criminal law. Because of the international setting, I spoke of human rights, as opposed to civil rights, but drew on the civil rights experience in the United States during the 1960s, seeking to extract from that experience certain general and enduring lessons about the criminal law. I invited the officials present to look beyond the guilt of individuals for particular wrongs and to consider the more systemic sources of human rights abuses and then fashion the remedies accordingly. I urged a greater emphasis on forward-looking remedies like the injunction. After all, President Alfonsín was not seeking retribution but rather structural reform of a very special character—to rebuild democracy. This chapter is the paper I then presented, which was first published in the February 1989 issue of the *Human Rights Quarterly* (volume 11, page 1).

In December 1986 the Argentine Congress, at President Alfonsín's prompting, enacted a law (Punto Final) that set a sixty-day time limit within which prosecutions of military officers for human rights abuses could begin. Many in the human rights community, including some of the participants in the April conference, saw this measure as a compromise with the military and denounced the president for sponsoring it. In fact, rather than being a compromise with the military, within the sixty-day period the number of prosecutions against the military swiftly escalated. This, in turn, provoked the military. On Thursday, April 15, 1987, two days after the conference had ended and just before the beginning of Semana Santa (Holy Week), a rebellion broke out within a number of garrisons. The citizenry responded with massive demonstrations in support of democracy, but the mutiny continued. On Easter Sunday President Alfonsín met with the rebels on his own. Eventually the rebels put down their arms and returned to the barracks. No one knows what deal, if any, was struck between the president and the rebels. In June 1987, however, the president introduced a statute (*Obediencia Debida*), soon enacted into law, that made obedience to higher orders a defense in criminal prosecutions, thus bringing to a halt virtually all prosecutions against the military for crimes committed during the dictatorship.

Although the conference at which I presented this essay took place two days before the Semana Santa rebellion, this unfortunate turn of events came as an utter surprise to all the participants, including me and my good friend Carlos Nino. It was hardly what I had in mind when I spoke of the awkwardness of the criminal law.

THE criminal law is the law's strong arm, and it derives its strength from two different sources. One is the severity of its sanctions: fines, imprisonment, and, in some countries, execution. Another source of strength is the social opprobrium that comes from being convicted of a crime and thus being labeled a criminal. Implicit in every criminal conviction is the judgment that the individual has engaged in conduct that is sufficiently wrongful to warrant a punishment.

There is some ambiguity as to what is meant by human rights, but most would agree that these rights are the most basic or fundamental of all rights. It would therefore seem that any violation of such a right should be met with a strong response by the state, indeed the strongest, and that there is a natural fit between the criminal law and the protection of human rights. It is taken today as axiomatic by those engaged in the international protection of human rights that each and every violation of a human right should be criminally prosecuted.

The fact is, however, that during the 1960s—a period sometimes referred to as the Second Reconstruction—we in the United States had an experience that did not conform to this expectation. The criminal prosecution was rare and exceptional, even though our commitment toward the protection of human rights was then firm and unequivocal, perhaps more so than in any other period of U.S. history. It was the injunction, not the criminal law, which became the primary legal tool for the extension and vindication of human rights. The purpose of this essay is both to explain and to justify this practice, and thus to suggest that the fit between the criminal law and the protection of human rights is not as natural as it might at first seem.

Procedural Difficulties

Virtually every legal system requires a higher burden of proof in a criminal prosecution than in a civil suit. Conviction requires proof beyond a reasonable doubt, precisely because the sanctions are punitive and severe. Thus if the state is to use the criminal prosecution effectively, it must be prepared to shoulder this burden. Law enforcement agencies sometimes shy away from the criminal law because they fear they cannot meet this burden. This is not, however, the whole story or, for that matter, even an important part of it. Even when the proof is clear and dramatic, two other features of the U.S. procedural system discourage the use of the criminal law, and these led, during the Second Reconstruction, to the use of the injunction. One concerns the jury trial, and the other relates to the method of activating criminal proceedings.

The Constitution guarantees trial by jury in all serious criminal cases, and part of the reluctance to use the criminal law in the 1960s stemmed from this procedural requirement. Prosecutors feared that no matter how gross the violation, the jury would not convict. The jury is not required to explain or otherwise justify its decision and thus can take the law into its own hands more easily than a judge. Of course, any prosecution, even an unsuccessful one, has some value: It educates the public and places a burden on the defendant, which might itself be seen as a form of punishment. Yet going forward with a prosecution when conviction is not likely poses difficult ethical problems and might well become counterproductive. An acquittal might be understood as a license for others to engage in similar conduct.

In the 1960s the risk of jury nullification was particularly pronounced in southern communities, where the human rights victim typically was black and the accused white. The racial polarization of the community could easily be exploited to devalue the life of the black victims or to exonerate or excuse the defendant. The risk of nullification was, to some extent, tied to the all-white jury, which persisted throughout the Second Reconstruction, but even when the jury more adequately reflected a cross section of the community this problem was not entirely eliminated. Since the jury's decision has to be unanimous or, in some jurisdictions, nearly unanimous, a conviction could be blocked by one or two jurors who were determined to hold out.

The effective use of the criminal law was also stymied by the fact that in the United States the power to initiate a criminal proceeding is vested exclusively in the hands of government officials. This method of allocating prosecutorial power proved especially problematic during the 1960s, because the human rights pursued during that period were to protect against governmental rather than private interferences.

The term *human rights* sometimes is used to refer to those rights deriving from the concept of personhood and, as a purely formal matter, a private citizen can violate them. An example would be the right to life. During the period I am referring to, however, the term *human rights* was taken as the equivalent of civil rights and primarily referred to rights that protect against abuses of government power. What made a lynching, to take one example, a violation of a human right or a civil right was not the taking of human life simpliciter, which would have been murder, but rather the complicity of government officials in the action. If that is so, and if it could be further assumed that where the official vested with the power of initiation is part of the very same governmental structure as the officials involved in the human rights violations, the chances of a prosecution would be remote. It would be a rare and surprising event, for example, to find a local district attorney prosecuting a local police chief or, for that matter, even individual police officers. The local prosecutor is likely to be dependent on the power possessed by the accused or the agency to which he or she belongs. The prosecutor is also likely to be subject to the same electorate that empowered the accused.

The peculiar federal structure of the U.S. government—the existence of overlapping and concurrent government jurisdictions, one belonging to the states and the other to the national government—created new possibilities: A federal prosecution of the municipal police chief may be more likely than one initiated by the local district attorney. On the other hand, not even federal officials are insulated from local political pressures or from the network of dependencies that immobilized local prosecutors. True, the attorney general of the United States and his or her other intermediate staff, all located in Washington and appointed by the president, may owe their first duty to a national rather than a local constituency. But, for the most part, the power to initiate federal criminal prosecutions and the resources necessary to bring them to successful completion are vested in the field agents of the attorney general—the various U.S. attorneys who are distributed throughout the nation and are very responsive to local politics. The U.S. attorneys are appointed by the president (one to a judicial district) but are usually proposed or cleared by the U.S. senators from the state. Senators hold national office but are elected on a local rather than a national basis.

Both these factors—the jury trial right and the scheme for allocating the power of initiation—rendered the criminal prosecution a rather blunt and ineffective instrument for protecting human rights during the Second Reconstruction. These factors played a more important role in discouraging the use of the criminal law than issues involving burden of proof. They also made the injunction more attractive, for an injunctive suit, because of an odd turn of history, does not require a jury and private parties can initiate it. I do not believe, however, that this exhausts our inquiry, for some evidence suggests that even had there been no jury trial right and the power of initiation had been more widely distributed, the injunction still would have been the primary instrument for vindicating and promoting human or civil rights.

One strand of evidence consists of the fact that the criminal law was not used even where there was no jury right, that is, when the penalty was less than six months of imprisonment. Second, the criminal law was not used even in those cases arising in communities where there was little risk of racially based jury nullification. The criminal prosecution for human rights violations was about as frequent in Oakland, California, as in Jackson, Mississippi. Third, the federal government was often the initiating agency in civil rights injunctive litigation. As a historical matter, the power to initiate an injunctive proceeding was vested in private citizens, but during the early 1960s the attorney general increasingly resorted to the injunction to protect national interests, including civil rights. Not only did the injunction become the primary legal instrument for the protection of human rights in general, but it also became the specific instrument for furthering the civil rights policy of the U.S. Department of Justice. It therefore seems hard to explain the non-use of the criminal law largely in terms of a technical feature of the procedural system, specific to the United States and perhaps some other countries, which give government officials a monopoly over the initiation of the criminal prosecution. We need to search for more general and compelling explanations.

The Individualism of the Criminal Law

The criminal law has an individualistic orientation. Punishment is imposed on an individual for an intentional wrong. It is assumed that the individual acted out of some mean spirit and that the infliction of a sanction —hopefully a severe one—will be appropriately vengeful and also effective as a means of discouraging others from committing similar wrongs. These individualistic norms might have had some plausibility during the formative era of the criminal law, but they are not in accord with the contemporary social arrangements found in the United States or, for that matter, anywhere else.

Imagine a typical case of police brutality. Two police officers are killed in the course of a holdup in some large American city.[1] The killers are identified as young black males. Police officers, mostly white, then fan out in a poor black neighborhood and arrest blacks without probable cause.

Homes are invaded without a warrant and searches occur at times and under circumstances that terrorize families and disrupt their personal lives. The arrestees are physically abused. It may seem appropriate in these circumstances to prosecute those police officers engaging in the unlawful action, but, remember, in order to do so, it will be necessary to identify the individual officers engaged in these practices and then establish the normal prerequisites of criminal responsibility, specifically, that the individual officer harmed the victim or violated his or her rights and also that the officer intended to do so.

Now and then these requirements can be satisfied. There are evil people on the police force—officers who are inflamed by racial hatred and whose conduct is so atrocious as to leave no doubt in anyone's mind about the appropriateness of blaming and punishing them. Provided the victim survives and recognizes a face or a badge, or is otherwise able to overcome the conspiracy of silence, it may even be possible to identify these individual officers. Under these circumstances the criminal law can be used. The problem is, however, that only in the rare case can these conditions be satisfied, and in no way could such cases account for the bulk of the abuses that minorities suffer at the hands of the police officers, day in and day out. In most instances the perpetrator cannot be identified, and when he or she can, the responsibility for the wrongdoing tends to be blurred, because the violation is not the product of racial animus or any other psychological dynamic that might justify the attribution of personal blame required by the criminal law.

Some of the factors responsible for the violation are tied to the general social context: the polarization of the races and the tendency of whites, in a less than fully conscious manner, to devalue the rights and interests of blacks. A second group of causal factors are organization-specific, relating to such matters as staffing patterns or information systems. Job requirements and recruitment practices tend to introduce a class, ethnic, and racial gap between the members of the police force and the population they come into contact with. Supervising officers may be unable to supervise line officers adequately, because they lack information about what the line officers are doing. Finally, some account must be taken of the institutional network of which the police department is only one part. It is the legislature that controls the financial appropriations to the department, and it might set funding at such low levels as to stretch the manpower to the breaking point, thereby making human rights abuses almost inevitable —overreaction tends to follow overwork.

Of course, these situational or structural factors do not explain all abuses. There is always room for the individual factor. But it was the judgment of those in charge of the U.S. Department of Justice in the 1960s, and it seemed to me to be a sound judgment, that these structural or situational factors were the dominant ones, for most of the cases most of the time, and, as such, made the vigorous enforcement of the criminal law a near impossibility. It was hard to point an accusing finger at any individual, at least in the manner required by the criminal law.

Arguably, the individualistic norms of criminal responsibility could have been revised to account for the new social reality, but that was not an option readily available to prosecutors. They had to take the law as they found it. Moreover, even if change were possible, and the concept of criminal responsibility were somehow adjusted so as to facilitate a prosecution of the officer whose conduct has a structural or situational explanation, then the very point of preferring the criminal law as a legal remedy would have disappeared; the social meaning of the label and the punitive practice would change dramatically. The attractiveness of the criminal law derives, in part, from the fact that it is strongly accusatory and thus permits the imposition of the harshest sentence on that individual, but these advantages would, I believe, largely disappear if systematic adjustments were made to the criminal law so as to permit conviction in the face of more attenuated notions of responsibility. We could extend the reach of the criminal law only by trivializing and rendering incoherent its most fundamental concepts.

The presence of the larger structural or situational explanations for rights violations not only diminishes individual responsibility, making conviction unlikely and less normatively appropriate, but it also creates doubts about the efficacy of the criminal law in changing future behavior, even assuming a successful prosecution. True, a conviction would create especially powerful incentives for the convicted officers to obey the particular norm in the future and also to resist the pressures that led to the violation (specific deterrence). Conviction might even result in the removal of those individual officers from the police force (incapacitation). But what effect would the conviction have on others? Officers not prosecuted might well be influenced by the reaffirmation of the norm entailed in the prosecution (the social norm would become internalized); and they might also be influenced by the fact that one of their colleagues had been punished for violating a citizen's rights (general deterrence). In that way it could be said that other officers would be given an incentive to resist the situational and structural pressures. It is hard to gauge how strong that incentive would be, but of even greater significance is the fact that the criminal conviction would leave the underlying situational or structural factors undisturbed.

Altering the target of the prosecution was considered. For example, some argued that the criminal prosecution should focus on a supervisory officer rather than on line officers and that a change would enhance the effectiveness of the criminal law. The supervisory officer would then have reasons to make the necessary changes in organizational structure so as to decrease the chance of future violations by line officers. Such a strategy, however, has problems of its own. For one thing, it would be hard to affix criminal responsibility to the supervising officer. Only if the line officer were acting under direct and explicit commands from the supervisory officer—or, alternatively, if the higher-level official initiated and inspired the program of abuses—could the supervisor be held criminally responsible for the misdeeds of line officers. A failure to find out what line officers were doing, or a failure to take necessary disciplinary action when he or she had reason to know of wrongdoing, would not be sufficient to establish the requisite criminal responsibility. As a moral matter, the chief should certainly try to find out what his or her line officers are doing, and perhaps even be removed from office for a failure to do so; yet it would be presumptuous, if not unfair, to condemn that failure with the harshness of the criminal law.

Moreover, while the prosecution of supervisory officers may be more efficacious than prosecuting line officers because it gives incentives to those with the power necessary to effect organizational reform, this remedial strategy does not adequately deal with those causal factors that lie outside the organization, such as the social context (e.g., the polarization of the races) or the institutional network in which the organization is embedded (e.g., inappropriate funding by the legislature). The supervisor who is prosecuted may point an accusing finger at these other extra-organizational forces (as well as the line officers), but the criminal prosecution against the supervisory officer provides no incentive whatsoever for these other agencies to alter their behavior. Indeed, the criminal prosecution tends to divert attention from those causal forces because it tends to personalize responsibility—it suggests that it is only the chief's fault.

A criminal prosecution against the organization itself might seem even more promising than the strategy of placing criminal responsibility on supervisory personnel. An organization could not be imprisoned, but heavy fines could be imposed. These fines might provide the necessary incentives for the legislature to undertake appropriate reform action, since the legislature (and the taxpayers) would have to foot the bill. Fining the organization might also give the managers of the organization incentives to institute the necessary reforms. This remedial alternative is not, however, without its own problems. The criminal statutes available to the prosecutors in the 1960s to deal with rights violations were aimed at persons, not organizations, and could have been used only if the courts were willing to take the tendency of anthropomorphizing organizations to new and unthinkable lengths. It would abuse a metaphor.[2]

The attractiveness of the injunction during the civil rights era largely stemmed from the fact that it permitted the state to avoid many of these difficulties. It is a wholly prospective remedy and thus need not be based on a finding that the party to which it is addressed, whether it be an organization or an individual, did something wrong. The injunction does not even require a showing that the party to be enjoined is about to do something wrongful (in the strong accusatory sense of that word). What it does require is a showing that sometime in the future a violation of rights will probably occur and that the party enjoined has the power to prevent that violation from occurring. This means, for example, that the injunction sought could be addressed to supervisors, requiring them to collect data on the action of line officers and to take necessary disciplinary action. Or the injunction could require the governor or the legislature to appropriate more funds to enhance training programs or to increase manpower. Such an injunction could be predicated on the theory that the court has the power to require whatever actions are needed to protect the rights of the citizens.

Prosecutors had to take the criminal law as they found it, but the injunction allowed more innovation. Sensitive to the larger situational and structural factors that might be responsible for the pattern of abuse, adjustments were made to the injunction. In its classical form, the injunction was an order that prohibited some discrete act from occurring in the future, say, the dumping of waste into a river. But during the civil rights era, the injunction was transformed into an instrument—referred to in this book as the structural injunction—by which the courts managed the reconstruction of an ongoing bureaucratic organization.

Typically one part of the structural decree restated the basic legal norm, such as requiring, for example, no discrimination on the basis of race; no cruel and unusual punishment; respect for the security of persons and their homes; and the like. Then the court order spelled out the steps to be taken to restructure the organization so as to eliminate or reduce the threat posed to the full exercise of constitutional rights. An injunction designed to prevent the harassment of minorities by the police force, for example, might have required the establishment of a grievance board within the department. The order might specify who is to serve on the board, how these persons might be selected, the ways citizens can file complaints, the notice the citizen should be given, time limits on such filings, the procedures to be followed by the board, the scale of disciplinary action, and so forth.

Aside from these changes in the content of the decree, the attempt to cope with the larger structural and situational factors also altered the basic methods by which those decrees were enforced. Traditionally the basic method was contempt, but judges quickly understood that frequent resort to the contempt power would return the court to a search for individual wrongdoing and the conundrums of the criminal prosecution. As a result, the typical method of enforcing the structural decree was through the modification of the initial decree and the issuance of supplemental orders.

The court usually began with a general command to obey the law, hoping to capitalize on whatever goodwill or professional integrity remained within the organization. When violations persisted, the court did not use its contempt power, but usually called on the supervisory personnel to submit a plan for reorganization. Once that plan was submitted, it was duly tested in court. At the conclusion of the hearing, the court would write the proposed plan or some variant of it into the decree. The court might, for example, at first proscribe certain general practices, like conducting searches for suspects on the basis of anonymous tips. If this remedy failed and abuses recurred, the court, once again anxious to avoid the contempt power, might enter a third stage of supplemental relief. Now the decree would acquire a more structural character, by requiring the establishment of an internal review board and specifying some of the steps that would be needed for the achievement of organizational reform. Even here the series of supplemental orders might not end. Typically jurisdiction of the court was maintained to see whether further relief was necessary, for example, to make certain that the board operated fairly and effectively, had the necessary funding from the legislature, and so on.

Of course, at any point in this process the court could use its contempt power, and might be tempted to do so, if the disobedience were sufficiently flagrant. For the most part, however, the disobedience was not of that character, but instead consisted of predictable human and institutional failure. Accordingly, the court once again shied away from the contempt power, as prosecutors had shied away from the criminal law. The court merely sought to alter the terms and methods of the injunctive intervention and experimented until a solution was found.

Inchoate Rights

The preeminence of the injunction during the Second Reconstruction was attributable not only to the changing nature of social reality and recognition of the structural and situational explanation for the violation of rights. It also reflected a more sophisticated understanding of the nature of rights itself. It had a philosophic as well as a sociological basis.

In speaking of the protection of rights during the 1960s, I am generally referring to those rights founded on the Constitution, specifically the Bill of Rights and the Thirteenth, Fourteenth, and Fifteenth Amendments. This species of rights might seem to have a more positivistic foundation and thus be more concrete than human rights, which, after all, are those derived from a notion of personhood. The fact is, however, that the Constitution operates at a rather high level of abstraction—not as abstract as the concept of personhood but abstract nonetheless. The Constitution is a charter of governance. It establishes at the highest levels of generality the institutions of government and prescribes the norms, standards, and principles that should govern the operation of these government institutions. These norms tend to be formulated abstractly and await a sociopolitical practice and complementary interpretive process to become fully operative. In this context, legally enforceable rights emerge as the product of the process of trying to give concrete meaning to these norms and the values they embody.

At any time a finite set of rights exists, simply because some portion of the process of actualization has already run its course. In 1954, for example, at the very beginning of the Second Reconstruction, the lynching of a black person (in which a sheriff actively participated) clearly would have been regarded as a violation of a constitutional right. This was so because for some time the Equal Protection Clause had been interpreted to include a right that protected individuals from such racially based forms of state terror. It is equally true, however, that before 1954 most of the other constitutional rights we take for granted today, even the right to a racially non-segregated education, had never been clearly articulated. To a philosopher, these rights may have always existed, but only in the limited sense that if any court had correctly spoken to that issue it would have declared that such a right exists. The fact is, however, that the history of the law in the United States, or for that matter anywhere else, is filled with mistakes or, even more, with silences. Until the mistake is corrected or the silence filled, the list of constitutional rights remains incomplete and inchoate.

During the Second Reconstruction the list of constitutional rights was greatly expanded. It was a period in which the right to a non-segregated education was formulated, promulgated, and then subsequently elaborated. For example, the courts also announced a right not to be discriminated against on the basis of wealth, a right for an indigent to have counsel appointed, a right to notice and a hearing before welfare benefits are terminated, a right to consult counsel before being questioned by the police, and a right to equal representation in voting. Even if the right had been previously articulated, during this period it gained a new and richer meaning.

Sometimes this process of articulating and elaborating rights occurred in the context of passing on a defense to a criminal prosecution. A citizen prosecuted for violating a general criminal statute might try to exclude a confession from the trial because he or she was not allowed to consult with counsel during the interrogation.[3] In ruling on that defense (at trial, on direct appeal, or in a collateral attack through the writ of habeas corpus) the court would have to interpret the Fifth Amendment privilege against self-incrimination and, at the conclusion of that interpretive process, might announce that a suspect has the right to consult counsel during a police interrogation. The court then had to decide whether the newly articulated right should be applied to all previous convictions.

It was therefore not strictly necessary to use the injunction for the process of rights articulation and elaboration, but the fact remains that the injunction proved to be a much more congenial instrument for that purpose than the criminal defense. Once again, crucial in this regard was the injunction's prospective character—the fact that the injunction looked to the future. Although at times it required an undoing of established practices, it offered an opportunity for voluntary compliance with the newly declared rights. Indeed, as we found out in the second *Brown* case, where the Court announced the "all deliberate speed" formula, that opportunity could be expanded.[4] Problems of retroactivity, as confronted in declaring rights in the criminal defense context, were thus minimized. Moreover, as I suggested before in my discussion of the process through which structural decrees are enforced (supplemental relief), the injunction allowed the court to return time and time again to the institutional practices and to measure them against constitutional ideals and thus introduced a more dynamic element into the interpretive process. Each request for supplemental relief created another opportunity for the court to consider the shape and terms of the right it had articulated and, if necessary, to alter the previous formulation.

In contrast to the injunctive process, the criminal prosecution had little flexibility. In fact, it presupposed that the rights in question had been fully and sharply articulated. During the 1960s there were two federal criminal statutes that seemed to reach as far as the Constitution.[5] They provided criminal penalties (one a felony, the other a misdemeanor) for forcible interferences with—and here is the catch—"rights secured by the Constitution and laws of the United States." What are these rights? Until some relatively clear response could be made to that question, there would be, in the minds of the prosecutor and the jurors, an obvious difficulty and an obvious unfairness in prosecuting someone for violating those statutes. The need for a rights-articulation process would not, of course, arise if the conduct in question were so gross as to violate the most elementary understanding of what rights we have—for example, when the contested conduct consisted of a racially based lynching organized by state officials or the crudest form of police brutality. But once you moved beyond such cases, or varied one of elements, as you invariably did when their more complex and subtle forms of behavior were challenged, the criminal law seemed inappropriate, at once too crude and too blunt an instrument. To affix blame, label conduct as criminal, and impose a punishment, the rights violated must be clearly known and clearly articulated.

Of course, once the injunctive process has run its course, and the list of rights has been fully elaborated, new opportunities may be created for an increased reliance on the criminal law. From this perspective, the criminal law might thus be seen as a supplement to the injunction (rather than the other way around). Such interaction occurred in April 1968, shortly after the assassination of Martin Luther King Jr., when Congress passed a new criminal statute in the civil rights field.[6] The measure greatly extended the reach of the criminal law in its protection of civil rights. It was made possible, however, by the fifteen prior years of injunctive litigation, where the crucial battles as to the nature, shape, and reach of the right to equal protection were fought. Indeed, the 1968 statute can be understood as a codification of the declared rights with the addition of a new sanction. The statute extended the protection of the criminal law to the rights that had previously emerged in the course of injunctive litigation (and, to a lesser extent, in the defense of a criminal prosecution). But with respect to rights not yet declared, we continued to look primarily to the injunctive process for the continuation of the process of rights-articulation that had begun in 1954 with *Brown v. Board of Education.*

The Wrongs of Everyday Life

Moving beyond some special technical features of the U.S. procedural system, I have identified two different and quite general reasons that account for an awkward fit between the criminal law and human rights. One has to do with the changing nature of social reality, and the difficulty of locating that element of individual responsibility required by the criminal law; the other has to do with the inchoate nature of rights and the need for a process to render them concrete. Common to both explanations has been the distinction between the ordinary and the extraordinary, the banal and the demonic.[7]

Extraordinary events—the murder of Viola Liuzzo in 1965 during the Selma March or the murder of three civil rights workers in Mississippi a year earlier at the outset of Freedom Summer[8]—tend to capture the public's attention in a swift and dramatic way. They demand a stern response by law enforcement agencies, which is often in the form of a criminal prosecution. Such a response seems to me to be entirely appropriate, and yet our willingness to applaud and accept such measures should not obscure two other facts.

One is that for most citizens, most of the time, the true source of oppression is not the activities of the Klan or similar paramilitary organizations but rather the accepted violence of everyday life—school segregation, job discrimination, and the indignities of Jim Crow; the small but persistent abuses by the police, inflicted on a day-to-day basis as they go about their work; the overcrowding of prisons and the use of trustee systems to deal with budgetary shortages; warehousing of patients who have nowhere else to go. The appropriate remedy for these sources of oppression is the injunction, not the criminal law, both because the rights to govern these situations still need to be articulated and because the violations are largely attributable to structural or situational factors; indeed, that is why they are part of our ordinary everyday life.

Second, although a criminal prosecution might respond to the felt necessities of some highly charged situation, it also risks creating a misunderstanding. It suggests that the violations are personal and the remedial problems are simple. It leads us to believe that, because we are punishing some individuals, we have done all that needs to be done to protect rights. The need for structural reform appears less urgent. In fact, the criminal prosecution may also divert our critical energy. A criminal prosecution focuses our attention on the extraordinary and sometimes gives to the ordinary, simply because it is ignored, a patina of legitimacy that is ill deserved.

The criminal prosecution and the injunction are not mutually exclusive. The same incident may be subject to both remedies—indeed, earlier I suggested that, over time, one may operate as the supplement of the other. It is best to recognize, however, that a measure of competition exists between the two, and that within the budget or program of any law enforcement agency it will be necessary to establish priorities, if for no other reason than because the economic, temporal, and emotional resources that are consumed by one are diverted from the other. A number of criminal prosecutions for brutal violations of rights were launched during the 1960s, but each criminal prosecution taxed the Civil Rights Division of the Department of Justice to the breaking point, in terms of time, manpower, and organizational resources. Granted, in some cases the criminal prosecution should be the remedy of first recourse. However, that, I believe, is the exception rather than the rule. To see such a need within every human or civil rights violation, or even the bulk of them, would be to place the appropriate government agency in an unfortunate straitjacket and inevitably cause a reversal of the proper priorities. A fixation on the criminal law would result in a thunderous condemnation of the extraordinary but would nonetheless leave the ordinary unexamined and, as a result, leave most of our rights unprotected.

9

Objectivity and Interpretation

Of all the jurisprudential movements spawned since the 1970s, I feel a special affinity for Critical Legal Studies. I share the egalitarianism that inspired the movement and that initially drew so many to its ranks. What I object to is its theoretical excesses—its determination to obliterate the line between law and politics and to deny that objective law is ever possible.

On a purely practical level, the claims of Critical Legal Studies scholars seem fanciful. Only the most naïve or those unfamiliar with the distribution of power in America could believe that debunking law could possibly serve the cause of equality. Although the Second Reconstruction depended on the activism of the Civil Rights Movement and the efforts of the Executive and Congress, the great transformation never would have come to be without *Brown v. Board of Education* and the judgment that racial segregation was unacceptable as a matter of law, not just politics.

Although the flaws of Critical Legal Studies as a political movement were clear, coming to terms with its underlying theory—above all, the claim that all interpretation is necessarily and thoroughly indeterminate—was more difficult. For that purpose I found myself turning to the work of a number of philosophers and literary theorists. Much to my surprise, however, some of these theorists, especially the ones located in New Haven, only lent support to the claims of Critical Legal Studies and the indeterminacy thesis. I thus needed to address Deconstructionism as well as Critical Legal Studies. The essay that follows necessarily draws on literary theory as well as philosophy, and it tries to identify the distinctive features of law that make objective interpretation possible.

This essay was spurred by Professor Thomas Heller's invitation to participate in the series of lectures to inaugurate the Stanford Humanities Center. The lecture was delivered on May 12, 1981, and was later published, together with a response by Paul Brest, then a professor at Stanford University and arguably more sympathetic to Critical Legal Studies than I. His response was entitled "Interpretation and Interest," and, together with my essay, appeared in the April 1982 issue of the *Stanford Law Review* (volume 34).

$\sim$ ADJUDICATION is interpretation: It is the process by which a judge comes to understand and express the meaning of an authoritative legal text and the values embodied in that text. Interpretation, in the law or literature, is neither a wholly discretionary nor a wholly mechanical activity. It is a dynamic interaction between reader and text, and meaning is the product of that interaction. Interpretation affords proper recognition of both the subjective and objective dimensions of human experience; for that reason, it has emerged in recent decades as an attractive method for studying all social activity.[1] The idea of a written text, the standard object of legal or literary interpretation, has been expanded to embrace social action and situations, which are sometimes called text-analogues. In one of the most significant works of this genre to date, Clifford Geertz's *Negara*, a nineteenth-century Balinese cremation ceremony, is taken as "the text."[2]

Admittedly, to treat everything as a text might seem to trivialize the idea of a text, but the appeal of the interpretive analogy stems from two facts: that interpretation accords a proper place for both the perspective of the scholar and the reality of the object being studied, and that interpretation sees the task of explicating meaning as the most important and most basic intellectual endeavor. This appeal is considerable and, as a consequence, liberties have been taken with the notion of a text, and interpretation is now accepted as central to disciplines that were once on the verge of surrendering to the so-called scientific ethos, such as politics and history (though interestingly, not economics—there the surrender to the pretense of science seems complete). The behaviorists or social scientists have hardly quit the field, but a new humanistic strand has emerged, and, when pushed to define that strand, one would speak, above all, of interpretation.

To recover, then, an old and familiar idea, namely, that adjudication is a form of interpretation, will build bridges between law and the humanities, and suggest a unity among mankind's many intellectual endeavors. A proper regard for the distinctive social function of adjudication, and for the conditions that limit the legitimate exercise of the judicial power, will require care in identifying the kinds of texts to be construed and the rules governing the interpretive process; the judge is to read the legal text, not morality or public opinion, not, if you will, the moral or social texts. But the essential unity between law and the humanities will be reinforced and the judge's vision will be enlarged.

Recognizing the interpretive dimensions of adjudication and the dynamic character of all interpretive activity and its capacity to relate constructively the subjective and objective will also deepen our understanding of law and, in fact, might even suggest how law is possible. It might enable us to come to terms with a new nihilism, one that doubts the legitimacy of adjudication—a nihilism that appears to me to be unwarranted and unsound but that is gaining respectability and claiming an increasing number of important and respected legal scholars, particularly in constitutional law. They have turned their backs on adjudication and have begun a romance with politics.[3]

This new nihilism might acknowledge the characterization of adjudication as interpretation, but it then would insist that the characterization is a sham. The nihilist argues that for any text—particularly such a comprehensive text as the Constitution—there are any number of possible meanings, that interpretation consists of choosing one of those meanings, and that in this selection process the judge will inevitably express his or her own values. All law is masked power. In this regard the new nihilism is reminiscent of the Legal Realism of the early twentieth century. It, too, sought to unmask what was claimed to be the true nature of legal doctrine, particularly the doctrine that insulated laissez-faire capitalism from the growth of the activist state and the reforms pressed by Progressives and the supporters of the New Deal. It saw law as a projection of the judge's values.

In the decades following World War II, particularly in the 1960s, at the height of the Warren Court era, a new judicial doctrine arose to replace the one associated with laissez-faire capitalism. It embraced the role of the activist state and saw equality, rather than liberty, as the central constitutional value. Scholars turned to defending this new doctrine and, in so doing, sought to rehabilitate the idea of law in the face of the Realist legacy.

The nihilism of today is largely a reaction to this reconstructive effort of the 1960s. It harks back to the Realist Movement of an earlier era, and coincides with a number of contemporary phenomena—the end of the Warren Court; a social and political culture dominated by the privatization of all ends; and a new movement in literary criticism, and maybe even in philosophy, called Deconstructionism, which expands the idea of text to embrace all the world and at the same time proclaims the freedom of the interpreter.[4]

The Idea of Bounded Objectivity

The nihilism of which I speak fastens on the objective aspiration of the law as a distinguishing feature of legal interpretation. The judge, the nihilist reminds us, seeks not just a plausible interpretation but seeks one that is objectively true. Judges may not project their preferences or their views of what is right or wrong, or adopt those of the parties or of the body politic. The judge must say what the Constitution requires. The issue is not whether school desegregation is good or bad, desirable or undesirable, to the judge, the parties, or the public, but whether it is mandated by the Constitution. The law aspires to objectivity, so the nihilist observes, but the nature of the constitutional text makes this impossible. The text is capable of any number of possible meanings, and thus it is impossible to speak of one interpretation as true and the other false. It is impossible to speak of law with the objectivity required by the idea of justice.

The nihilist stresses two features of the legal text in explaining why objectivity is impossible. One is the use of general language. The Constitution does not, for example, contain a specific directive about the criteria for assigning students among the public schools, but provides that no state shall "deny to any person within its jurisdiction the equal protection of the laws." There is no further specification of what is meant by "state," "person," "jurisdiction," "protection," "laws," or, most important, "equal." The potential of "equal" is staggering, and the nihilist is confounded by it.

A second feature of the text is its comprehensiveness. The Constitution is a rich and varied text. It contains a multitude of values, some of which potentially conflict with others. It promises equality and liberty. In fact, at times it seems to contain almost every conceivable value, especially when one refers to such provisions as the Privileges and Immunities Clause of Article IV or the Fourteenth Amendment, or the provision of the Ninth Amendment that reserves to the people rights not otherwise enumerated in the Constitution.

In coming to terms with this nihilism, one must begin by acknowledging the generality and comprehensiveness of the constitutional text, and by insisting that in this regard the Constitution is no different from a poem or any legal instrument. Generality and comprehensiveness are features of any text. Though the Constitution may be more general and comprehend more than a sonnet or a contract, it is comparable in this regard to an epic poem or some national statutes. Few, if any, statutes touch as many activities as the Constitution itself (which, after all, establishes the machinery of government), but many, if not most, embody conflicting values and are in that sense comprehensive. It should be understood that generality and comprehensiveness do not discourage interpretation but are the very qualities that usually provoke it. Interpretation is a process of generating meaning, and one important—and very common—way of both understanding and expressing the meaning of a text is to render it specific and concrete.

Some legal theorists would limit legal interpretation to highly specific constitutional clauses. This school, misleadingly called "interpretivism" but more properly called "textual determinism," operates under a most arid and artificial conception of interpretation.[5] Proponents of this school hold that only a specific text can be interpreted. Interpretation is thus confused with execution—the application of a determinate meaning to a situation—and is unproblematic only with regard to clauses like the one requiring the president to be at least thirty-five years old. Most interpretivists, including Justice Hugo Black, would recognize the narrowness of such a perspective and want to acknowledge a role for less specific clauses, like freedom of speech; but, in truth, such provisions are hardly obvious in their meaning and require substantial judicial interpretation to be given their proper effect. Does "speech" embrace movies, flags, picketing, and campaign expenditures? What is meant by "freedom"? Does it, as Isaiah Berlin wondered, pertain exclusively to the absence of restraint, or does it also embrace an affirmative capacity for self-realization?[6]

This endorsement of active judicial interpretation of specific clauses, while cautioning against judicial interpretation of the more general and potentially more far-reaching clauses like due process and equal protection, represents an attempt at line drawing that itself cannot be textually justified. It is, instead, motivated by a desire—resting on the most questionable of premises—to limit both the role of constitutional values in American government and the role of the judiciary in expressing those values. The line itself is illogical. It would require that small effect be given to the comprehensive constitutional protections while full effect is given to the narrow ones. I reject this attempt at line drawing because I reject the premises and the result. Yet it must be emphasized that, for purposes of this essay, the critical question is not whether judicial interpretation of specific clauses, understood in any realistic sense, is legitimate and that of general clauses is not, since, as we saw in the case of the First Amendment, both require substantial interpretation. Rather, the question is whether any judicial interpretation can achieve the measure of objectivity required by the idea of law.

Objectivity in the law connotes standards. It implies that an interpretation can be measured against a set of norms that transcend the particular vantage point of the person offering the interpretation. Objectivity implies that the interpretation can be judged by something other than one's own notions of correctness. It imparts a notion of impersonality. The idea of an objective interpretation does not require that the interpretation be wholly determined by some source external to the judge, but only that it be constrained. To explain the source of constraint in the law, it is necessary to introduce two further concepts: One is the idea of disciplining rules, which constrain the interpreter and constitute the standards by which the correctness of the interpretation is to be judged; the other is the idea of an interpretive community, which recognizes these rules as authoritative.

The idea of objective interpretation accommodates the creative role of the reader. It recognizes that the meaning of a text does not reside in the text, as an object might reside in physical space or as an element might be said to be present in a chemical compound, ready to be extracted if only one knows the correct process. It recognizes a role for the subjective. Indeed, interpretation is defined as the process by which the meaning of a text is understood and expressed, and the acts of understanding and expression necessarily entail strong personal elements. At the same time, the freedom of those who interpret is not absolute. Interpreters are not free to assign any meaning they wish to the text. They are disciplined by a set of rules that specify the relevance and weight to be assigned to the material (e.g., words, history, intention, consequence), as well as by those that define basic concepts and that establish the procedural circumstances under which the interpretation must occur.

The disciplining rules may vary from text to text. The rules for the interpretation of a poem differ from those governing the interpretation of legal material. Even within the law, there may be different rules depending on the text—those for contractual interpretation vary from statutory interpretation, and both vary from those used in constitutional interpretation. Though the particular content of disciplining rules varies, their function is the same. They constrain the interpreter, thus transforming the interpretive process from a subjective to an objective one, and they furnish the standards by which the correctness of the interpretation can be judged. These rules are not simply standards or principles held by individual judges but, instead, constitute the institution (the profession) in which judges find themselves and through which they act. The disciplining rules operate similarly to the rules of language, which constrain the users of the language, furnish the standards for judging the uses of language, and constitute the language. The disciplining rules of the law may be understood, as my colleague Bruce Ackerman has suggested, as a professional grammar.

Rules are not rules unless they are authoritative, and only a community can confer that authority. Accordingly, the disciplining rules governing an interpretive activity must be seen as defining or demarcating an interpretive community consisting of those who recognize the rules as authoritative. This means, above all, that the objective quality of interpretation is bounded, limited, or relative.[7] It is the existence of a community that recognizes and adheres to the disciplining rules used by the interpreter, and is defined by its recognition of those rules, that bounds it. The objectivity of the physical world may be more transcendent, less relativistic, though the Kuhnian tradition in the philosophy of science throws considerable doubt on that commonsense understanding;[8] but as revealed by the reference to language, and the analogy I have drawn between the rules of language and the disciplining rules of interpretation, the physical does not exhaust the claim of objectivity nor does it make this bounded objectivity of interpretation a secondary or parasitic kind of objectivity. Bounded objectivity is the only kind of objectivity to which the law—or any interpretive activity— ever aspires and the only one we care about.[9] To insist on more, to search for the "brooding omnipresence in the sky,"[10] is to create a false issue.

Nihilism is also fashionable in certain literary circles and is represented there by what I referred to as the Deconstruction Movement. Deconstructionists exalt the creative and subjective dimension of interpretation. For them, interpretive freedom is absolute. Deconstructionists reject the idea of objectivity in interpretation, presumably even the bounded objectivity of which I speak, because they would deny that an interpretive community possesses the necessary authority to confer on the rules that might constrain the interpreter and constitute the standards of evaluation. Deconstructionists consider competing interpretive communities and the freedom of the literary critics to leave one community to join or establish another, inconsistent with the authoritativeness that rules need in order to constrain. They hold that authority that depends completely on members' agreement is not authority at all.

I will not attempt here to dispute the notion that literary critics are so unconstrained that no claim of objectivity can be made for any of their interpretations, though my instinct is to be wary of this form of nihilism, too.[11] For my purposes, it is sufficient to recognize the distinctive feature of legal interpretation: In law the interpretive community is a reality. It has authority to confer because membership does not depend on agreement. Judges do not belong to an interpretive community as a result of shared views about particular issues or interpretations but by virtue of their commitment to uphold and advance the rule of law itself. They belong by virtue of their office. There can be many schools of literary interpretation, but, as my student Jordan Flyer once put it, in legal interpretation there is only one school, and attendance is mandatory. All judges define themselves as members of this school and must do so in order to exercise the prerogatives of their office. Even if their personal commitment to the rule of law wavers, the rule continues to act on judges. Even if the rule of law fails to persuade, it can coerce. Judges know that if they relinquish their membership in the interpretive community or deny its authority, they lose their right to speak with the authority of the law.

Nothing I have said denies the possibility of disagreement in legal interpretation. Some disputes may be centered on the correct application of a rule of discipline. For example, a dispute may arise over a rule that requires the interpreter to look to history. Some may claim that the judge has misunderstood the history of the Fourteenth Amendment or that the judge is using a level of generality that is inappropriate for constitutional interpretation.[12] These critics may claim, for example, that the focus should not be on the willingness of those who drafted and adopted the Fourteenth Amendment to tolerate segregated schools but on the framers' desire to eradicate the caste system and the implication of that desire for segregated education today. Disputes of this kind are commonplace, but they pose little threat to the legitimacy of the disciplining rules; they pose only issues of application.

Other disputes may arise, however, and they may involve a challenge to the very authority or existence of a rule. Some judges or lawyers may, for example, deny the relevance of history altogether in constitutional interpretation.[13] Disputes of this type pose a more serious challenge to the idea of objectivity than those over the application of a rule, for such disputes threaten the source of constraint itself. It should be remembered, however, that there are procedures in the law for resolving these disputes—for example, pronouncements by the highest court and perhaps even legislation and constitutional amendments. The presence of such procedures and a hierarchy of authority for resolving disputes that could potentially divide or destroy an interpretive community is one of the distinctive features of legal interpretation. One should also be careful not to exaggerate the impact of such disputes. The authority of a particular rule can be maintained even when it is disputed, provided the disagreement is not too pervasive; the integrity of an interpretive community can be preserved even in the face of a dispute or disagreement as to the authority of some particular disciplining rule. The legal community transcends cliques; some cliques may dissolve over time, others may come to dominate the community.

Just as objectivity is compatible with a measure of disagreement, it should also be stressed that objectivity is compatible with error: An objective interpretation is not necessarily a correct one. *Brown v. Board of Education* and *Plessy v. Ferguson*[14]—one condemning segregation, the other approving it—may both be objective and thus legitimate exercises of the judicial power, though only one is correct. To understand how this is possible, we must first recognize that legal interpretations can be evaluated from two perspectives—the internal and the external.

From the internal perspective, the standards of evaluation are the disciplining rules themselves, and the authority of the interpretive community is fully acknowledged. The criticism, say, of *Plessy v. Ferguson*, might be that the judges did not correctly understand the authoritative rules or may have misapplied them; the judges may have failed to grasp the constitutional ideal of equality imported into the Constitution by the Fourteenth Amendment or may have incorrectly assumed that the affront to blacks entailed in the Jim Crow system was self-imposed. Though such a criticism argues that the interpretation is mistaken, it might nonetheless acknowledge the objective character of the interpretation on the theory, borrowed from Wittgenstein,[15] that misunderstanding is a form of understanding, that a judge could misunderstand or misapply a rule and still be constrained by it. An objective but (legally) incorrect interpretation partakes of the impersonality or sense of constraint that the idea of law implies. Not every mistake in adjudication is an example of lawlessness.

The internal perspective permits still another type of criticism in which both the objectivity and the correctness of the decision may be challenged. The charge may be that the judge utterly disregarded well-recognized disciplining rules, such as those requiring the judge to take account of the intentions of the framers of the Fourteenth Amendment or those rules prohibiting the judge from being influenced by personal animosities or bias. If these are the bases of criticism of the judicial decision, and arguably they may have some relevance to *Plessy*, then the claim is that the interpretation is both wrong and non-objective. I imagine it is also possible for an interpretation to be both non-objective and correct, as when a judge simply decides to do what he or she wishes; that is, once again the judge utterly disregards the disciplining rules and yet, in this instance, gives the text the same meaning—in a substantive sense—as would a fair and conscientious judge constrained by all the appropriate rules. Such a situation does not seem to be of great practical importance, but it once again illustrates the analytic distinction between objectivity and correctness, even from the wholly internal perspective. Both qualities arise from the very same rules: Objectivity speaks to the constraining force of the rules and whether the act of judging is constrained; correctness speaks to the content of the rules and whether the process of adjudication and the meaning produced by that process are fully in accord with that content. From the internal perspective, legitimacy largely turns on objectivity rather than correctness; as I emphasize in the last chapter of this book, judges are allowed to make some mistakes. Judicial reason is fallible.

The internal perspective does not exhaust all evaluation of legal interpretation. Someone who stands outside the interpretive community and thus disputes the authority of that community and its rules may provide another viewpoint—an extended one. A criticism from this so-called external perspective might protest *Plessy* on the basis of some religious or ethical principle (e.g., denying the relevance of any racial distinction) or on the grounds of some theory of politics (e.g., condemning the decision because it will cause social unrest). In that instance, the evaluation is not in terms of the law; it matters not at all whether the decision is objective. It may be law, even good law, but it is wrong—morally, politically, or from a religious point of view.

External critics may accept the pluralism implied by the adjectives "legal," "moral," "political," and "religious," each denoting different standards of judgment or different spheres of human activity. External critics may be able to order their lives in a way that both acknowledges the validity of the legal judgment and preserves the integrity of the view, based on non-legal standards, about the correctness of the decision. They may render unto the law that which is the law's. Conflict is not a necessity, but it does occur, as it did over the extension of slavery in the 1850s and over the legalization of abortion in the 1970s. Those who criticize from this perspective will then have to establish priorities. They may move to amend the Constitution or engage in any number of lesser and more problematic strategies designed to alter the legal standards, such as packing the court or enacting statutes that curtail jurisdiction. Failing that, they remain free to insist that the moral, religious, or political principle take precedence over the legal. They can disobey the law.

One of the remarkable features of the American legal system is that it permits such a broad range of responses to external criticism, and that over time—maybe in some instances over too much time—the legal system responds to this criticism. The law evolves. There is progress in the law. An equally remarkable feature of the American system is that the freedom of external critics to deny the law, and to insist that their moral, religious, or political views take precedence over the legal interpretation, is a freedom not easily exercised. Endogenous change is always preferred, even in the realm of the wholly intellectual. External critics struggle to work within the law, say, through amendments, appointments, or inducing the Supreme Court to recognize that it had made a mistake. An exercise of the freedom to deny the law, and to insist that the favored moral, religious, or political views take precedence, requires critics to dispute the authority of the Constitution and the community it defines. That is a task not lightly engaged. The authority of the law is bounded, true, but, as de Tocqueville recognized more than a century ago, in America those bounds are almost without limits.[16] Commitment to the rule of law is nearly universal.

The Special Needs of the Law

Viewing adjudication as interpretation helps to stop the slide toward nihilism. It makes law possible. We can find in this conceptualization recognition of both the subjective and the objective—the important personal role played by the interpreter in the meaning-giving process, as well as the possibility of an inter-subjective meaning rooted in disciplining rules and an interpretive community that both legitimates those rules and is defined by them. I have explained how objective interpretation becomes possible in the law, even if it is not possible in literature. But a number of other distinguishing features of adjudication remain to be considered: the prescriptive nature of the text, the claim of authoritativeness for the interpretation, and the desire for efficacy. These differences seem to deny the essential unity between the ways of the law and those of the humanities, and may well cast doubt on my claim about the existence of constraint in the law.

The question is whether we can insist that adjudication is an interpretive activity and still find that it possesses an objective character in the face of these differences. I think we can.

The Prescriptive Nature of the Text

Legal texts are prescriptive. Though they presuppose a state of the world, and employ terms and concepts that are descriptive or representational, their purpose is not to describe but to prescribe. For example, the statement in the Fourteenth Amendment that "no State shall . . . deny to any person within its jurisdiction the equal protection of the laws" is not meant to depict what is happening, much less what has happened, but to prescribe what should happen. It embodies a value, namely, equality, and I see adjudication as the process by which that value, among others, is given concrete meaning and expression.

Adjudication and morality both aspire to prescribe norms of proper conduct. Both state the ideal. The ultimate authority for morality is some conception of the good. The ultimate authority for a judicial decree is the Constitution, for that text embodies public values and establishes the institutions through which those values are to be understood and expressed. When a lawyer is asked to justify why the schools of a community must be desegregated, reference will first be made to some lower court decision, then to a Supreme Court decision, and finally to the Constitution itself, for it is the source of both the value of equality and the authority of the judiciary to interpret that value.

The prescriptive element in adjudication and legal texts does not preclude objective interpretation. Prescriptive texts are as amenable to interpretation as descriptive ones. Those who might think otherwise would point to the profound and pervasive disagreement that often characterizes moral life—that people disagree about what is right and good, as, for example, whether the separate-but-equal doctrine is consistent with equality or whether the state should be allowed to interfere with the freedom of a woman to decide to have an abortion. The existence of this disagreement cannot be denied, but I fail to see why it precludes interpretation or is inconsistent with objectivity.

Interpretation does not require agreement or consensus, nor does the objective character of legal interpretation arise from agreement. What is being interpreted is a text and the morality embodied in that text, not what individual people believe to be the good or right. Individuals are, as I have already noted, morally free to dispute the claim of the public morality embodied in the Constitution and its interpretation—they can become renegades—but that possibility does not deny the existence or validity of either that morality or its interpretation. Neither the objectivity nor the correctness of *Brown v. Board of Education* depended on the unanimity of the Justices, and much less on the willingness of the people—all the people or most of the people—then or even now—to agree with that decision. The test is whether that decision is in accord with the authoritative disciplining rules. Short of a disagreement that denies the authority of the interpretive community and the force of the disciplining rules, agreement is irrelevant in determining whether a judicial decision is a proper interpretation of the law.

Moreover, though the celebration of disagreement in the realm of morality has become commonplace, it is far from clear that disagreement is more pervasive in the interpretation of prescriptive texts than descriptive or representational ones: Consensus as to the meaning of a play by Shakespeare, a novel by Joyce, or a historical text by Thucydides seems no more likely than it does in the interpretation of the Constitution. Consensus becomes possible in the interpretation of descriptive or representational texts only if we trivialize those texts (e.g., reduce them to statements like "There is a tree in my back yard"). That move is equally available in the treatment of prescriptive texts (e.g., "Equality is good"), though I see no value in insisting on it.

The prescriptive nature of the text, therefore, should not be seen as a bar to objective interpretation, but it does have an important impact on the content of the disciplining rules through which the law is defined. Legal interpreters are under constant pressure to abide by the constraints governing moral judgments, for both law and morals seek to establish norms of proper behavior and attempt to describe the ideal by similar concepts, such as liberty and equality. Law borrows from morals (and, of course, morals from law). The borrowing is sometimes substantive; more often it is procedural.

Different schools of interpretation contemplate different degrees of borrowing. The natural law tradition, for example, demands that courts give morality the decisive role in the interpretation of the legal text or, to put the same point somewhat differently, that judges read the legal text in light of the moral text, the so-called unwritten constitution.[17] In this instance the substantive borrowing would be most pronounced, but, in fact, the natural law tradition has never dominated American jurisprudence.

That school has remained a clique. It has been largely overshadowed by legal positivism, which emphasizes the analytical distinction between law and morals, between what is legal and what is good. Legal positivism celebrates the "written constitution" and stresses factors like the use of particular words or the intent or beliefs of the framers, all of which have little or no moral relevance.

Positivism tries to separate law from morals, and keeps the substantive borrowing to a minimum, but as I suggested in my account of the so-called external criticism, and my depiction of the pressures forcing external critics to work within the law, the separation will, in fact, never be complete. Two forces modulate the commitment to positivism and thus minimize the separation. The first derives from the fact that the judiciary is trying to give meaning and expression to public values (those that are embodied in a legal text) and that the judicial understanding of such values—equality, liberty, property, due process, cruel and unusual punishment—is necessarily shaped by the prevailing morality. The moral text is a prism through which judges understand the legal text. The second force relates to an intellectual dilemma of positivism: A too rigid insistence on positivism will inevitably bring into question the ultimate moral authority of the legal text—the justness of the Constitution.

Judges ardently committed to legal positivism will ultimately be asked —as they were in the debates over the constitutionality of slavery before the Civil War[18] and in response to the judicial efforts to protect industrial capitalism in the early part of the twentieth century[19]—to justify the public morality embodied in that text and the processes by which those values are expressed. Slavery may be protected by the Constitution, and so may industrial capitalism and the inequality of wealth and privilege it invariably produces; but why must we respect the Constitution? The answer to such a question is not obvious or easily discovered, for one must transcend the text and the rules of interpretation to justify the authority of the text; to justify the Constitution itself or explain why the Constitution should be obeyed, one must move beyond law to political theory, if not religion. Such questioning can itself become a moment of crisis in the life of a constitution, and, since it is occasioned by a rigid insistence on the principles of positivism and the separation of law and morals, judges have an incentive to temper their commitment to that legal theory and thus to read the moral as well as the legal text. A judge quickly learns to read in a way that avoids crises.

An even more pronounced measure of borrowing occurs in formulating the disciplining rules that govern the procedures of legal interpretation. Above all, it is the procedures of morals that the law borrows.[20] An alluring vision of the procedures of morals is conveyed by the vivid and powerful image created by John Rawls of the original position—of a group of people deliberating behind a veil of ignorance and reaching agreement on the principles of justice in a situation that entails divorcement from interests, a willingness to engage in rational dialogue, and a willingness to universalize the principles agreed on.[21] Rawls was speaking of morals, but we can see in the law an insistence on an analogous set of procedural norms to discipline the interpreter: Judges must stand independent of the interests of the parties or even those of the body politic (the requirement of judicial independence); judges must listen to grievances they might otherwise prefer not to hear (the concept of a non-discretionary jurisdiction) and must listen to all who will be directly affected by the decisions (the rules respecting parties); judges must respond and assume personal responsibility for the decisions rendered (the tradition of the signed opinion); and judges must justify their decisions in terms that can be universalized (the neutral principles requirement). These rules reflect the inherently prescriptive character of the legal text and the identity of concepts used by law and morals to describe the ideal.

These procedural constraints are not, mind you, mere techniques of administration, to be dispensed with whenever the need or desire to do so arises. They are an essential component of the body of disciplining rules that govern the interpretive process known as adjudication and that constitute the standards for evaluating a legal interpretation. The correctness of any interpretation is relative to a set of standards, and in law those standards are composed of procedural as well as substantive norms. This is partly owing to the prescriptive nature of the text and the fact that the judge is trying to state the ideal, which has the effect of blending the idea of "correctness" into "justness": A just interpretation speaks to process as well as outcome. The role of procedure is also attributable, though perhaps in a secondary way, to certain institutional facts. The judiciary is a coordinate agency of government, always competing, at least intellectually, with other agencies for the right to establish the governing norms of the polity. The judiciary's claim is largely founded on its special competence to interpret a text such as the Constitution, and to render the public morality embodied in that text specific and concrete. This competence stems not from the personal qualities of those who are judges—judges are not assumed to have the wisdom of philosopher kings—but rather from the procedures that limit the exercise of their power. It is as though they operate under the procedural constraints of the original position and from that fact obtain a measure of authority over the other branches.

The Claim of Authoritativeness

I have pictured the judge as an individual essentially engaged in interpretive activity. I have also suggested a moral dimension to legal interpretation—the judge interprets a prescriptive text and, in so doing, gives meaning and expression to the values embodied in that text. The judge seems to be a combination of literary critic and moral philosopher. That, however, is only part of the picture. The judge also speaks with the authority of the Pope.

Some literary critics aspire to a kind of authority: They not only search for a plausible interpretation of the text but for the correct one. The same is true for moral philosophers: They do not simply express what they believe to be good but try to identify principles of morality that are objective and true. Both literary critics and moral philosophers aspire to a kind of authority we might term *intellectual*, an authority that comes from being right in their intellectual endeavor. Judges also attempt to achieve intellectual authority, yet this is only to supplement a powerful base of authority that they otherwise possess. Judicial interpretations are binding, whether or not they are correct. *Brown v. Board of Education* was not only right but had the force of law; *Plessy v. Ferguson* may have been wrong, from either the internal or external perspective, in 1896 as well as now, but it was nonetheless binding.

In what ways is the interpretation of the judge uniquely authoritative? There are two answers to this question. The first, emphasized in the work of John Austin,[22] is based on power: By virtue of the rules governing their behavior, the officers of the state are entitled to use the power at their disposal to bring about compliance with judicial interpretations. Sometimes the power is brought to bear on the individual through contempt proceedings; sometimes through criminal prosecutions and police action; sometimes through supplemental civil proceedings. Sometimes, as with the desegregation of the public schools at Little Rock or the admission of James Meredith at Ole Miss, the power is expressed through brute force—bayonets, rifles, clubs, and tear gas.[23] A judicial interpretation is authoritative in the sense that it legitimates the use of force against those who refuse to accept or otherwise give effect to the meaning embodied in that interpretation.

The second sense of authoritativeness, suggested by the works of other positivists, namely Herbert Hart[24] and Hans Kelsen,[25] stresses not the use of state power but an ethical claim to obedience—a claim that an individual has a moral duty to obey a judicial interpretation, not because of its particular intellectual authority (i.e., because it is a correct interpretation) but because the judge is part of an authority structure that is good to preserve. This version of the claim of authoritativeness speaks to the individual's conscience and derives from institutional virtue, rather than institutional power. It is the most important version of the claim of authoritativeness because no society can depend on force, exclusively or even heavily, to secure compliance; it is also the most tenuous one and vitally depends on recognition of the value of judicial interpretation. Denying the worth of the Constitution, the place of constitutional values in the American system, or the judiciary's capacity to interpret the Constitution dissolves this particular claim to authoritativeness.

Belief in the institutional virtue of judicial interpretation may proceed from a variety of theories. One theory stresses the importance of having questions of public values settled with some finality through procedures unique to the judiciary. Another centers on the desirability of maintaining continuity with our traditional values and sees adjudication as the process best designed to promote that end. A third theory emphasizes the need to maintain the stability of the larger political system, and the role of the judiciary in maintaining that stability.

Taken together, or maybe even separately, these theories have sufficient force, at least to my mind, to create a presumption in favor of the authoritativeness of judicial decisions. Any interpretation of a court, certainly that of the highest court, is prima facie authoritative. On the other hand, none of these theories, taken individually or collectively, can assure that this presumption will withstand a decision that many, operating from either the internal or external perspective, perceive to be fundamentally mistaken, an egregious error. In such a situation, the judiciary may be unable to ground its claim to obedience on a theory of virtue but may have to assert the authoritativeness that proceeds from institutional power alone.

It is important to note that the claim of authoritativeness, whether it is predicated on virtue or power, is extrinsic to the process of interpretation. It does not arise from the act of interpretation itself and is sufficient to distinguish the judge from the literary critic or moral philosopher who must rely on intellectual authority alone. Moreover, though the claim of institutional authoritativeness is not logically inconsistent with objective interpretation, but rather presupposes it, the authoritative quality of legal interpretation introduces certain tensions into the interpretive process. It creates a strong critical environment; it provides unusually strong incentives to criticize and defend the correctness of the interpretation. Something practical and important turns on judicial interpretations. They are binding. Institutional authoritativeness also produces psychological strains in the interpreter. It at once oppresses and liberates the interpreter.

From one perspective, the claim of authoritativeness acts as a weight: It creates additional responsibility. The search for meaning is always arduous, but even more so when one realizes that the interpretation will become authoritative. *Brown* must have been agonizing. The Justices had to determine what the ideal of racial equality meant and structure its relation to liberty. This task was hard enough, especially given the legacy of *Plessy v. Ferguson*, but the difficulty was compounded because the Justices knew they were also charting the future course of the nation. They were authoritatively deciding whether more than one-third of the states could adhere to their long-established and passionately defended social order. Authoritativeness confers a responsibility that is awesome, probably at times disabling. It appears that, in at least one instance, when Justice Charles E. Whittaker had to decide the reapportionment issue finally resolved in *Baker v. Carr*,[26] this responsibility apparently produced a nervous breakdown.

The contrasting perspective is best captured by the work of Justice William O. Douglas and a judicial quip that became popular in the mid-1960s, at the height of the Warren Court era: "With five votes we can do anything." From this perspective, the claim of authoritativeness liberates judges, dangerously so; they work with the knowledge that their words will bind whether or not they have correctly interpreted the text. This sense of security is not completely well founded, for, as we saw, insofar as a judge claims authoritativeness based on the virtue of the institution, the claim can be overcome or defeated by what others perceive to be a particularly serious mistake. Even from the perspective of power, the judges must recognize that a serious abuse of the judicial office may also incline the Executive against using the force at its disposal to compel obedience. (President Eisenhower's hesitation in deploying the federal troops in Little Rock is ample warning on that score.) But these limitations on the claim of authoritativeness depend on a complicated chain of reasoning and presuppose the most egregious of errors and, as such, only circumscribe the judge's sense of freedom. The larger fact is the freedom itself: An interpretation is binding even if mistaken. The judge enjoys a protection not shared by the literary critic or the moral philosopher, which might allow a casual indifference to the integrity of the interpretive enterprise. The impact of the disciplining rules may be dulled. The search for meaning may be less than complete.

The mention of Justice Whittaker and Justice Douglas is not meant to suggest that each dimension of this conflicting dynamic finds expression in a different person. I assume that the psychological conflict resulting from the claim of authoritativeness is present in all judges, perhaps all the time. The existence of this conflict does not deny the interpretive character of judging or make that task impossible to perform. The great judge—I have Earl Warren very much in mind—is someone who can modulate these tensions, someone whom the specter of authority both disciplines and liberates, someone who can transcend the conflict.

Efficacy and the Element of Instrumentalism

The claim of authoritativeness, like the prescriptive nature of the text, complicates and defines the distinctive nature of legal interpretation. There is a third dimension that informs the judge's task and probably plays an even greater role in giving legal interpretation its distinctive cast: The judge tries to be efficacious. The judge seeks to interpret the legal text and then to transform social reality so that it comports with that interpretation.

Literary critics, no doubt, often find themselves anxious as to whether the audience will accept their interpretation as the true one. They will polish their rhetorical skills and participate in institutional politics to that end. But the personal anxiety literary critics experience is raised to a duty in the law. Judges must give a remedy; it is part of the definition of their office. The duty of the Supreme Court in *Brown* was to interpret the ideal of racial equality in terms of concrete reality and to initiate a process that would transform that reality so that it comports with the ideal—to transform, as the slogan reads, the dual school systems into unitary, nonracial ones.

The authoritativeness of a legal interpretation is an essential ingredient of this transformational process. Faced with the Little Rock school desegregation crisis, the Supreme Court felt compelled to reaffirm *Brown* and to put its authority on the line. Yet the reassertion of the authority of its interpretation, the achievement of *Cooper v. Aaron*,[27] did not itself desegregate the schools. The troops were also needed. Authoritativeness is a necessary, not a sufficient, condition of efficacy. Efficacy also requires measures that will transform social reality.

Part of that transformational process entails further specification of the meaning of the text, an explication of the ideal of racial equality in the context of a particular social setting: Does the commitment to racial equality allow freedom of choice as the method of student assignment in this particular city? Does it allow a neighborhood school plan? The answers to these questions depend, in part, on a further explication of the ideal of racial equality and a determination of its relation to other constitutional ideals, such as liberty. In this regard, the transformational process also entails interpretation, with, so to speak, one eye on the Constitution and the other on the world—the world that was and the one that should be. There is, however, another dimension of the transformational process that is not properly considered interpretive, and that is instrumentalism. The judge must know how to achieve specific objectives in the real world.

The meaning the court gives the constitutional value, in the general and in the specific, defines and structures the end to be achieved by this transformational process. The objective established in *Brown* is to desegregate the schools. The question, then, becomes one of deciding how to achieve this objective, and in resolving that question the judge will have to make certain technical judgments: choosing the schools to be paired, designing bus routes, deciding which teachers are to be reassigned, adjusting the curriculum and sports schedule, and so on. The judge may rely on the initiative of the parties and their so-called experts to help in these matters, but, in the end, he or she will have to assume responsibility for the technical judgments—the judge must be an architect and an engineer, redesigning and rebuilding social structures.

This is, however, only one facet of instrumentalism. We also know, especially from the history of *Brown*, that a deeper and more intractable set of obstacles may confront judges in their efforts to give the value of racial equality a practical meaning: resistance by those who must cooperate in order for the meaning to become a reality—parents, children, teachers, administrators, citizens, and politicians. Collectively, and sometimes even individually, these people have the power to frustrate the remedial process. In ways that are both subtle and crude, they may refuse to recognize the authoritativeness of the judge's interpretation. They can boycott the schools, attack the students crossing the color line, withdraw from the public school system and flee to the suburbs or private schools, or refuse to appropriate money needed for buses.

In the face of this resistance, judges can reassert their authority either by proclaiming the virtues of their office and the place of the judiciary in the political system or by employing the physical power at their disposal. When the resistance is deep and sufficiently widespread, however, such an action is likely to be hollow and unavailing. Then the court must be able to manage the opposition: The judge must transform resistance into cooperation and win the support of those who are needed. The judge must bargain and negotiate. To succeed in achieving the court's remedial objectives, the judge must be as much a political strategist as he or she is a social architect and engineer.

This journey into instrumentalism, perhaps most vividly symbolized by the "all deliberate speed" formula of the second *Brown* decision, may cause important departures from the interpretive paradigm, for the legal text cannot inform, in any important sense, the technical and strategic judgments that are an integral part of the remedial process. The Constitution establishes the values as well as the institutions for expressing those values, but it is not a significant source for understanding how those values might be effectively implemented. It is not a manual of the type Machiavelli might write. Of course, the judge can read another text, the one that legislators read, namely, public opinion, but it is not an authoritative text for the judiciary.

Moreover, there is no reason to assume that instrumental judgments should be or even could be constrained by the disciplining rules that characteristically govern judicial interpretation—for example, the rules assigning weight to precedent or requiring dialogue or independence of the judiciary from the political process. Indeed, it is not at all clear why the instrumental judgments are entrusted to the same officials who are charged with interpreting the constitutional text. At best, one can employ the argument of necessity outlined in "The Forms of Justice" (chapter 1): The instrumental judgments must be entrusted to the judge as a way of preserving the integrity of the meaning-giving enterprise, because the meaning of a value derives from its practical realization as well as its intellectual articulation.

The concern with efficacy may have even greater consequences. Instrumentalism may not only call for a departure from the interpretive paradigm, but it may actually interfere with the interpretive process. It may make judges settle for something less than what they perceive to be the correct interpretation. The technical and strategic obstacles to efficacy may be humbling. By revealing the practical limits of judicial authority, they remind judges that even with five votes they cannot do everything. There is, however, always the risk that the humility will be excessive. It may be crippling. Fearing they lack the ability—the technical expertise or political power—to implement the right answer and determined to avoid failure, even if it means doing nothing, judges may tailor both the remedy and the right to what they perceive to be possible, and that may be considerably less than what the text—the appropriate text—requires. That fear may drive judges to read a lesser text—public opinion; even worse, it may lead them to embrace what might be regarded as Felix Frankfurter's axiom—it is better to succeed in doing nothing than to fail in doing something. Doubting that they have the ability to change social mores or to implement desegregation plans that involve the suburbs as well as the city,[28] judges may modify their reading of the Equal Protection Clause in order to produce an interpretation of equality that tolerates separation.

The desire for efficacy may, as a result of this dynamic, corrupt, but it need not. The need to address complex social situations with creative and often complicated remedies and then to manipulate power so as to make them reality is undeniable, but these needs do not necessarily cause judges to compromise the integrity of the interpretive process. A secure concept of the judicial role and the priorities within that role, and a proper recognition of the source of legitimacy, may enable the judge to order and perhaps even reconcile tasks that may otherwise tend to conflict. The core of adjudication, objective interpretation, can be protected from the pressures of instrumentalism, as it can be protected from the tensions produced by the claim of authoritativeness. The multiple demands of adjudication often make law an elusive, partly realized ideal, for these demands mean that judges must manage and synthesize a number of disparate and conflicting roles—literary critic, moral philosopher, religious authority, structural engineer, political strategist; but it would be wrong to abandon the ideal in the face of this challenge. The proper response is increased effort, clarity of vision, and determination, not surrender.

The Denial of Meaning

The nihilism I have addressed is based on the premise that for any text there are any number of possible meanings and the interpreter creates a meaning by choosing one. I have accepted this premise but have tried to deny the nihilism by showing why the freedom is not absolute. I have argued that legal interpretations are constrained by rules that derive their authority from an interpretive community that is itself held together by the commitment to the rule of law. There may, however, be a deeper nihilism I have not yet addressed, and that also seems part of modern America.

For the Deconstructionist, it makes little difference whether a text is viewed as holding all meanings or no meaning: Either brand of nihilism liberates the critic as the creator of meaning. My defense of adjudication as objective interpretation, however, assumes that the Constitution has some meaning—more specifically, that the text embodies the fundamental public values of our society. I have confronted the nihilism that claims the Constitution means everything. But my defense does not work if the alternative version of the literary nihilism—that the Constitution has no meaning—is embraced as applied to the law, for there is no theory of legitimacy that would allow judges to interpret texts that themselves mean nothing. The idea of adjudication requires that there exist constitutional values to interpret, just as much as it requires that there are constraints on the interpretive process. Lacking such a belief, adjudication is not possible, only power.

The roots of this alternative version of nihilism are not clear to me, but its significance is unmistakable. The great public text of modern America, the Constitution, would be drained of meaning. It would be debased. It would no longer be seen as embodying a public morality to be understood and expressed through rational processes like adjudication; it would be reduced to a mere instrument of political organization—distributing political power and establishing the modes by which that power will be exercised. Public values would be defined only as those held by the current winners in the processes prescribed by the Constitution. Beyond that, there would be only individual morality or, even worse, only individual interests.

Against the nihilism that scoffs at the idea that the Constitution has any meaning, it is difficult to reason. The issue seems to be one of faith, intuition, or maybe just insight. This form of nihilism seems so thoroughly at odds with the most elemental reading of the text itself and with almost two hundred years of constitutional history as to lead me to wonder whether anything can be said in response. On the other hand, I believe it imperative to respond, in word and in deed, for this nihilism calls into question the very point of constitutional adjudication; it threatens our social existence and the nature of public life as we know it in America; and it demeans our lives. It is the deepest and darkest of all nihilisms. It must be combated and can be, though perhaps only by affirming the truth of that which is being denied—the idea that the Constitution embodies a public morality and that a public life founded on that morality can be rich and inspiring.

10

Judging as a Practice

When Bruce Ackerman and I first joined the Yale faculty in 1974, we began the Legal Theory Workshop. The workshop was a forum in which scholars from a broad variety of disciplines presented works-in-progress for comment and discussion. In 1983, when Ackerman was teaching at Columbia University, I directed the workshop alone and decided to invite Stanley Fish, then teaching at The Johns Hopkins University, to present a paper. "Objectivity and Interpretation" (chapter 9) had just appeared, and in the formulation of some of the key issues in that paper I had drawn on Fish's work, *Is There a Text in This Class?* (1980). Professor Fish quickly accepted my invitation.

The guests at the workshop have always been given complete freedom in deciding what paper they might present. I did not even know the topic until the guest's paper arrived in my office a week or two before the scheduled session. You can imagine my surprise when Professor Fish's paper arrived. It was entitled "Fish v. Fiss" and criticized "Objectivity and Interpretation." He, too, denied any distinction between law and politics, though for quite different reasons than those advanced by the proponents of Critical Legal Studies. The house was packed, and he commanded the floor. The evening was his—I hardly said a word.

By the mid-1980s literary theory and hermeneutics had become a subject of great interest to legal scholars. In 1984 the University of Southern California convened a conference on hermeneutics, and both Professor Fish and I were invited to participate. I used the occasion to respond to him. Fish's paper, which had not yet appeared, was published in the July 1984 *Stanford Law Review* (volume 36, page 1325). Mine was published in the January 1985 issue of the *Southern California Law Review* (volume 58, page 177), under the title "Conventionalism." These ideas were further elaborated in "The Jurisprudence [?] of Stanley Fish," *ADE* (*Association of Departments of English*) *Bulletin* (spring 1985) and in a lively panel discussion entitled "Legal Modes of Interpretation: Principled, Political, or Materialistic?" at the Law and Humanities section of the American Association of Law Schools. This panel, organized by Professor Richard Weisberg of Cardozo Law School, included Stanley Fish and my colleague, Robert Cover, and was held in San Francisco on January 7, 1984. A recording of the panel discussion is available from the Association. This remarkable encounter is described in Laura Kalman's *The Strange Career of Legal Liberalism*, published by Yale University Press in 1996.

~ CONVENTIONALISM is a viewpoint, most closely associated with the later writings of Wittgenstein, that emphasizes practice and context.[1] It holds, for example, that we understand a concept not when we grasp some fact but when we can successfully use that concept within a language game or a defined context, and that truth is a function of the agreement of those participating within a practice rather than the other way around. There's nothing "out there," and even if there were, we couldn't possibly know it.

What bearing, if any, does conventionalism have for legal interpretation or adjudication in general? Stanley Fish has developed a general theory of interpretation that also emphasizes practice and context, and, accordingly, might be seen as a branch of conventionalism. His concern was first with literary texts; in addition to being a Milton scholar, he also established his preeminence as a literary theorist with the publication, in 1980, of *Is There a Text in This Class?*. In a number of recent articles, however, he moved on to legal texts, and in one—"Fish v. Fiss"—he sought to criticize an account that I gave of constitutional interpretation in my essay "Objectivity and Interpretation" (chapter 9).[2]

In the spirit of conventionalism, Fish reminds us that both the judge and the Constitution are always contextualized—the judge is a thoroughly socialized member of a profession, and the Constitution is never "waiting around for interpretation" but is "always an already-interpreted object." This claim about the contextualized nature of text and reader, it seems to me, is entirely correct and I gladly embrace it, but I do not believe that it leads to or in any way supports Fish's theory of constitutional interpretation. One branch of his theory pictures the judge knowing immediately and without reflection what to do, simply by virtue of being a socialized member of the profession; the other denies that the Constitution embodies a public morality or, for that matter, anything else.

Freedom vs. Determinism in Interpretation

The disagreement between Fish and myself takes place against a background disagreement in the profession over the degree of freedom the interpreter is allowed. One faction that John Ely represents depicts interpretation as an intellectual process in which outcomes or decisions are determined by the specific words contained in the text (a process Ely sometimes terms *clause-bound interpretivism*).[3] Interpretation, for Ely, is confined to the highly specific clauses of the Constitution, such as the one requiring the president to be at least thirty-five years old; it cannot be used to characterize judgments under more general provisions such as the Equal Protection Clause.

In his book *The Constitution, the Courts, and Human Rights* (1982), Michael Perry displays a similar attitude toward interpretation but broadens its application.[4] He, too, allows the interpreter virtually no freedom but, in contrast to Ely, admits that it might be possible to speak of interpreting more general constitutional provisions. All that would be needed is a method of constraining the reader. Perry finds the source of constraint in a highly specific conception of authorial intent and, in the context of the general clauses, sees interpretation as a species of originalism.[5] *Brown v. Board of Education* could be understood as an interpretation of the Equal Protection Clause, Perry argues, only if the framers had intended to prohibit segregated schools and *Brown* was but an implementation of that wish.[6]

On the topic of originalism, Ronald Dworkin has said that the issue in constitutional interpretation is not whether to consider authorial intent but what should count as intent.[7] Dworkin sees two levels of intent—one denoted a "concept" (an abstract value) and the other a "conception" (a concrete application of that value)—and he argues in favor of the more abstract. He insists that the relevant inquiry in *Brown* is not whether the framers intended to prohibit segregated schools (the conception) but whether they intended to embody a value such as equality (the concept), which, in turn, could be understood by future generations to outlaw segregated schools. Perry, drawing on Stephen R. Munzer and James W. Nickel,[8] dismisses Dworkin's argument by saying that there is no empirical evidence that the framers had an abstract rather than a concrete intention (or that they wanted their abstract intention to govern). But Dworkin, in fact, provided the best evidence imaginable—the language of the clause itself. The framers had a choice between specific and abstract language, and their choice of the latter is, for Dworkin, a fairly good indication of which level of intent they thought should govern. Dworkin also claimed that the empirical evidence Perry sought was irrelevant, because the choice of the kind of intent that should govern (abstract rather than specific) should not itself turn on what the framers intended on that issue (for that would involve a circularity) but rather on a political theory (unfortunately one that Dworkin has not yet worked out). To this, Perry made no rejoinder: He seemed determined, in his effort to explicate the concept of interpretation, to reduce authorial intent to a more specific level.

In this determination Perry reflects the same impulse as Ely—seeing interpretation largely as a mechanical process that denies the reader a creative role.[9] Ely reduces interpretation to textual determinism, whereas Perry, addressing the more general clauses, sees it as a form of originalism. For Ely, the judge interpreting the Constitution is carrying out the specific directives of the Constitution. To use the familiar metaphor, the judge is the phonograph, and the words on the parchment are the record. For Perry, authorial intent is the record. A judge engaged in interpreting a clause such as equal protection is implementing original intent; to minimize the creative role of the judge, Perry formulates that intent to make it a wholly sufficient basis for resolving the case before the court—very specific and concrete. Perry, in fact, speaks of the framers' intent in terms of "value judgments" and of the Constitution as an embodiment of those judgments. He appears to conceive of the framers as judges (rather than political actors), distinguished from the Justices of the Supreme Court only by their multitude (hundreds of thousands, rather than nine) and their age (they formulated their judgments in 1787 or 1868 rather than 1954).

I take issue with the Ely-Perry conception of interpretation because it is excessively mechanistic. As I argue in "Objectivity and Interpretation" (chapter 9), such a conception confuses interpretation with execution. To me, an interpretation is determined neither by the specific words on the parchment nor by an assessment of the framers' specific concrete intentions, although each plays a role. Interpretation is not reducible to either textual determinism or originalism but, instead, contemplates a dynamic interaction between text and reader in which an analysis of the specific words of the text and of the concrete intent of the framers is only part of the process by which that meaning is understood.

Although I disagree with Ely's or Perry's account of interpretation, it needs to be emphasized that I do not take issue with their substantive views, inasmuch as each envisions a role for the Supreme Court that extends beyond what he calls interpretation. For Ely, *Brown* is an instance of "ultimate interpretivism"[10] (which he distinguishes from ordinary interpretation or "clause-bound interpretivism" and which is, for him, not a form of interpretation but a program for using the judicial power to perfect majoritarian processes). For Perry, *Brown* is an instance of "constitutional policy-making" under which the judge "reaches decision without really interpreting any provision of the constitutional text"[11] and, instead, writes into law his or her "own values (albeit, values ideally arrived at through, and tested in the crucible of, a very deliberate search for right answers)."[12] Given Ely's and Perry's positions on a case like *Brown*, so central to the modern understanding of the judicial power, it might seem that my disagreement with them over interpretation is only nominal; we all accept *Brown* as a legitimate exercise of the judicial power but use different words to describe the same intellectual activity.

It seems important, however, to recover the concept of interpretation and to avoid a mechanistic view of it. We need to appreciate that interpretation permits a measure of creativity to the judge or reader and that a decision such as *Brown* could be seen as an interpretation of the Constitution. Such an understanding would forge links between law and literature, and bring into our vision the work of literary theorists like Stanley Fish. It would remove some of the controversy and puzzlement surrounding the Supreme Court's role in our political system, for it allows us to conceive of the Court's function in the most elemental and widely accepted terms— as interpretation. Such an understanding would also emphasize the unity of constitutional adjudication, whether the Court is applying the First Amendment, the Equal Protection Clause, or the clause specifying the minimum age of the president. Although there may be more disagreement over the meaning of one clause than another, the function of the Court and the methods by which it discharges that function are the same and do not vary from clause to clause.

Ely and, to a large extent, Perry identify the countermajoritarian dilemma as their preeminent concern,[13] and I will concede that recovering the idea of interpretation and characterizing a decision such as *Brown* as an instance of interpretation will not resolve that dilemma. Interpretation is countermajoritarian, even if properly understood. On the other hand, a proper conception of interpretation will help us appreciate the pervasiveness of the countermajoritarian dilemma. All adjudication is countermajoritarian. The highly mechanical kind of activity that Ely and Perry characterize as interpretation is widely accepted, yet it puts the majority at risk—countermajoritarianism cannot pose that much of a dilemma if it is so integral to adjudication and so widely accepted. True, the role of the judge is trivialized under their conception of interpretation (the judge is the phonograph), but power is not transferred from the judge to the contemporary majority. Rather, it is given to the framers, as manifest in either the words scribbled in 1787 or 1868 or their concrete intentions. The countermajoritarian dilemma, as formulated and propounded by Alexander Bickel and addressed by Perry and Ely, focuses on the tensions between the Supreme Court and the preferences or desires of the current majority (as voiced by elected representatives).[14]

Standing at the other end of the spectrum from John Ely and Michael Perry is Professor Sanford Levinson.[15] He repudiates the Ely-Perry conception of interpretation as excessively mechanical and, in an effort to bridge the gap between law and literature, emphasizes the creative role of the judge. But Levinson errs in the other direction: His conception of interpretation is too dynamic. Whereas the Ely-Perry conception denies any freedom to the interpreter or reader, Levinson's exalts that freedom—too much for my taste.

Levinson is prepared to treat *Brown* as an interpretation of the Equal Protection Clause (without regard to the framers' intent) only because he believes that all interpretation is a constructive process. Levinson begins his account with the observation that the Constitution is capable of any number of readings, and then he characterizes the judicial task as one of choosing among these different readings. He also asserts that the judge is (relatively) free to choose among these readings and that there are no standards—distinctively legal standards—by which to evaluate that choice. Levinson, like Ely, Perry, and myself, and presumably Fish (and maybe the entire generation of scholars of which we are part), believes that *Brown* is a correct decision. But, for Levinson, the correctness of *Brown* derives simply from the fact that he shares the political or moral (but not legal) vision that guided the Justices' choice among the many possible readings of the Equal Protection Clause.

Just as I reject the Ely-Perry account of interpretation as too deterministic, I reject Levinson's account as too free. Although I start with the view that the Constitution embodies a public morality, including a commitment to racial equality, I recognize that this commitment, when applied to a particular situation, such as segregated schools, is capable of several readings, some of which may conflict with other constitutional promises, such as liberty. The judicial task is to choose among these readings, and this choice is, for me, as it was for Levinson, the core of the intellectual process known as interpretation (legal or literary). Unlike Levinson, however, I do not believe that the choice is unconstrained.

The judge's choice is constrained by a set of rules (or norms, standards, principles, guides, etc.)[16] that are authorized by the professional community of which the judge is a part and that define and constitute the community. A judge might be directed, for example, to pay particular attention to the wording of a text and to the intent of the framers, while a political actor might consider the impact of segregation on the conduct of foreign affairs. Adherence to the rules authorized by the professional community imparts a measure of impersonality to a legal judgment (its objective quality) and at the same time provides the standards for evaluating the correctness of the judgment as a legal judgment. I can say that *Brown* is a correct interpretation of the Fourteenth Amendment not because I subscribe to some political or moral tenet that condemns racial segregation but because it conforms to the properly authorized disciplining rules.

The Sources of Constraint

Stanley Fish and I are united in our effort to secure the middle ground. In another article he rejects Levinson's proclamation of freedom and I believe he would reject the Ely-Perry conception of interpretation as excessively mechanical.[17] Fish believes, as I do, that the interpretive process—whether it be of specific clauses or highly general ones, like equal protection—is neither wholly determined nor wholly free but is constrained. What we are divided over is the nature of the constraints and the account we give of them: Fish emphasizes practice, and I emphasize norms. Compared to my disagreement with those at the ends of the spectrum—Ely and Perry at one, Levinson at the other—this difference might seem trivial (and probably accounts for the play on the similarity of our names in Fish's title— "Fish v. Fiss"—and the difficulty some may have in remembering who's who). Yet I believe the difference between us is, in fact, important: Fish's account of these constraints trivializes the reflective moments of the law and, like Levinson's account (but for different reasons), blurs the distinction between law and politics.

In countering Levinson and others of his school, I thought it necessary to introduce two concepts in "Objectivity and Interpretation": One is the idea of disciplining rules, which constrain the judge; the other is that of an interpretive community, which is defined and constituted by, and confers authority on, the disciplining rules. Fish has claimed a proprietary interest in the idea of an interpretive community, and thus, not surprisingly, his criticism is addressed only to my notion of disciplining rules (although we use the concept of an interpretive community differently—I see it as a source of authority for the disciplining rules, and Fish sees it as the source of shared understandings). Fish makes two claims about the disciplining rules: first, that they will not work, and, second, that they are unnecessary.

The Usefulness of Disciplining Rules

Disciplining rules are, as I have said, to provide constraints. "Unfortunately," Fish comments, "rules *are* texts. They are in need of interpretation and cannot themselves serve as constraints on interpretation." I agree that disciplining rules must be interpreted, and, like Fish, I conceive of the interpretive process as a dynamic interaction between the text and the reader; but none of this renders these rules incapable of constraining the interpretive process.

To see this, let us return to *Brown*. The Justices' task was to determine whether segregated schools were consistent with the guarantee of equality in the Fourteenth Amendment. This seems like a rather open-ended judgment, one in which the Justices could have said many things or, as Levinson (invoking a notable image of Richard Rorty) might put it, they could have beaten the text into any shape that served their purposes.[18] I maintain, however, that their freedom was, in fact, bounded by certain disciplining rules: Some required the Justices to pay attention to precedents, others directed their attention to the purposes of the Civil War and the Fourteenth Amendment, and still others precluded them from favoring one side over the other simply because of the race of the parties. Under my view of interpretation, judges faced with an open-ended question (such as whether Jim Crow laws are consistent with equal protection) are increasingly circumscribed in their discretion by more particularized constraints (which direct their attention to the framers' intent, precedent, etc.). The image I have in mind is that of a judge moving toward judgment along a spiral of norms that increasingly constrain.

At any point in the spiral there might be a disagreement over the meaning of a rule (just as there might be disagreement over whether the conditions that make the rule applicable are present). There may, for example, be a dispute as to the level of authorial intent one must look to—whether it is the framers' particularized desires regarding segregated schools or, as Dworkin maintains, their general concept of equality. To resolve this dispute, the disciplining rules must be interpreted, and the process of interpreting those rules must itself be constrained by other norms further along or higher up the spiral. Of course, if the dispute about any norm is so pervasive as to return one to the previous level of constraint, then we have made no progress. The judge is as unconstrained as he or she was before we made any mention of disciplining rules.

In "Objectivity and Interpretation" I acknowledged the possibility of disputes over a disciplining rule but then confidently asserted, "The authority of a particular rule can be maintained even when it is disputed." To this Fish replies, "But how can 'it' be maintained *as a constraint* when the dispute is about what 'it' is or about what 'it' means?" I would answer: the same way that the Constitution or a statute or a common law rule can be maintained as a constraint even though there are disputes as to its meaning. Disputes over the meaning of a text do not deny either the existence of the text or that it has a meaning that can inform, guide, and constrain intellectual processes.

Some may insist that my account of constraint collapses because the disputes about the meaning or the application of the disciplining rules (such as the one about framers' intent) are more pervasive than I was originally willing to allow, so that there is no way to reduce the vast freedom Levinson claims for the judge. Maybe the judge has no guidance besides the spacious words of the Equal Protection Clause. I do not think so, but this is not the place to explore that problem because it is not Fish's point. He insists that disciplining rules cannot constrain even "where there is perfect agreement about what the rule is and what it means."

In insisting that the disciplining rules will not work, Fish is not making a claim about the pervasiveness of disagreement about the meaning of disciplining rules. He is not making a claim about indeterminacy but about contextualization. He notes that disciplining rules, like any text, are always situated within a practice and thus are always interpreted, even where there is perfect agreement as to what they mean. From this rather straightforward observation Fish concludes that these rules cannot constrain: "A so-called 'disciplining rule' cannot be said to act as a constraint on interpretation because it is (in whatever form has been specified for it) the product of an interpretation."

Of course, all texts are situated. I also agree with Fish that all disciplining rules, even where there is no dispute as to their meaning, are in need of interpretation and have, in fact, received that interpretation. Like all texts, disciplining rules are always contextualized and arrive in an "interpreted shape." That does not, however, reduce (in either a logical or practical sense) the content or meaning of a rule to its various interpretations,[19] nor does it mean that one text (disciplining rules) cannot constrain the interpretation of another text (the Constitution).

The Need for Disciplining Rules

Fish's intent, recall, is not simply to deny that disciplining rules will provide constraint but also to show that they are unnecessary: The freedom Levinson spoke of, and that I offered my disciplining rules to combat, does not exist. In denying this freedom, Fish does not revert to the mechanistic conception of interpretation that Ely or Perry offers. Rather, he tries, once again, to use the conventionalist emphasis on practice and context to give a new and different account of the middle ground.

One part of Fish's account relates to the position of the interpreter or judge. I picture the judge trying to choose, in a self-conscious and reflective manner, between the arguments of the contending lawyers and, in that process, thinking about and perhaps discussing with colleagues and clerks the rules or norms of the profession—What do they imply for the case at hand? Are they in conflict? Fish pictures the judge as an actor who is thoroughly socialized into the profession and who, by virtue of that socialization (and perhaps the life processes that make the judge the person he or she is), knows "not upon reflection, but immediately" what to do. For Fish, the judge is like a basketball player who plays the game beautifully and instinctively, without, so Fish says, reflecting on the rules of the game in any way.[20]

Fish introduces this peculiar picture of the judge in the course of his attack on the disciplining rules, for they are the professional norms and symbolize a kind of reflective or abstract knowledge or "knowledge that" (as opposed to "knowledge how").[21] Fish first makes a point about the method by which students are initiated into the legal profession:

The student studies not rules but cases, pieces of practice, and what he or she acquires are not abstractions but something like "know how" or "the ropes," the ability to identify (not upon reflection, but immediately) a crucial issue, to ask a relevant question, to propose an appropriate answer from a range of appropriate answers, etc.

In truth, the student learns both cases ("pieces of practice") and rules, and, for the remainder of his or her professional life, will use both. Fish acknowledges this (as he puts it, "Somewhere along the way the young student will also begin to formulate rules"), but then he takes a wrong turn. Rather than acknowledging the interactive nature of rules and practice—the rules will shape the practice just as the practice will shape the rules—he tries to establish a theoretical, as opposed to just a temporal, priority for practice.

Fish's argument for this priority rests on a single assertion: The student, lawyer, or judge, Fish insists, "will be able to produce and understand [the rules] only because he or she is deeply inside—indeed, is a part of—the context in which they become intelligible."[22] Fish may be right that only lawyers can understand and produce the norms of the profession (though he may be a glaring exception) and thus, with a nod toward conventionalism, I once again acknowledge the importance of practice. But Fish's point establishes neither the priority of practice nor the secondary nature of the rules (or "knowledge that"), for a reciprocal claim can be made on behalf of rules: A person could not continue to operate successfully within the practice and be considered a good lawyer without understanding and being able to articulate and critically evaluate the rules or norms that govern the practice. While it is true that one cannot fully understand the rules of grammar (or, to revert to Fish's favorite example, basketball) unless one also speaks and uses the language (or plays the game), one cannot fully participate in a practice, much less occupy an exalted place within a practice, especially the practice of law, without knowing the rules and being able to talk about them in an abstract or reflective manner. Practice informs the rules, and the rules inform the practice.

Admittedly the judge does not consult a judicial rule book on a daily basis in order to determine what factors to consider in reaching judgment, or otherwise to guide him or her to judgment, any more than the native speaker consults a grammar book before each utterance. For the professional, rules, norms, principles, standards, or other general normative propositions are internalized; a large part of the educational process of any profession is aimed at the internalization of its norms. In fact, sometimes the norms are so thoroughly internalized that a judge can decide without reflecting on or considering them in any conscious manner. Judges occasionally decide almost by instinct; the press of their work may sometimes force them to do so. But this is not always the case and, in any event, in introducing the concept of disciplining rules in "Objectivity and Interpretation," my intent was not to provide an empirical report on the thoughtfulness of the judiciary but, rather, to construct a conceptual framework that would render coherent the central ideal of the profession—decision according to law. I was trying to explain how law is possible.

At the highest levels of the judicial process—as we get closest to the ideal—debate, discussion, and deliberation about the professional norms (the disciplining rules) are, in fact, commonplace and are understood to be central to the decisional process. Moreover, even when judges operate short of the ideal and move to judgment almost by instinct, the norms that I speak of have a role similar to that of rules of grammar. Although they are internalized, they are also objects of self-conscious reflection. Judges who in fact had decided cases by instinct can wonder later whether they did the right thing and can measure their performance against the norms of their profession. Even before their decision, judges can check their initial inclinations and wonder whether their instincts are in accord with those norms.

Fish often speaks of "tacit knowledge," and it may seem to some that the issue dividing us is one of human psychology: On this account, I see the norms which I call "disciplining rules" "outside" the judge, whereas Fish believes they are "inside." But that's not it. I concede that these norms might be internalized. In any event, Fish is not trying to locate norms within the human psyche but, rather, is trying to get away from norms altogether. In order to sustain his position—that judges do not enjoy the freedom that Levinson postulated and that I try to curb through my disciplining rules—Fish must argue for a form of knowledge of a very special kind. Not only must it be internal, as the term *tacit knowledge* suggests, but, even more important, it must propel action or govern decision almost instinctively. It cannot be in need of interpretation, for Fish has argued that anything that needs interpretation cannot constrain. The kind of knowledge Fish seeks cannot be the object of analysis, discussion, or reflection.

Fish appears to broaden his account of "tacit knowledge" when he speaks of certain "understandings" of the judge, for example, the judge's "sense" or "view" of "what the Constitution is for." Fish suggests that these understandings are an important, even decisive, source of decision. Although this addendum appears to render his account of judging more plausible, it does so only on the assumption that these understandings are viewed as "internalized disciplining rules" or other forms of knowledge that he earlier denounced. This is strongly suggested by Fish's examples of these understandings, for they sound like our old disciplining rules, though even more abstract and general than I ever imagined. One understanding depicts the Constitution as "an instrument for enforcing the intentions of the Framers"; another claims the Constitution is "a device for assuring the openness of the political process"; and a third holds that the Constitution is "a blueprint for the exfoliation of a continually evolving set of fundamental values." Clearly any of these understandings must be interpreted; they are texts, just as much as my disciplining rules or any norms are. Thus, under Fish's own argument (texts cannot constrain because they are in need of interpretation), these understandings cannot do the work he assigns them—to provide a basis of decision that denies the possibility of freedom and thus make the constraint that disciplining rules would supply unnecessary. To accomplish that, Fish must reduce these understandings to an instinctive form of knowledge, another form of "know how," a non-text or an object that needs no interpretation.

In a final turn of the argument, introduced as a parenthetical aside, Fish says, "When I use phrases like 'without reflection' and 'immediately and obviously' I do not mean to preclude self-conscious deliberation on the part of situated agents." This sounds odd to my ear, a distortion of ordinary language and, in any event, renders unintelligible his entire argument. Most anyone would assume that "without reflection" means "without self-conscious deliberation." At this point I start wondering what Fish could possibly mean by his disclaimer. But, alas, he continues: "It is just that such deliberations always occur within ways of thinking that are themselves the ground of consciousness, not its object."

Thus far, Fish has situated the judge within a practice; soon he will situate texts within a practice; but now he is trying to situate deliberations within a practice of their own, and that practice turns out to be "ways of thinking." Deliberation is for me a way of thinking, and, consequently, I do not understand what it would be for deliberations to be situated within ways of thinking (and, even less, what it would be for ways of thinking to be, as he claims, a ground of consciousness"). But these puzzlements need not be resolved, for this nesting of cognitive processes will not advance

Fish's case. Even if deliberations were somehow situated within ways of thinking, it would not follow that the deliberations are not real or important, or that the judge knows immediately and without reflection what to do, or that the judge's deliberations are so constrained as to render the disciplining rules superfluous.

In the end, I find that Fish's parenthetical aside, like the talk about understandings, leads nowhere. The exaltation of "tacit knowledge" is nothing more than a celebration of judgment by instinct. Fish's purpose has been to explain why disciplining rules are unnecessary, and he has searched for a way to deny the freedom that Levinson proclaimed and that I offered my disciplining rules to combat. But he has achieved his purpose by trivializing the self-conscious and reflective moments of decision (when the judge thinks about the norms of the profession and their implications for the case at hand). These moments may not be as deep and as full as they should be, especially in this age of mass justice, but they are at the core of our professional ideals and probably explain the special appeal of adjudication as a distinctive form of institutionalized power.

In his account of the judge, Fish reflects the conventionalist emphasis on practice (but takes it to false extremes): The judge is "always and already" situated in a practice (the profession). Fish also gives an account of the text that might be seen as another facet of conventionalism: The Constitution is also situated. Fish argues that all texts are part of a context and "never appear in any but an already contextualized form."

By situating a judge within a practice, Fish hoped to show that the freedom I worried about does not exist and that there is therefore no need for disciplining rules because the judge is already constrained. By situating the text within a context or practice, Fish once again tries to allay my fears, but now he wants to show that the problem of the Constitution that I worried over—namely, that it is a text with many meanings—is without basis. I have assumed that the Constitution embodies a public morality, that this morality is capable of many meanings (when applied to a specific situation like segregated schools, and when account is taken of the whole Constitution), and that the task of judging is one of choice. The disciplining rules are supposed to be the standards to govern that choice. To this Fish responds: "There are . . . no texts that have a plurality of meanings, so that there is never a necessity of having to choose between them."

Fish's assertion seems to contradict the most elemental understanding of the Constitution (or, for that matter, any other legal or literary text I can think of). If it were merely a proposition that might be tested by everyday experience or our ordinary understanding of language, it could be rejected out of hand. But Fish is not proceeding in such a straightforward manner, as becomes quite evident a moment later, when he couples his assertion that there are no texts that have "many meanings" with an assertion that there are "no texts that have a single meaning." How can it be that there are no texts with a single meaning and no texts with many meanings? Fish answers by explaining that meaning is a property or quality or attribute not of a text but rather of the context in which the text is located. The Constitution, for Fish, is not the repository or embodiment of a public morality or of any meaning whatsoever.[23] When we speak of a text such as the Constitution and say it has many meanings, we are, according to Fish, really talking about a situation in which people disagree about the meaning of the text (because they are reading it with different interpretive assumptions, etc.). When we speak of a text with a single meaning, we are talking about a situation of agreement.

I do not believe that this view (which makes the meaning of a text the property of a context rather than a text) in any way follows from the conventionalist tenet—which I believe to be true—that every text is "always and already" embedded in a context and "is always an already interpreted object." Fish simply seems to be taking conventionalism to illogical extremes and confounding a situation (context) with an object located in that situation (the text), or confusing the act of interpretation with the object of interpretation. Moreover, I fail to see what is to be gained from his strategy of making meaning a property of a context rather than of a text. The theoretical problem we confront, you will recall, is one of constraint: The question is whether there is a need for a concept such as disciplining rules. Fish sought to deny that there is any such need by proclaiming that there are no texts with many meanings, but all he has done is *re-characterize* the problem of choice and thus the need for constraint. Choices still must be made, though now it is not a choice between several "meanings of a text" (for texts have no meanings) but rather between "different interpretive assumptions" (for example, about the purpose of the text). Admittedly the Constitution, in Fish's words, is an "always and already interpreted object," but that does not deny the need to interpret it, to reinterpret it, or to choose between conflicting interpretations.

At one point in "Fish v. Fiss," Fish concedes that even though the Constitution is "always an already interpreted object," conflicts will arise and choices will have to be made. He then poses the question of method: "How are these conflicts to be settled?" My answer to this question makes reference to the disciplining rules, which are, you recall, the authoritative norms of the interpretive community, but Fish is determined not to introduce into his account any such norms or standards and, as a result, blurs whatever distinctions might flow from such norms. "How are these conflicts to be settled?" he asks himself and then continues:

> The answer to this question is that they are always in the process of being settled, and that no transcendent or algorithmic method of interpretation is required to settle them. The means of settling them are political, social, and institutional, in a mix that is itself subject to modification and change.

Is this an adequate answer?

Adjudication may be subject to two different attacks. One is based on a moral vision that condemns the institutionalized relationships that are necessarily entailed in adjudication and that seek new institutional forms. Adjudication is condemned because it is evil. A prominent intellectual and political movement of our times, Critical Legal Studies, often aspires to so radical a critique, but it fails in its delivery because it does not explain how we could meet the genuine needs adjudication now serves and yet avoid the excesses of that institution. However, the Critical Legal Studies Movement mounts another, somewhat lesser critique of adjudication. This one claims not so much that adjudication is evil but that it is incoherent. This critique theorizes that the judge lacks any distinctive legal standards to guide or constrain his or her judgment, and that the judge, by choice and of necessity, draws on values or viewpoints that are either personal or rooted in the various social groups that he or she belongs to. This theory is similar to that espoused by Levinson and is encapsulated in the movement's slogan, "law as politics."

Stanley Fish is not, by any stretch of the imagination, a member of the Critical Legal Studies Movement. He believes in professionalism, as do most conventionalists. He does not seek to undermine adjudication: He does not claim that it is evil nor even that it is incoherent. The problem, however, is that he offers an account of that institution and answers the question of method in a way that blurs the line between law and politics. His point is not so much to dispute the existence of legal norms or standards but to deny a role for any norms or standards. All is practice. But once you enter Fish's "normless" world, you have lost the basis—other than instinct or "know how"—for separating good judgments from bad ones or legal judgments from political ones. All you can say is that there

are conflicting interpretations and that "the means of settling them are political, social, and institutional, in a mix that is itself subject to modification and change"—which, in my judgment, is not saying much at all.

Under my account, professional norms constrain judges in choosing
between conflicting interpretations and are the standards for assessing the
correctness of their decisions. My reference to disciplining rules allows me
to see an inner coherence to the law, and to speak about the legal correctness of *Brown* or countless other constitutional decisions. As explained
in "Objectivity and Interpretation," I also envision a role for an external
critic of a decision, who stands outside the law and operates on some other
standards, such as those rooted in moral or political principles. Fish insists
that this distinction between the internal and external critic is "less firm
and stable" than I suggest. He also belittles the distinction I draw between
the various strategies open to a critic of a judicial decision—amending the
Constitution as opposed to packing the Court or enacting statutes that
curtail jurisdiction:

> In calling these latter strategies "lesser" and "more problematic," Fiss once
> again assumes a distinction that cannot finally be maintained. Presumably
> they are "lesser" and "more problematic" because they are more obviously
> political; but in fact the entire system is political, and the question at any
> moment is: From which point in the system is pressure being applied, and
> to what other points?

Too often in the law we transform differences in degree into differences
in kind; lawyers tend to see lines where there are only gradations of gray
(so my students and friends often remind me). Fish's brand of conventionalism may be a healthy corrective for this tendency, but I cannot help but
believe that in the end it is a bit too much, and that Fish is destroying distinctions that comport with the way we think and talk about the law and
that have served us well. For those in the profession, and maybe even for
those outside, it seems terribly important—not just as a psychological
matter but also for the purpose of figuring out what you can and cannot
do—to know the difference between a legal argument and a political one,
that is, to know that passing a constitutional amendment is a more legitimate response to a detested decision than packing the Court. Of course, all
these distinctions are made in terms of an ongoing system—a certain discourse and set of institutions that we know all too well—and it might be
that the entire system, viewed from some transcendental perspective, is

political. But that seems to be beside the point. We work and live within this world, not at some point of transcendence (as any conventionalist should know). Adjudication is an ongoing institution, and the purpose of "Objectivity and Interpretation" or, for that matter, any other exercise in legal theory is to identify those features that distinguish adjudication from other institutions, and that call forth and justify the special normative discourse that surrounds it.

Let me also note, on perhaps a more technical level, that Fish's assault on the distinction between law and politics does not in any way flow from his views about the contextualized nature of texts or any of the other insights of conventionalism. It simply flows from his unwillingness to allow any place in his system for disciplining rules or any other form of generalized norms. I see them as essential because, for me, adjudication is a process that calls on judges to choose between many conflicting interpretations (or "meanings" or "interpretive assumptions" or whatever) of some authoritative text and because the law assumes that these choices are made pursuant to standards. The distinction between law and politics arises from the fact that the standards for judges are not necessarily the same as those for political actors or moral prophets. The distinction assumes different standards for different actors.

In "Objectivity and Interpretation" I tried to identify the forces that tend to make legal and political standards converge—the judge's desire to avoid crises, the sharing of similar normative concepts such as equality, and so on. I acknowledged the considerable convergence of law and politics that has, in fact, occurred in American society, and I indicated that this convergence might be one of the most distinctive features of our legal system. But I did not suggest that the convergence was complete. Even more to the point, I do not believe that whatever convergence exists is in any way attributable to the fact that texts—whether the Constitution itself or disciplining rules—are always contextualized or that judges are situated within a practice. Wittgenstein tried to give an account of meaning that employed the idea of a language game, but he always insisted on the multiplicity of language games.[24]

The Stakes

In the final paragraph of his paper, Fish announces "that nothing turns on Fiss's account or, for that matter, on my account either." With this assertion

Fish once again reveals his love for the paradoxical, but also, and more significant, he reflects the conventionalist emphasis on practice and context. As Wittgenstein put it, "Don't think, but look."[25] As a conventionalist, Fish believes that everything is in place: The judge is situated; the text is situated; so what possible significance could there be to a theoretical dispute about adjudication?

This may be a real problem for Fish (I doubt it) but not for me. I do not believe that everything is in place. It is indeed important to look, but I also believe that it is important to think, and that there is a crucial place in the profession of law for the theoretical. Professional training does try to instill "know how," but that is not all there is to the law (nor perhaps even to basketball). Ideas do matter. Indeed, the interest the profession has shown in Fish's own theoretical work suggests that not all is practice (although Fish assures me that this interest is a passing fad which will last for only seven years—which seven?). I mention this now not to find another ground for impeaching Fish's account but only to explain why I believe it is important to figure out whether Fish is right (and I, wrong).

Theory informs practice, just as surely as practice informs theory, and, in my view, Fish's theory threatens two important practices of the profession. One is the value placed on self-conscious reflection—those moments when a judge considers the interpretive choices, and identifies and weighs the norms of the profession that are to guide that choice. Fish denies that such moments exist ("a judge always knows in general what to do"),[26] and that denial both legitimates and invites a certain thoughtlessness. Those who judge by instinct are told not to worry, because that is what they must of necessity do. The others—the great judges—only believe that they are deliberating.

Fish's account also jeopardizes the special pull that the norms of the profession have—and should have—on the judge. Anything goes. Fish tells the judge that "the entire system is political" and all that differs is the "point in the system" where the pressure is applied. Some judges might take these words seriously (although I have explained why they shouldn't), and, if so, they might generate a set of practices that would turn law into politics. Judges who listen to Fish would see no reason to be especially faithful to the norms of the profession and would believe instead that they are entitled to do whatever they think best. The discipline so prized by the law would be gone and, with it, much of the law's special claim for our respect. Judging is a practice, but a very special kind.

11

The Death of Law?

Although I devoted much of my intellectual energy in the 1980s to arguing against Critical Legal Studies, then at its peak, I felt that the widespread public criticism directed against that movement unfairly and unfortunately overlooked the threat that a more honored and respected jurisprudential movement posed to law, a movement that achieved its ascendancy during the same period, Law and Economics.

Law and Economics began earlier. Its origins can be traced to the work of Henry Simons and Aaron Director at the University of Chicago. It reflects the longstanding commitment of that university to the interdisciplinary study of law. Yet Law and Economics achieved a new prominence starting in 1969, when Richard Posner joined the Chicago faculty, which then included such economists as Ronald Coase, Gary Becker, and George Stigler. Posner began the series of articles that portrayed "law as efficiency" and that culminated in the publication of *Economic Analysis of Law* (1972). From 1968 until 1974 I was a member of the Chicago faculty and was thus especially attuned to all these developments.

I was fascinated by the interplay of Law and Economics and Critical Legal Studies and, during the early and mid-1980s, taught, with my colleague and friend Anthony Kronman, a number of seminars at Yale that touched on these issues. (One bore the title of this chapter, while others were posted as "The Tyranny of Kant," "Not By Reason Alone," and so on; you get the drift.) The invitation to deliver the Robert S. Stevens Lecture at Cornell Law School created an opportunity to put my thoughts together in a more systematic fashion. The lecture was delivered on April 9, 1986, and was published soon thereafter in the *Cornell Law Review* (volume 72, page 1).

"The Death of Law?" appeared to have touched a live nerve. It became the subject of a panel discussion at the January 1988 meeting of the American Association of Law Schools. The other panelists were Clare Dalton, Duncan Kennedy, Frank Michelman, and George Priest. The chair was Gary Minda. By that time the Feminist Movement had taken hold of a generation of law students, and, for reasons indicated in the concluding passages of "The Death of Law?" I saw that as an encouraging sign. My remarks at the American Association of Law Schools meeting were distinctly (and perhaps naively) upbeat. They were later published in the January 1989 issue of the *Cornell Law Review* (volume 74, page 245), as "The Law Regained." Laura Kalman, in chapter 4 of *The Strange Career of Legal Liberalism,* published by Yale University Press in 1996, describes the place of "The Death of Law?" in the academic debates of its day.

T HE 1970s were an exciting and unusual time for legal education in America. The period was marked by the emergence of two jurisprudential movements that filled classrooms and law reviews with a remarkable spirit and energy. Everyone talked about theory.

One of the movements is Critical Legal Studies, which, during the late 1970s and 1980s, became deeply entrenched in two of the most prestigious law schools in the country, Harvard and Stanford. This movement became the subject of a number of unfriendly articles in a wide variety of popular journals and even the national newspapers.[1] It was considered largely responsible for the institutional turmoil tearing Harvard Law School apart in the 1980s. Critical Legal Studies also provoked an unnerving and widely publicized response by Paul Carrington, then the dean of Duke, who argued, in 1984, that the members of the Critical Legal Studies Movement have no place in the modern law school.[2]

Critical Legal Studies engendered fierce and sometimes misguided resistance. Because I share the egalitarianism that inspires much of the movement, I am sorry about that. However, I will not draw back from my criticism of that movement, as adumbrated in "Objectivity and Interpretation" (chapter 9); instead, I will try to strengthen and broaden that criticism. I will try to place Critical Legal Studies in a larger cultural and intellectual framework, and attempt to link it with the other jurisprudential movement, Law and Economics, that arose almost contemporaneously.

The success of Law and Economics is not of the kind that generates articles for popular journals, but it is important to bear in mind that it arose roughly at the same time as Critical Legal Studies and became even more firmly entrenched within the legal academy. By the mid-1980s, hardly a major law school did not have a full-time economist on its faculty; Yale had two, as well as five or six lawyers who had considerable training in economics and who self-consciously defined themselves as practitioners of Law and Economics. Much to my embarrassment (I have no taste for Carrington's purge), the Critical Legal Studies Movement was virtually unrepresented on the Yale faculty during the 1980s. Several of the leading practitioners of Law and Economics—Richard Posner, Frank Easterbrook, Ralph Winter, and Robert Bork—were appointed to the federal bench by President Ronald Reagan, thereby achieving a measure of power that lies far, far beyond the reach of any Critical Legal Studies scholar.

The practitioners of Law and Economics tend to be better behaved; their mission more closely accords with the traditions of the academy than does that of Critical Legal Studies scholars. The politics of the two movements also tend to be different. Law and Economics is a movement of the Right, whereas Critical Legal Studies is one of the Left. Despite these differences, however, and others I will try to elaborate, what strikes me as even more significant is how much they share. Both movements can be understood as a reaction to a jurisprudence, confidently embraced by the bar in the 1960s, that portrays adjudication as the process for interpreting and nurturing public morality. Both Law and Economics and Critical Legal Studies are united in their rejection of the notion of law as public ideal. One school proclaims "law as efficiency," the other "law as politics." Yet neither is willing to take law on its own terms, and to accept adjudication as an institutional arrangement in which public officials seek to elaborate and protect the values we hold in common.

Law as Efficiency

Law and Economics has a descriptive dimension and, as such, might be understood as a continuation of the social scientific tradition in the law that began with Roscoe Pound and the Realists. It seeks a patterned description of the case law. The most prominent hypothesis generated by such an inquiry asserts that the law is efficient or, more particularly, that in defining or shaping rights judges have tended to create rules that maximize the total satisfaction of preferences. Richard Posner's academic career was made by going through one body of judicial decisions after another—torts, contracts, property, and so on—in an effort to show how each and every decision might be understood in such instrumental terms.[3] He began with private law, but has not been so confined, and saw all as serving efficiency.

The efficiency hypothesis always seemed weak. The evidence marshaled has not been wholly convincing;[4] the exceptions seemed almost as important as what purported to be the generalization. Although a story might be told as to how a particular rule (e.g., the fellow servant rule) served efficiency,[5] it also seems possible to tell a similar story about the opposite rule. Even more important, no explanation was ever given for how the law might work in the wondrous way Posner hypothesized,[6] namely, that it would always, or generally, produce the efficient result. An explanatory mechanism was needed to render the hypothesis plausible (and thus to compensate for shoddy empirical work). It was also needed to give the hypothesis some predictive power and thus to fulfill the highest scientific aspirations of this school. Posner and his colleagues claimed not only that the law *was* efficient, but that it *will be*.

On one occasion, at a workshop at Yale in the late 1970s, Posner was pressed on this point. He was asked how a body of judicial decisions might be understood as an instrument for maximizing the total satisfaction of preferences when the judges responsible for those decisions were not trained in economics, did not justify their decisions in those terms, and did not give much evidence that they even thought about such matters. In fact, it appeared that the judges thought about everything else but maximization. Posner responded by describing the work of a colleague who sought to explain the behavior of rats in terms of maximizing their satisfaction. What was critical, Posner insisted, was that the rats behaved "as if" the maximization of their satisfaction was their objective, and it was not important for the validity of such an explanation that the rats actually thought about maximization, economics, or, for that matter, anything else.

To many the analogy seemed far-fetched, if not downright insulting, but the general theoretical point Posner made was well taken. "As if" explanations might have predictive validity and do not require self-awareness or any kind of consciousness. It is possible to say that judges are acting "as if" they were trying to maximize the satisfaction of preferences, even though it could be assumed that they never thought in those terms. "As if" explanations do require, however, identifying some dynamic (e.g., a structure of incentives) that would explain the behavior in question and render the empirical hypothesis plausible, or even credible. In the case of the rats there was the cheese; for judges there was no explanation as to why they might behave "as if" they were maximizing the total satisfaction of preferences. No reason was given for why we should disbelieve the justification the judges offered for their behavior.

Subsequently Posner turned away from an "as if" explanation, toward what might be termed a *sensible objectives* one. According to this theory, devising rules for maximizing the satisfaction of preferences is the only "sensible" (or "rational") thing for judges to do. Posner postulated two types of rules—those that maximize and those that redistribute—and then further assumed that courts cannot effectively redistribute and that legislatures can. Under these circumstances, the only "sensible" thing for a court to do is to promulgate rules that maximize the total satisfaction of preferences and are, in that sense, efficient. As Posner put it, "Courts can do very little to affect the distribution of wealth in a society, so it may be sensible for them to concentrate on what they can do, which is to establish rules that maximize the size of the economic pie, and let the problem of slicing it up be handled by the legislature with its much greater taxing and spending powers."[7] This sentence comes from an article written after Posner became a judge and, as such, has special biographical value. In an earlier paper, he advanced a similar theory to explain the behavior of litigants. They are likely to fight for efficient rules in the courts, Posner claimed, because that is the only sensible thing for them to do: "By doing so they increase the wealth of the society; they will get a share of that increased wealth; and there is no alternative norm that would yield a larger share."[8]

Each and every step in this argument is contestable: the division of judge-made rules into two (and only two) types, the allocations of competencies among various institutions, the assumption that we all do what is "sensible," and so forth. In one of the great understatements of his long and distinguished career, Posner said of his own effort to provide the requisite explanatory mechanism: "Some of the links in the chain are obscure."[9] For our purposes, however, what must be stressed is that a "sensible objectives" theory would never suffice for a thoroughgoing positivist, especially an economist. Scientific theories are not built on claims about what is the "sensible" or "rational" thing for someone to do; rather, they require an identification or description of those observable features of the environment that systematically lead people to behave as they do (regardless of what they say about their beliefs or anything else). That is something Posner and his colleagues never provided.

The theory of "sensible objectives" fails to supply the explanatory mechanism needed to give the "law as efficiency" hypothesis predictive validity, or even descriptive credibility. In that sense, it takes us no further than Posner's talk about rats and "as if" explanations did. However, the theory of "sensible objectives" does advance our understanding of the Law and Economics Movement in general, for it makes it abundantly clear that the efficiency hypothesis rests largely on a normative assumption—that judges *should* decide cases in a way that serves efficiency. Such a normative assumption cannot, of course, save an enterprise that purports to be descriptive and predictive—the pretense of scientism must be abandoned—but this assumption can stand on its own and, in fact, has given rise to what might be regarded as a second branch of the Law and Economics Movement, a normative one, which has turned out to be predominant.

The aim of this second, or normative, branch of Law and Economics is not to describe or explain how judicial decisions were actually made or predict how they will be made but, rather, to guide them. It depicts the normative concepts judges employ—for example, equality or reasonableness—as a hopeless jumble of intuitions, and offers an intellectual structure to order those intuitions and give them content. That structure is the market. According to this branch of Law and Economics, the normative concepts of the law should be construed and applied in such a way as to make the judicial power an instrument for perfecting the market.

The normative branch of Law and Economics relativizes all values. Values are reduced to preferences, and all preferences are assumed to have an equal claim for satisfaction. The struggle between neighbors in the typical nuisance case (to take an example that is at once central to the economic analysis of the law and most congenial to it) is not a conflict between peace and recreation, which are understood as public values that have to be harmonized and ordered; rather, it is a conflict between those who prefer to use the land for recreation and those who prefer peace and quiet. There is no way, moreover, of judging one preference as more worthy than the other, any more than there is a way of judging the preference for one flavor of ice cream over another. Any choice between the two would be arbitrary or, to use the jargon of this school, merely a matter of "distribution" (which means that the choice does not depend on any universally acceptable criterion but, instead, amounts to favoring the interests of one group over another).

Having thus reduced all values to preferences, and having established that a choice between preferences would be arbitrary, it then follows that social institutions can have one purpose and only one purpose, which is to maximize the total satisfaction of preferences. In the ordinary situation, bargaining and exchange are presumably the best means for achieving that end. Individuals know best what their preferences are and how much they are worth, and thus they should be free to bargain with one another to obtain the means (or conditions) of satisfying them, for example, cash for ice cream. The exchange will take place only when the positions of both parties will be improved. In this way, free exchanges between individuals keep us moving toward the goal of maximizing the satisfaction of preferences.

With the ordinary commercial transaction, say, between a retailer and a customer, the contribution of market exchanges to the satisfaction of preferences seems clear and obvious. What the new Law and Economics Movement did, under the leadership of Ronald Coase,[10] was to perceive a role for market exchange even in noncommercial contexts, such as nuisance cases. In a nuisance dispute, the argument goes, the desires of the parties could not be fully satisfied because there was a conflict or, to introduce more jargon, a "costly interaction" between the two, but an exchange might maximize the total value realizable; either the raucous sports club that destroys the tranquility of the neighborhood could buy out the adjoining homeowners (which would leave both parties better off—one with the game, the others with money) or the bargain could work inversely if the cost would be less to move the club than to buy out the homeowners.

Under this account, law appears to have two purposes. One is to provide the conditions necessary for effective bargaining (demarcating property rights, assuring bargains are enforced, preventing fraud, etc.). The law is an indispensable backdrop for the market. A second mission for the law arises only when bargaining breaks down or is not possible, as when too many people are involved. In such a case, often described as one in which there are "transaction costs," the law takes a more active role, serving as a supplement rather than a backdrop for the market. It corrects for market failure. The purpose of law or adjudication in particular is to remove the obstacles to exchange and, if that is not possible, to replicate the market outcome. The just result is one that either brings the parties together for exchange or gives them approximately what they would have received had they been able to bargain.

For some theorists, mostly in Chicago, the role of law as an institution that supplements and thus perfects the market in this second way is minor, for they assume that market failure (because of, say, high transaction costs) is the exception and sporadic. Law and Economics merely becomes the handmaiden of laissez faire, though perhaps with a special twist. Law is not only unnecessary, but, as emphasized by Harold Demsetz[11] and the others who have pursued Coase's essential insight, it is also redundant: No matter how the case is decided, as long as bargaining remains possible, an exchange between the parties after judgment will maximize the satisfaction of preferences and move us closer to the efficient allocation of resources.

In contrast to the Chicago school, some practitioners of Law and Economics (originally based in New Haven) contemplate a larger role for the state and for adjudication. They see market failure almost everywhere. They acknowledge the power of the market paradigm, in which all values are treated as relative and the maximum satisfaction of preferences is the end of all social institutions, yet they insist that the need for supplementary institutions is all-pervasive. Through the most ingenious of arguments they are able to embrace both the market and the activist state.

The New Haven school is, in my judgment, closer to the truth than the Chicago school, especially if the focus shifts, as it invariably does, from nuisance cases to the great public law cases of our day. The "transaction costs" in the typical desegregation case are staggering, if I may engage in something of an understatement. It seems to me, however, that the problem is deeper and that all practitioners of Law and Economics—whether they are in New Haven or Chicago—are on the wrong track. The issue is not quantity but quality: It is not that a larger role for law must be assumed but, rather, that its role should be understood in qualitatively different terms. The role of the law is neither to perfect nor to replicate the market; instead, it is to make those judgments that the adherents of Law and Economics claim are only arbitrary, that is, a mere matter of distribution. The duty of the judge is not to serve the market but to determine whether it should prevail.

This account of law reflects actual practices, how we think and talk about the law. It also reflects the judiciary's self-understanding. Judges do not see themselves as instruments of efficiency but rather as engaged in a process of trying to understand and protect the values embodied in the law. But, as you recall, at this juncture the claim of Law and Economics is normative, not descriptive: As a statement of what the purpose of the law should be, the efficiency principle is not defeated by the simple (and well-taken) objection that it contradicts the actual social practices or self-understanding of judges by depicting the law in crudely instrumental terms (as a means of satisfying preferences). The normative claim of Law and Economics can be defeated only by challenging its first premise, namely, that all values are relative, and, as the rest of this book makes abundantly clear, I, too, am happy to do that. I do not believe that all values are reducible to preferences and that all have an equal claim to satisfaction. Values are values.

The proponents of Law and Economics would have us believe that the typical nuisance case, or, for that matter, a case such as *Brown v. Board of Education,* is simply a conflict over preferences and that it arises because the preferences of all the parties cannot be fully satisfied. They assign the judge the task of trying to devise some scheme for maximizing the satisfaction of these conflicting preferences. It seems to me, however, that the conflict before the court is of a different character altogether—not a conflict arising from a divergence of preferences or tastes but one between the various ethical commitments implicit in that body of shared understandings known as the law. From that perspective, the assigned task of the judiciary should not be to devise schemes for maximizing the satisfaction of preferences; rather, it should be to give concrete meaning and expression to the values made authoritative by the law. Judges should order, interpret, and establish a regime of state power for protecting these values.

As emphasized previously, the right of the judiciary to give meaning to our public values does not rest on the moral expertise of the persons who happen to hold office but on the procedural norms that simultaneously constrain and liberate those who exercise the judicial power—judges are insulated from the political process and are required to engage in a special kind of dialogue over the meaning of those values. This dialogue is arduous and taxing, at times almost beyond anyone's powers, but it is an essential part of the process through which a morality evolves and retains its public character.

Law as Politics

Like Law and Economics, Critical Legal Studies starts by emphasizing the openness of the normative concepts used by the judiciary. The purpose here, however, is not affirmative, but negative. Critical Legal Studies scholars do not try to transcend the uncertainty—they revel in it. Rather than impose an intellectual structure on all the conflicting intuitions embraced within these normative concepts, these scholars accept this openness or (to use their favorite term) *indeterminacy* as a given. Consequently, they argue, there can be no standards for constraining judges or for determining whether a decision is correct as a matter of law. To revert to the example of Law and Economics, there is no basis for saying one use of the land is more reasonable than another; or, to move to the public law cases that have been much more central to Critical Legal Studies, there is no basis for saying that one judicial interpretation of the Equal Protection or Due Process Clause is truer than another. The purpose of this exercise is to deny the distinctive claim that law is a form of rationality.[12] Law is not what it seems—objective and capable of yielding right answers; rather, it is simply politics in another guise. Judges speak the way they do because that is the convention of their profession and is needed to maintain their power, but their rhetoric is all a sham.

The Legal Realists of the 1920s and 1930s were also intent on demystifying the law, insisting that the law's claim to determinacy and objectivity was a sham, but their critique was aimed at freeing law from the past (in particular, from its commitment to laissez faire). Their critique was a prelude to having the law become an effective instrument of good public policy. There is a strain of Feminism that also seeks to unmask the law—to show how the privileged position of men in the legal profession has tended to skew the law, and how neutral-sounding concepts or principles have often served as a cloak for patriarchy.[13] These Feminists, like the Realists, are moved by an affirmative vision—if not liberty, then a true and substantive equality—and they appreciate how the law can be used to further that vision. But that is not critical legal scholarship.[14] Critical Legal Studies scholars are distinguished (if at all) from Feminists and from the Legal Realists of an earlier generation by the purity of their negativism. When these scholars insist on "law as politics," they mean something quite different and more nihilistic than either Realists or Feminists. They want to unmask the law, but not to make law into an effective instrument of good public policy or equality. The aim of their critique is critique. Critical Legal Studies scholars realize that any normative structure created to supplant law would be subject to the very same critique they used to attack the law.

A few have tried to go further. They have tried to construct an affirmative program and to explain what law could become once it is unmasked, but in each instance the affirmative program offered is rather empty and unattractive. Indeed, it turns out to be another form of negativism. One such program has been put forth by Duncan Kennedy,[15] generally considered to be the Abbie Hoffman of the movement.[16] Kennedy's program contemplates a particularized form of adjudication, where judges look at the totality of circumstances and simply make a decision, without the guidance of rules or principles (which, of course, would be vulnerable to the critique) but with a full understanding of their historical position and a willingness to assume complete responsibility for their decisions. Another so-called affirmative program has been advanced by Roberto Unger, whose work I consider to be the true inspiration of the movement.[17] He urges us to use the judicial power as an instrument of destabilization—of tearing down whatever structure happens to exist at the time—not as a means of moving us closer to nirvana (which, given the distortions of existing social structures, cannot be specified) but as a way of revealing our capacity to transcend the particular context we happen to find ourselves in.

Critique that lacks a vision of what might replace what is destroyed strikes me as both politically unappealing and politically irresponsible. Some suggest that such fears are unwarranted. They claim that adjudication has a place in these so-called affirmative programs and that for the first time it will become "responsible," "intelligible," and "democratic." But this is simply word play. Of course, I would have to accept the critique and live with its political consequences, however unpleasant they might be, if I thought for a moment that the critique was intellectually compelling. But, in fact, it is not. The freedom of the judge that is posited by Critical Legal Studies and that serves as its central premise simply does not exist. The concepts of the law may be open-ended, in the sense that one cannot reach judgment by a simple process of deduction, but that is not what the law or objectivity requires or even aspires to. What is required is that judges be constrained in their judgment, and indeed they are.

When I read a case like *Brown v. Board of Education*, for example, what I see is not the unconstrained power of the Justices to give vent to their desires and interests but, rather, public officials situated within a profession, bounded at every turn by the norms and conventions that define and constitute that profession. There is more to judging than simply confronting the bare words of the Fourteenth Amendment, which commands that "no State shall . . . deny to any person within its jurisdiction the equal protection of the laws." The Justices start with the amendment's legislative history and a body of cases that struggled to make sense out of the amendment's commitment to racial equality. Guided by years of training and experience, they read earlier cases and sense which way the law is moving.

They consider the role of the state, and the place of public education in particular, in the life of the nation and weigh the evidence developed at trial on the impact of segregative practices. They also know what constitutes a good reason for distinguishing *Plessy v. Ferguson* or for deciding the case one way or another.

As explained in "Objectivity and Interpretation" (chapter 9) and again in "Judging as a Practice" (chapter 10), the Justices are disciplined in the exercise of their power. They are caught in a network of so-called disciplining rules that, like a grammar, define and constitute the practice of judging and are rendered authoritative by the interpretive community of which the Justices are a part. These disciplining rules provide the standards for determining whether some decision is right (or wrong) and for justifying it (or contesting it). They constrain, not determine, judgment. Of course, disagreement can still take place, as it has throughout history. But disagreement—at least within modest proportions—is not destructive of law. Rather, it is generative of it: Disagreement is an essential part of any collaborative moral enterprise within a complex and changing society.

In this account of adjudication I recognize that I am making an empirical assumption about the richness of the legal system in this country. I am assuming that our legal culture is sufficiently developed and textured so as to yield a body of disciplining rules that constrains judges and provides the standards for evaluating their work. This assumption is, of course, open to a factual challenge, as any empirical claim must be. The proponents of Critical Legal Studies are not prepared, however, to disagree with me on these (mundane) terms. For their claim is not that, as a factual matter, in some particular legal system or at some historical phase, judges are not constrained by law, but rather that law, by its nature, can never provide the constraint needed to achieve objectivity. Their idea is not that there is no right answer but rather that there *never* can be a right answer. To support so ambitious and extravagant a claim, most proponents of Critical Legal Studies resort to Duncan Kennedy's theory of the "fundamental contradiction"[18] (though some, like Gerald Frug[19] and Sanford Levinson,[20] believe —quite falsely—that the key may be found in the work of Jacques Derrida, Paul de Man, Stanley Fish, Hillis Miller, and other literary theorists of the deconstructive bent).

According to Kennedy's theory of the "fundamental contradiction," all normative concepts are infected with a conflict that cannot be resolved. They deconstruct into two (or more) antithetical and competing forces, impulses, or desires, such as the desire for others and the fear of others.

So infected with contradictions, a normative concept (or any rule, principle, or standard generated out of it) cannot act as a restraint on the judge, for it always affords the judge a choice. The judge can favor one antipode over the other and nonetheless be said to be (honestly) applying the rule. The "fundamental contradiction" creates a freedom, a choice, and thus renders everything normative indeterminate, that is, unable either to constrain the judge or provide any standards of evaluation. It creates this freedom almost as a matter of logical necessity. There is nothing contingent, limited, or empirical about the "fundamental contradiction." It is no mere "tension."

There is no proof or even an argument on behalf of the "fundamental contradiction." Professor Kennedy simply asserts its existence in the midst of an exceedingly long analysis of the table of contents of Blackstone's *Commentaries*. I am not even sure whether the existence or validity of the "fundamental contradiction" can be proved or demonstrated, given its universal scope. Operating much like a moral axiom, it ultimately rests on an appeal to common experience. In response, one can always appeal to a different understanding of that very same experience and assert with equal fervor that the normative structures of the law are not riddled with "fundamental contradictions." I am prepared to do just that. Moreover, I might point out that the stakes are greater than they at first appear. What is at issue as one starts down the road of the "fundamental contradiction" is not simply the law but morality as well, or, for that matter, any practice or institution that rests on or otherwise incorporates normative structures. There is no way to confine the "fundamental contradiction" to law. Everything normative must go. There can never be a right answer in morals, just as certainly as there can never be a right answer in law.

Some have claimed to the contrary, and once Professor Frank Michelman—not a member of the movement but obviously drawn to it—insisted that although there could never be a right answer in the law, there could be (indeed must be) right answers in morals.[21] This view fails to account for the full sweep of the "fundamental contradiction." It also seems to be at odds with common intuitions. Given the institutional apparatus of the law, and the shared understandings that bond and animate the profession, I think it is far more likely that there are right answers in the law than in morals. Of course, morality does not require "the compulsion of a transcendent rule," to use a phrase of Michelman's,[22] but neither does law. As I argued in "Objectivity and Interpretation," it requires only constrained judgment. An insistence on the contrary, and an attempt to depict the law in other terms, as "transcendent," "mechanical," or "unitary," strikes me as a strained attempt to restrict the critique of Critical Legal Studies to the law and to render credible a jurisprudence that rests not on any fancy theory about the "fundamental contradiction" or anything else but on a special strain of utopianism, one that rightly aspires to a true and substantive equality but fails to accord a proper place for the institutional arrangements needed to bring that ideal into being.

Law as Public Reason

Critical Legal Studies and Law and Economics differ in many important respects—their politics, the intricacies of their arguments, the definition of their scholarly mission, and, of course, their antics. To depict "law as efficiency" is quite different than heralding "law as politics." I believe, however, that these movements have something in common and that what they share is as important as their differences. I have tried to show that they both start from a rejection of law as an embodiment of a public morality and thus have a common baseline. Critical Legal Studies denies that there is such a morality (or, for that matter, any kind of morality) when it argues that *all* our normative structures embody an irresolvable contradiction. Law and Economics strikes at the notion of law as public morality, too, but not through the "fundamental contradiction." It does this by considering all values as relative and claiming for itself what Bork, in a gesture that trivializes the jurisprudence of the sixties, calls the "Equal Gratification Clause."[23] Under Law and Economics the idea of a public morality once again becomes untenable because values are transformed into preferences, and each preference is assumed to have an equal claim to satisfaction.

From this perspective it is no surprise that both Law and Economics and Critical Legal Studies achieved their ascendancy in America within the same period of history. Nor is it surprising that this period was the 1970s —a time of difference and disagreement, in which the emphasis was not on what we shared, our public values and ideals, but on how we differed and what divided us. Although in the 1960s we undertook the Second Reconstruction and tried to build the Great Society, and we were drawn to law as public ideal, in the next decade we took refuge in the politics of selfishness. All normative matters became subjective. The prospect of understanding and nourishing a common morality seemed hopeless.

Locating these two jurisprudential movements within a specific historical context may also help us to understand how law might be regained.
Law has been threatened by the disintegration of public values in the
larger society, and its future can only be assured by the reversal of those social processes. In order to protect the law, we must look beyond the law.
We will never be able to respond fully to the negativism of Critical Legal
Studies or the crude instrumentalism of Law and Economics until a regen-
erative process takes hold, until the broad social processes that fed and
nourished those movements are reversed. The analytic arguments wholly
internal to the law can take us only so far. There must be something more
—a belief in public values and the willingness to act on them.

Where will that belief come from? In speaking of a public morality and
the judiciary's responsibility to give meaning and expression to those values, I am sustained by a historical vision—namely, the 1960s and the role
the law played in the struggle for racial equality. But for a generation born
after *Brown,* after Ole Miss, after Birmingham, after Freedom Summer,
and after Selma, this vision does not work. It is not fought but only toler-
ated as a quaint, even touching remembrance of a time past.

The Feminist Movement, as it gained sway in the 1980s, provoked powerful memories of this historical experience. Feminism mobilized a new
generation of law students and sought a reexamination of existing social
arrangements. But in order for Feminism to become, like the Civil Rights
Movement before it, the instrument of social regeneration that the law
awaits, we—both the bearers of the cause and the community under criticism—must not view gender issues as a matter of individual or group interests; rather, we must recognize the claim to sexual equality as an expression of the ideals and values we hold in common.[24]

Beyond that, it is difficult to know how a belief in public values might
be regenerated. Such a process of social regeneration depends on events
that are beyond our control and are even hard to imagine. It seems to me,
however, that law itself might have an important role to play in this process, for law appears to be as generative of public values as it is dependent
on them. The Warren Court and the transformative process it precipitated
in American society not only presupposed a belief in the existence of public values, it was also responsible for it. The Court's decision in the *Brown*
case assumed that the Constitution embodied a commitment to racial
equality, and that this value was so real and so important as to warrant
moving mountains (almost). It also generated and nurtured a commitment to racial equality that far transcended the law.

An appreciation of law as a generative force of our public life does not make the task we confront any easier. In truth, it compounds the complexity and magnitude of our challenge, for it suggests that we are caught in a circle: Law is, alas, both agent and object. Yet an understanding of the generative force of law can make us acutely aware of the dangers posed by Law and Economics and Critical Legal Studies, and thus strengthen our resolve to resist them. We need public morality to have law, true, but, even more, we need law to have a public morality. Of course, law will exist even if the two jurisprudential movements of which I have spoken have their way, in the limited sense that there will be people who wear black robes and decide cases, but it will be a very different kind of law. For Kennedy, adjudication will be entirely particularistic; for Judge Posner it will be wholly instrumental. In neither case will it be capable of sustaining or generating a public morality. It will be law without inspiration. This will mean the death of law, as we have known it throughout history and as we have come to admire it.

12

Reason vs. Passion

Goldberg v. Kelly represented one of the great achievements of the Warren Court era. Even though it was decided in March 1970, shortly after Earl Warren had stepped down and Warren Burger was appointed Chief Justice, the changes in personnel and outlook in the High Court, which would soon mark the end of one era and the beginning of another, had not yet taken place. Justice William Brennan wrote the opinion. It held that welfare recipients had a right to be heard before their benefits could be terminated. It thus promised a transfer of the due process revolution launched by the Warren Court from the criminal to the civil domain.

The Court's decision soon became a centerpiece in many first-year procedure courses, including mine. *Goldberg v. Kelly* is the first (and some say, the last) case that students read in my course. I use it to expose students to judicial reasoning and the difficulties courts encounter trying to decide what procedure is fair. Brennan's affirmation of procedural values strikes most students as appealing, yet it is difficult to formulate the principle that would justify the imposition of additional procedural safeguards when they might cause a diminution of substantive welfare benefits. Moreover, although Justice Brennan seemed to favor procedural values when it came to the timing of the hearing, he did not believe that those values required welfare recipients to receive the assistance of state-funded lawyers in the termination proceedings. What might account for this distinction? For me, questions like this are the challenge of public reason.

In 1987, some seventeen years after the opinion was rendered, Justice Brennan offered another interpretation of his opinion altogether. He insisted that *Goldberg v. Kelly* was not an exercise in public reason but rather an instrument of the judge's passion, and he extolled the role of emotion and passion in judicial decision making. He invoked Justice Benjamin Cardozo for this view—Brennan gave the lecture as part of the prestigious lecture series in Cardozo's honor at the Association of the Bar of the City of New York. Yet his views seem to have a greater affinity with the work of more contemporary legal scholars, including some Critical Race Theorists, Feminists, and the proponents of an even newer theoretical movement—Law and Literature. Brennan's lecture was hailed in such circles.

In the spring of 1990 Brooklyn Law School invited me to participate in a symposium to celebrate the twentieth anniversary of *Goldberg v. Kelly*. I used the occasion to criticize Justice Brennan's gloss of his original opinion, even though, as the audience well knew, the Justice was a man I knew and loved, and for whom I once worked. (See "A Life Lived Twice," 100 *Yale Law Journal* 1117 [1991].) My remarks, and those of other participants in the symposium, were published in the fall 1990 issue of the *Brooklyn Law Review* (volume 56). The essay was then entitled "Reason in All Its Splendor." A slightly modified version of the essay appears, under the title "The Other Goldberg," in *The Constitution of Rights: Human Dignity and American Values*, edited by M. Meyer and W. Parent (1992).

GOLDBERG *v. Kelly*[1] extended the due process revolution of the 1960s from the criminal to the civil domain and promised that the less fortunate would enjoy procedural protections traditionally provided to the privileged. In its March 1970 ruling the Supreme Court held that a state cannot terminate welfare benefits without first providing an additional hearing to welfare recipients.

Although the outcome in *Goldberg v. Kelly* was singular and, in that sense, remarkable, its underlying method or jurisprudence was not. Justice William J. Brennan Jr. wrote for the majority and, in doing so, employed a method that had characterized the Court's work for the prior twenty-year period. The Court's method was, I believe, entirely rational: The Justices used reason to understand what our constitutional ideals require in the practical world they confronted. In *Brown v. Board of Education*, for example, the Justices had to give content to the ideal of racial equality embodied in the Fourteenth Amendment and to ascertain whether the dual school system was consistent with that ideal, that is, whether segregated schools were inherently unequal. In *Goldberg v. Kelly* the value was not racial equality but procedural fairness—the nature of the process due a citizen before the state could deprive that citizen of liberty or even property —but the decisional process was essentially the same.

In calling this jurisprudential method rational, I mean to underscore its deliberative nature: The Justices listen to arguments about a broad range of subjects—the facts, the history surrounding the law in question, earlier cases, and the precise wording of the text. This argument goes on with the lawyers, between the Justices and their clerks, and between the Justices themselves. The Justices also think about all that they heard and try to evaluate the strengths and weaknesses of the arguments. Thinking itself is an interiorization of the discursive process, a continuation of the argument but now wholly within the individual. Thinking is, as Hannah Arendt put it, "the soundless dialogue . . . between me and myself."[2] The process of deliberation comes to a conclusion at the moment of decision, at which time the decision is publicly announced and the Justices set forth their reasons for it.

Given its deliberative character, the judicial decision may be seen as the paragon of all rational decisions, especially public ones. It differs from other decisions only by virtue of the rules or standards that determine what counts as a good as opposed to a bad reason. A member of the city council trying to decide what should be done with public funds, or the superintendent of a park confronting a similar predicament, might consider facts, reasons, or arguments that a judge would not, because of differences in their offices. But each is obliged to decide questions rationally and thus engage in the deliberative process that is the essence of judging and, for that matter, of law itself.

Some portion of this deliberative process is addressed to the elaboration of ends, some to the means for achieving those ends. The latter goes by the name of instrumental rationality: A particular end is stipulated, and the decision maker tries to identify the best means for achieving that end. These judgments are almost technocratic in nature and, as we saw in "The Forms of Justice" (chapter 1), tend to dominate the remedial phase of a lawsuit, in which the judge formulates a plan for bringing a recalcitrant reality into conformity with the norms of the Constitution. What kind of decree, the judge might ask, would most effectively instill within the welfare bureaucracy a proper regard for procedural fairness? On the other hand, the explication of the ideal of procedural fairness—a judgment as to whether due process requires a hearing prior to termination of welfare and what might be the components of such a hearing—is not technocratic or instrumental but deeply substantive or normative. It focuses on ends, not means, and on the relationship of these ends or values to social practices, in this instance, the welfare system.

While instrumental reasoning dominates the remedial phase, substantive rationality—that is, the refinement and elaboration of ends through the process of deliberation—is the essence of the right-declaring phase of adjudication. In my view, that aspect of adjudication is foundational, for, as also explained in "The Forms of Justice," the authority of the judiciary is linked to substantive rationality. The independence of the judiciary and its commitment to public dialogue are the source of the judiciary's special claim to competence, and thus the source of its authority, yet the competence that is produced by independence and public dialogue has more to do with normative than technocratic judgments. We give power to the judiciary because it is "the forum of principle," to use Ronald Dworkin's phrase,[3] not because it has a corner on the social technologies of the world, not because it is more adept than the legislature or the executive in devising the best means for realizing some stipulated end. In fact, we allow the judiciary the power to make instrumental judgments and to be decisive in that domain—to be supreme in the formulation and administration of the remedy—only as a way of protecting or safeguarding its declarations of principle or right. In celebrating the Warren Court, and the doctrine it created, one has in mind more what that institution said about substantive ends—equality, free speech, religious liberty, and procedural fairness —than the technologies it devised to achieve those ends. This is true of *Goldberg v. Kelly*, which was, in my judgment, largely an exercise in, and a triumph of, substantive rationality.

Triumph it was, but the travails of that case, and of the entire jurisprudence it exemplified, began in the early 1970s, at the very moment the decision was rendered. *Goldberg v. Kelly* marked the end of an era. It was announced as American culture turned inward, and we began to lose faith in the Constitution as an embodiment of a public morality to be known and elaborated through the exercise of reason. In the academy the doubts that characterized the 1970s informed and accounted for the rise and extraordinary success of the Law and Economics Movement, a movement that, as explained in the previous chapter ("The Death of Law?"), believes in reason, but only of the instrumental variety.

Law and Economics is premised on the idea that there are no public values or ideals about which judges should reason. Ideals exist but only at a personal or individual level and, as such, are not fundamentally different from an individual's interests, desires, or preferences—none of which are especially amenable to reasoned elaboration. Law and Economics also assumes that it is arbitrary for any social institution, but especially the judiciary, to choose between these preferences; all preferences are entitled, to use Robert Bork's formula, to equal gratification. In practical terms this means that there can only be one end for social institutions: the maximization of the total satisfaction of individual preferences or, as Richard Posner has characterized it, increasing the size of the pie, as opposed to deciding how it should be divided. The task that remains for the judiciary under this formulation is essentially technocratic: to devise or choose the rules that are the best means for increasing the size of the pie. To view "law as efficiency," as Law and Economics does, implicitly hypothesizes a single, uncontested end and relegates the judge to formulating rules—the instruments—that best serve that end.

Law and Economics, and its special brand of instrumentalism, has not been confined to the academy. It has had a significant impact on private law and has even managed to find its way into constitutional doctrine. For example, the three-prong test Justice Lewis Powell announced in *Mathews v. Eldridge*[4] for deciding due process questions bears a striking similarity to a formula that Richard Posner had proposed earlier. For Posner, the judge who is confronted with a claim for new procedure must compare the cost of the proposed procedural innovation against the benefits it is likely to produce, and those benefits are to be calculated by multiplying the costs of an error by the chance of it occurring if the proposed procedure is not instituted.[5] In *Mathews v. Eldridge*, Justice Powell wrote:

> More precisely, our prior decisions indicate that identification of the specific dictates of due process generally requires consideration of three distinct factors: First, the private interest that will be affected by the official action; second, the risk of an erroneous deprivation of such interest through the procedures used, and the probable value, if any, of additional or substitute procedural safeguards; and finally, the Government's interest, including the function involved and the fiscal and administrative burdens that the additional or substitute procedural requirement would entail.[6]

As can be seen, Justice Powell's formula confuses the matter slightly by adding to the equation a term that was already there (the value to the individual of the new procedure was already reflected in the error costs), but, in spirit and conception, Powell's formula is the same as Posner's. Both understand procedure in purely instrumental terms, as though it is a machine dedicated to reducing erroneous outcomes. They believe the machine should be acquired if the costs of buying and operating it are less than the benefits likely to be produced. The machine should be acquired only if it is more efficient.

Such a model for deciding procedural questions can be criticized, and has been, on the ground that it assumes an intellectual capacity that simply does not exist. Operationalizing the cost/benefit methodology requires quantifying factors that cannot be quantified, and any attempt to engage in such an exercise will be worse than useless—it will tend to drive out of the decisional process the so-called soft variables, those values that are most important to any understanding of procedural fairness.[7] For me, however, the failure of Law and Economics and the *Mathews v. Eldridge* approach is of another order: It derives not simply from the attempt to quantify that which cannot be quantified but from the reduction of due process and, for that matter, the entire judicial judgment to instrumental terms.

From my perspective, a Justice charged with the duty of construing the due process clause, as Justice Brennan was in *Goldberg v. Kelly*, should be seen as engaged in a process of trying to understand what it means for a society to be committed to procedural fairness, and to elaborate that understanding in a certain practical context. According to Law and Economics and *Mathews v. Eldridge*, however, the judicial task is transformed into one of choosing an instrument, a means, or a technology that would serve some specific and relatively uncontested end, such as reducing the number of erroneous outcomes. Such a view trivializes and distorts the judicial task entailed in the explication of due process and can be faulted on that ground; it also should be noted that it puts the authority of the judiciary into question. The instrumentalization of reason eradicates that portion of the judicial decision that is the foundation of its authority—the deliberation about ends and values. There is no good reason for the judiciary to second-guess the legislature or the executive on purely instrumental questions, and, as a result, an attitude of deference and passivity on the part of the judiciary becomes all the more appropriate.

Goldberg v. Kelly denies the instrumentalization of reason of *Mathews v. Eldridge* and stands as a tribute to substantive rationality. Such a reading of the decision became complicated when, in 1987, a second version of *Goldberg v. Kelly* appeared, not in the United States Reports but in the Record of the Association of the Bar of the City of New York.[8] I am referring to Justice Brennan's speech before the Bar Association in September 1987, a speech in which he gave another account of the underlying jurisprudence of that case. He stayed clear of the instrumentalism of Law and Economics and *Mathews v. Eldridge* but nonetheless challenged my understanding of *Goldberg v. Kelly* as an expression of substantive rationality. He introduced a new element into the decisional process: passion.

Justice Brennan did not deny any role for reason (either of the instrumental or substantive kind), but nonetheless he insisted that any account of *Goldberg v. Kelly* that did not include room for the emotional or affective elements would be incomplete and inadequate. He also quoted a passage from one of the briefs describing the plight of some of the welfare recipients involved in the case, and he characterized that passage in terms of a form of discourse that seems especially tied to the emotive faculty. He saw the brief as telling "human stories."[9] While arguments, of fact or principle, seem especially addressed to the faculty of reason, storytelling seems more suited to stirring emotions.

The principal burden of Justice Brennan's discussion of *Goldberg v. Kelly* before the Bar Association was to criticize the welfare bureaucracy for having become captured by "the empire of reason,"[10] but I understand him to be making a point about all government officials, including judges. He said as much, and underscored the role of passion in judicial decision making— in *Goldberg v. Kelly* itself—by taking Justice Cardozo as his point of departure. Of Cardozo, Justice Brennan said, "He attacked the myth that judges were oracles of pure reason, and insisted that we consider the role that human experience, emotion, and passion play in the judicial process."[11]

Many factors account for the tremendous stir caused by Justice Brennan's speech, not the least of which is that it coincided with the emergence of a new jurisprudential movement in the academy—spearheaded by Critical Race Theorists[12] and some Feminists[13] and by the practitioners of Law and Literature[14]—that also places a premium on passion and storytelling. These scholars tend to be leftist critics of the Court's work and appear to be the natural successors to Critical Legal Studies, which also emphasized the role of passion.[15] Unlike the practitioners of Critical Legal Studies, however, the scholars I am referring to believe in rights, and in the redemptive possibility of law, and draw their inspiration from a broad range of theoretical works that gained great ascendancy in the academy during the 1980s.[16] I am sure that Justice Brennan would be surprised to learn that his speech lent comfort and support to a new jurisprudential movement, especially one so hostile to much of the Court's work,[17] but it has turned out that way, and a number of these scholars have reciprocated by endowing his speech with a measure of visibility and energy that is indeed stunning. Judging from the reaction of my students and some of the commentary published in response to Justice Brennan's speech,[18] the second version of *Goldberg v. Kelly* stands at the verge of supplanting the original.

Mention of Justice Cardozo makes it worth emphasizing at the outset that I do not believe that Justice Brennan was engaged in an exercise in Realism and thus merely restating the obvious: Judges are people, and as hard as they strive to be rational, emotion and passion inevitably creep into the judicial process. If that were all that were involved, I would have no objection. The presence of passion could be safely acknowledged, though on the understanding that it must always be disciplined by reason. My concern arises, however, from the fact that Justice Brennan was not content with repeating the Realist's observation but, instead, quickly moved from the descriptive to the normative. He celebrated passion as a factor that *should* enter the decisional process, and he criticized Cardozo for not sufficiently encouraging or valuing, as opposed to merely acknowledging, the "dialogue between heart and head."[19] In his Bar Association address Brennan argued that passion must be seen as a part of the judicial ideal.

Rational deliberation, about ends or means, is no easy endeavor. It requires an enormous amount of mental and physical effort, and it always leaves one with an uneasy feeling: Have I done the right thing? I speak from rather mundane personal and professional experiences, but I am sure the agony of decision increases with the magnitude of the responsibility. The sense of uncertainty a Justice must feel, either at the moment of decision or when he or she is reflecting on past decisions, must be excruciating. It always struck me as a measure of Justice Brennan's greatness that he was not overwhelmed by self-doubt. Tireless, he was able to push on to judgment, day in and day out, for more than thirty years, although he acknowledged, in a paraphrase of Cardozo that dramatically understates the matter, that "judging is fraught with uncertainty."[20]

The temptation to look for ways of curbing that uncertainty is always great. This was, I believe, one of the driving forces behind the rise of Law and Economics and, by implication, the *Mathews v. Eldridge* formula. Evoking the scientism that surrounds economics and the formal language of mathematics associated with that discipline, the practitioners of Law and Economics promised a method—cost/benefit analysis—that might reduce the uncertainty of judging. Their method was to be determinate and certain. There was, of course, nothing to this promise. It presupposed an end that is either vacuous or deeply contested, and, in any event, as a method, Law and Economics depended on a capacity to quantify values or contingencies that cannot be quantified. But the appeal of the offer could not be denied, and passages in Justice Brennan's speech suggest that his turn to passion might have been impelled by a similar consideration. It may be viewed as an attempt to move the judge to judgment in the face of uncertainty or, to use a familiar jurisprudential metaphor, to fill the gaps of the law that might remain if there were nothing but reason.

A number of aspects of the original *Goldberg v. Kelly* decision remain shrouded in uncertainty even today. One arises from the risk, and it is only a risk, that the introduction of pre-termination adversarial hearings might reduce the funds available for actual or potential welfare benefits. Is that a sufficient risk for declining to require pre-termination hearings? I consider this one of the central dilemmas of *Goldberg v. Kelly,* and, although reason gives no easy answer to it,[21] neither does passion.

In his speech Justice Brennan focused on the hardship that would be imposed on the individuals whose benefits might be wrongly terminated and, in the name of passion, specifically invited an empathetic under-standing of their situation. Of course, those people deserve our sympathy, but no more nor less than those whose welfare checks might be reduced by the institutionalization of the pre-termination procedure, assuming that the risk I spoke of were to materialize. Sympathetic figures appear on both sides of the issue, a fact underscored by the division among the Justices. Justice Brennan, the author of the majority opinion, is indeed a passionate person, but so was Justice Hugo Black, who, in dissent, spoke out on behalf of those whose welfare checks might be reduced as a consequence of the new procedural requirement. It may be that one group of recipients is more deserving of our sympathy than another, but, even if that is so, there is no reason to believe that the question of desert—of determining who is more deserving of our sympathy—would itself be resolved on the basis of some feeling.

Often, but not always, our passions seem directed toward, or attached to, particulars: More often than not, we love particular people or activities, rather than abstract ideas. Building on this insight, one might be tempted to say that passion helps to resolve the uncertainty present in *Goldberg v. Kelly* because it suggests favoring, or at least protecting, the particular indi-viduals whose welfare benefits were about to be terminated—the plaintiffs in the suit. This might explain why, in his Bar Association speech, Justice Brennan quoted at length one of the briefs describing the hardship suffered by four welfare recipients (Angela Velez, Esther Lett, Pearl Frye, and Juan DeJesus) and their families.

Although mention was indeed made in the briefs of these four welfare recipients, the Justices knew little about them other than their names. These persons did not function as particulars that the Justices might have become passionately attached to; rather, they were treated as legal mannequins, stand-ins for a group of persons consisting of all welfare recipients. That is why, in the case itself, Justice Brennan could so easily dispose of the mootness objection arising from the fact that some or all the named plaintiffs had already been restored to the welfare rolls. In dissent, Justice Black expressed concern for those who might be in desperate straits because of the newly imposed requirement of pre-termination hearings, and, though he did not use proper names to make his point, his concerns were no more general or particularized than Justice Brennan's. Both were speaking of aggregates or classes of people. *Goldberg v. Kelly* was no more about particular named persons, who might suitably be the object of our affections, than *Brown v. Board of Education* was about Linda Brown. Both were about social groups and what the Constitution promises them.

In suggesting that passion is no more a determinate guide to judgment than reason, thus far I have focused on the multiplicity of the objects of our affections; I have assumed that the passion was singular (sympathy) but that it may be distributed on both sides of the issue. The indeterminacy of impassioned judgment becomes even more pronounced, however, when we vary that assumption and acknowledge the multiplicity of passions as well: Like all of us, judges are complicated human beings who harbor not only feelings of sympathy but also feelings of fear, contempt, even hate. A sympathetic attitude toward the recipient whose welfare is about to be terminated might point in one direction, perhaps in favor of the pre-termination hearing, as Justice Brennan hypothesized. Imagine, however, the judge (also) feeling that those recipients claiming a right to the hearing might well be the troublemakers who are driving the welfare system into bankruptcy. Once our horizons are thus enlarged, so as to account for both sympathy and its antithesis, the uncertainty of decision will be as acute and as profound as it is under "the empire of reason"; the gaps of the law will remain as large as ever.

A proper acknowledgment of the multiplicity of passions not only reinforces doubts about the usefulness of introducing passion in the decisional process, but it also brings into focus the special danger entailed in celebrating passion as a basis, even a partial basis, for judicial decisions. The danger I allude to arises from the rather obvious fact that while some passions are good, others are quite bad. In a comment on Justice Brennan's speech, Professor Edward de Grazia draws a distinction between the passions to be allowed and those to be disallowed.[22] He calls one "humanistic" and the other "authoritarian," and then uses "respect for human dignity" as the standard for distinguishing the two categories. Love is to be allowed; hate is not.

As a gloss on what Justice Brennan had in mind, Professor de Grazia's scheme seems unobjectionable. However, one must wonder at the utility of the entire exercise because it can rescue passion only by reference to an ideal—"respect for human dignity"—that is itself in need of rational elaboration. We need to know, for example, whether fear shows disrespect or whether it might be a special form of respect. The need to answer questions like this, or otherwise elaborate the ideal of "respect for human dignity," adds a new element of uncertainty in the decisional process. Even more important, it renders the entire turn to passion redundant. Once we come to understand what it means to respect human dignity it is unlikely that we need to have recourse to passion in the first place. Human dignity will become the standard, and reason the method by which it is explicated.

Even assuming that somehow we could sort the passions in the way that Justice Brennan or Professor de Grazia proposed, and thus be certain we are permitted only love, not hate, there is still reason to worry about encouraging or valuing passion as a basis for public action. By its very nature, love, or at least earthly love, not only invites a certain partisanship (nepotism in all its forms) but allows the person possessed by love to favor one individual over another for purely arbitrary reasons, for no reason at all, or for reasons that are ineffable.[23] An unanalyzed and unanalyzable sentiment—passion in all its glory—should not only be acknowledged but encouraged and valued in choosing a friend or a lover, or deciding why I might give more of my resources to my child than some charity, or deciding why I might garden rather than write an article. Nevertheless, it seems to be a highly questionable basis for decision for a court of law.

Allowing passion to play a role in the decisional process of the Supreme Court—even if the passion is the most beneficent imaginable or even if the role is a modest or partial one—is inconsistent with the very norms that govern and legitimate the judicial power and constitute its central disciplining mechanism: impartiality and the obligation of the judiciary to justify its decisions openly and on the basis of reasons accepted by the profession and the public. These features of the judicial process are not infallible, obviously, but they do at least place the judiciary under a discipline that is gone once passion becomes an appropriate basis of decision. Why, we are left to ask, should the passions of those who happen to wield the judicial power rule us all?

At several points in his lecture, Justice Brennan seemed to be making a point not about passion but about social reality and the perception of reality. He criticized "*formal* reason"[24] or "*pure* reason"[25] and, speaking of *Goldberg v. Kelly* itself, he said that "the Court . . . sought to leaven reason with experience."[26] In this regard, he seemed to be recommending that decisions should be based on a full and true appreciation of social reality. If that is what he was proposing, I am in complete agreement. It is important, however, to distinguish this insistence on empiricism from his claim that reason be leavened with passion or that the commitment of the judge to reason be qualified by allowing a role for passion.

Passion is not experience, nor a privileged means of gaining access to experience, even if the experience in question is the suffering of those on welfare. Experiences may trigger passions, but experiences may also stir thoughts, and be the subject of reflection and deliberation. Granted, reason sometimes operates at a totally abstract level, wholly removed from experience, as it does in mathematics, but it need not. When it comes to making practical judgments, as in the case of ethics or law or politics, abstract reasoning is hardly the ideal. In these domains, the best judgment is one that is fully sensitive to, and cognizant of, the underlying social reality.

As I already acknowledged, passion tends toward the particular and, in that sense, does not pose the same danger of abstractness or remoteness as certain formal systems of reason like mathematics do. But it is important to understand that passion, and, even more, its associated form of discourse, storytelling, might create the opposite danger: becoming so thoroughly involved in the particular as to confuse the particular with social reality. The description in appellees' brief of the plight of Angela Velez, Esther Lett, Pearl Frye, and Juan DeJesus and their families—in truth, no more a story than a letter to Ann Landers is a work of literature—might have triggered an emotional response, but it would have been a mistake of the first order for the Court to have let these so-called human stories stand for the social reality over which it governs.

Because it lays down a rule for a nation and invokes the authority of the Constitution, the Court necessarily must concern itself with the fate of millions of people, all of whom touch the welfare system in a myriad of ways: some on welfare, some wanting welfare, some being denied welfare, some dispensing welfare, some creating and administering welfare, some paying for it. Accordingly the Court's perspective must be systematic, not anecdotal: The Court should focus not on the plight of four or five or even twenty families but should consider the welfare system as a whole—a complex network embracing millions of people and a host of bureaucratic and political institutions.

The methods by which a court comes to know and understand a system as far-ranging and as complex as welfare are complicated and, as in the case of *Goldberg v. Kelly* itself, always in need of further refinement and improvement. But to describe these informational methods as storytelling, as the practitioners of Law and Literature or Critical Race Theory do, trivializes what is at stake, unfairly disparaging the enormous progress modern society has made in developing sophisticated techniques for assembling, presenting, and evaluating empirical information. It also throws into doubt the basic aspirations of all these informational processes, namely, finding the truth.[27] A story is a story, sometimes a very good one, even if completely untrue.

For decades now *Goldberg v. Kelly* and its jurisprudential method have been embattled, as has the entire legacy of the Warren Court. As I noted, it largely had to be protected from the instrumentalism of Law and Economics that found concrete expression in *Mathews v. Eldridge*. Justice Brennan's Bar Association speech, as well as the work of Critical Race Theorists and practitioners of Law and Literature, can be seen as a response to Law and Economics and *Mathews v. Eldridge*. They all grasped the profound inadequacy of what, for the controlling majority of the Supreme Court in this period, passed as reason.

On this view, Justice Brennan's speech and the new version of *Goldberg v. Kelly* should be embraced and applauded by all who care about law. I am troubled, however, by Brennan's response, for by valorizing passion rather than calling for the enrichment of its antithesis, Justice Brennan appears to have surrendered reason to the instrumentalists and left the idea of substantive rationality more exposed than ever. His celebration of passion not only seems unresponsive to the needs of the law, which call for more, not less, reflection and deliberation, but endangers so much that is good about the law. Qualifying the judiciary's commitment to reason undermines its authority and weakens the principal means we have for guarding against abuses of the judicial power. It reduces the pressure on the Justices to reflect deliberately and systematically on the issues before them and to justify their decision in each and every particular.

Of course, on the issue of what actually moved the Justices in *Goldberg v. Kelly*, Justice Brennan will have the last word (I guess) but only by putting the authority of that decision into question. *Goldberg v. Kelly* is indeed a great case, but I believe that no part of its grandeur derives from the possibility that some of the Justices were emotionally responding to the so-called human stories of Angela Velez, Esther Lett, Pearl Frye, and Juan DeJesus. The issue before the Court was whether the welfare system as a whole was being operated in accordance with the ideal of procedural fairness, and the Court's judgment should be assessed on the assumption that the Justices were guided by reason and reason alone. Despite Brennan's gloss, *Goldberg v. Kelly* stands as a tribute to our own little Enlightenment —that extraordinary age of American law when we understood the promise of public reason and boldly acted on that understanding.

13

The Irrepressibility of Reason

Throughout the twentieth century the study of law became increasingly interdisciplinary. This tradition started with sociology and economics but then branched out to include political science and psychoanalysis, and, more recently, embraced literary theory and philosophy. Although professors of jurisprudence have always appreciated philosophy, the use of philosophy to address the kind of pragmatic issues that fascinate American lawyers can be traced to the work of John Rawls. The publication of *A Theory of Justice* in 1971 was immediately hailed as a singular event in the history of American philosophy, and lawyers began to apply its many insights to the issues they confronted.

A decade later, Rawls was on the defensive. A number of important works began to appear in philosophy challenging many of Rawls's methodological assumptions, above all, the idea that abstract reason and reason alone could resolve the many questions of justice that divide society. Among such works I would include Michael Walzer, "Philosophy and Democracy," published in *Political Theory* (1981); Alasdair MacIntyre, *After Virtue* (1981); Michael Sandel, *Liberalism and the Limits of Justice* (1982); Bernard Williams, *Ethics and the Limits of Philosophy* (1985); and Martha Nussbaum, *The Fragility of Goodness* (1986). Soon enough, lawyers turned away from Rawls and borrowed many of the ideas in these more recent essays to give expression to their disenchantment with law and its commitment to reason.

In the chapter that follows I respond to the work of two of the philosophers—Alasdair MacIntyre and Martha Nussbaum—who spearheaded this turn from reason. MacIntyre and Nussbaum were among the many scholars invited to Yale for a symposium in 1991, entitled "Constructing Traditions: Renovation and Continuity in the Humanities," that was to mark the tenth anniversary of the Whitney Humanities Center. Over the years, that institution and the many personal and professional relationships it spawned have been important for the development of my ideas. The papers presented at the anniversary symposium can be found in the spring 1992 issue of the *Yale Journal of Criticism* (volume 5). Mine appears as a comment to the paper by Martha Nussbaum, "Emotions as Judgments of Value." Subsequently, Professor Nussbaum presented her argument on behalf of passion in a significantly expanded form, under the same title, as chapter 1 of *Upheavals of Thought: The Intelligence of the Emotions* (2001).

THE publication in 1971 of *A Theory of Justice* by John Rawls was a singular event in American intellectual life. This work, hailed by many as one of the greatest works of American philosophy,[1] produced the theoretical justification for the egalitarianism of the 1960s and, even more relevant for our purposes, reflected a faith in reason as the universal mechanism for resolving questions of justice. The book seemed to deliver all that the Enlightenment promised.

On its publication, all eyes focused on the substantive moral position taken by Rawls—above all the difference principle, which allowed inequalities only to the extent that they improved the position of the worst off. At first Rawls's egalitarianism was the principal subject of commentary, and, as in the case of Robert Nozick's *Anarchy, State, and Utopia* (1974), extolling a kind of libertarianism, the resulting criticism was sometimes spirited and stirring. In time, however, as the egalitarianism of the 1960s waned and the difference principle increasingly became politically irrelevant, the focus of the debate shifted from the ethical to the meta-ethical level. Philosophic discussion in the late 1970s and 1980s turned to the rational method that underlay Rawls's work, so much so that, for many, it then appeared that we had moved into what has been referred to as a post-Enlightenment era.

This new era has produced changes in philosophy one can only marvel at. Pick up almost any philosophy book and you encounter concepts and terms—*narrative, tradition, character,* and *passion*—that rarely appeared when *A Theory of Justice* was first published. Although many philosophers are responsible for this transformation, few have made as significant a contribution, or are as widely respected, as Alasdair MacIntyre[2] and Martha

Nussbaum.[3] Much of their work is intended to undermine (albeit in very different ways) the rational premises of Rawlsian liberalism, and to suggest methods of resolving ethical questions that are quite different from Rawls's.

From the perspective of a lawyer, concerned with the ways in which citizens and judges use reason to adjudicate practical questions, neither MacIntyre nor Nussbaum is as far from Rawls as they seem. When forced to describe the dynamics of practical choices, both MacIntyre and Nussbaum introduce an understanding of reason not very different from the one Rawls advanced. I would suggest that their inability to recognize their own reliance on rationality stems from their failure to recognize that substantive rationality—impartial, dispassionate reasoning about ends—can and does play a crucial role in our public lives.

Through his writings Professor MacIntyre presents himself as a foe of the Enlightenment, yet what he attacks is not reason itself but reason that is abstract and universal. For MacIntyre, reason is not denied but is socially embedded and thus rendered plural,[4] and he introduces the notion of a tradition in order to situate reason. A tradition has two components, the ideational and the material. A tradition is both a way of thinking and a way of life, and MacIntyre insists that these components are linked.[5] Reason can provide guidance in moral matters but only by working within a shared understanding, which evolves through a historical process that defines and creates a specific community.

At first reading, MacIntyre's argument might seem plausible enough as an account of how we actually reason about moral matters or how we start to address a moral issue. But on further reflection we can see that his argument is incomplete, because it renders all moral truths relative to some specific tradition.[6] What is right and good within one tradition will not be so from another tradition's perspective. This is no small problem for moral theory, for in a world such as ours, where there is a plurality of diverse traditions, a tradition-based theory of ethics will yield a multitude of moral directives, some conflicting with others, none entitled to a priority.

MacIntyre fully understands the danger of relativism that stems from the contextualization of reason, and he seems determined to avoid it; indeed, he faults the Enlightenment for the uncertainty that it gives to all matters moral, for failing, for example, to provide any basis for choosing between Nozick and Rawls.[7] Admittedly MacIntyre hopes for the demise of the now dominant tradition, which he identifies as liberalism and associates with Rawls, but he does not look forward to a situation where there is a multitude of traditions, all equally good. For MacIntyre, there *is* a right answer. MacIntyre must therefore believe that some traditions are superior to others; but how, we are left to ask, are we to make that judgment?

Given his attack on abstract reason, and his effort to contextualize reason within traditions, we would expect MacIntyre to offer a method of adjudicating between traditions or of choosing the correct course of action that is itself tradition-bound. An individual considering the conflicting truths offered by various traditions would have to choose between them from the perspective of his or her own tradition. Such a method would not, however, solve the problem of relativism; it would only give it new form. A tradition evaluated from the perspective of a particular tradition will not demonstrate the superiority of one tradition over another, but only that one tradition looks better than another from that vantage point. If you are a Thomist, as Professor MacIntyre is, certainly liberalism looks degenerate, empty, and hollow, but that is not likely to be the case if you are a liberal, and, in any event, what a Thomist thinks about liberalism does not establish the truth of the matter.

In the closing pages of *Whose Justice? Which Rationality?* (1988), Professor MacIntyre describes an intellectual process—what he calls "acts of empathetic conceptual imagination"[8]—that might be thought to resolve the problem of relativism. I read these passages to suggest that we should not judge other traditions from the perspective of our own tradition but, rather, that we should imagine what it would be to live in all other traditions, and only then make the judgment about which tradition is superior. Such a mental exercise is admirable, indeed heroic, for it requires us to imagine what it would be to live quite a large number of other lives. Such an exercise might even be sufficient to overcome the problem of relativism, but only if the imagining were so rigorous and so thoroughgoing as to become a species of rational reflection, which is, after all, nothing more than an intellectual process in which we try to free ourselves from the distorting influence of our particular attachments and circumstances.

In rejecting the abstract reason of the Enlightenment, MacIntyre criticizes Rawls's talk of an "original position," where individuals deliberate about the principles of justice behind a "veil of ignorance" that shields them from any knowledge about their interests. MacIntyre is most emphatic in his criticism, yet it is difficult to perceive the great difference between Rawls's rationalistic method and MacIntyre's "acts of empathetic conceptual imagination." True, MacIntyre's method is additive, while Rawls's is subtractive, but both aspire to an intellectual process that is free from the limitations imposed by the person we happen to be and where we might find ourselves. Indeed, Rawls's "veil of ignorance" might well function as a technique to effectuate MacIntyre's "acts of empathetic conceptual imagination." The view from everywhere *is* the view from nowhere; in either case, you end up with white light.

Martha Nussbaum does not explicitly attack the Enlightenment, and she would probably take exception to being described as one of its critics. In fact, however, she challenges one of the central tenets of the Enlightenment: the sovereignty of reason. Unlike MacIntyre, Professor Nussbaum does not insist that reason be socially embedded; instead, she argues for a place for emotions in our moral judgments, not as an ineluctable residue, not as a factor that must inevitably be present in judgment simply by virtue of the fact that we are human, but rather as something that *should* enter into the process of judgment and serve as a basis for it. Her claim is normative, not descriptive.

If all that were involved were the choice of a friend or a lover, then there would be little reason to be concerned with Nussbaum's brief for the emotions. No one—not even the most ardent defender of the Enlightenment—would maintain that all is reason or that emotions do not have an important role to play in such personal judgments. But Professor Nussbaum's claim is far more ambitious. She envisions all ethical or normative judgments, even those having a distinctly public dimension, like those of Agamemnon or, to address my professional concerns, those of Earl Warren or William Rehnquist, as properly having an emotional component, that is, as properly being based on some mixture of reason and passion.

In "Emotions as Judgments of Value," Professor Nussbaum describes reasoning as purely calculative or quantitative, and she makes reference to cost-benefit analysis, Law and Economics, and utilitarianism.[9] In all these methods, a quantitative end is postulated, like the maximization of welfare or wealth; the human mind is then left to devise the best method for achieving this end. Reason is instrumentalized. Professor Nussbaum rejects this form of reason as the proper basis for normative judgments. So do I, yet I do not believe that such a view leads us to embrace emotions as a proper basis of judgment. There is an overlooked alternative, namely, substantive rationality.

Substantive rationality is an intellectual process in which we deliberate about ends, about what is just or fair or equal or, to invoke some cases from my profession, whether the maintenance of a dual school system is a form of unequal treatment or whether it would be fundamentally unfair to try an indigent person for a serious crime without providing that person with a lawyer paid by public funds. As emphasized in the previous chapter, substantive rationality is deliberative and discursive. Decision makers look to the facts and consider a wide range of ethical arguments, not for the purpose of choosing the most efficient means to achieve postulated ends but to determine the meaning of shared values and what they require of us. In doing so, the decision maker should be, I would insist, "cool" and "detached" or, as a lawyer might say, impartial and just, but, to break Nussbaum's string of adjectives, not "calculative" or "quantitative."[10]

Concerned with ends, not means, substantive rationality should not be confused with the instrumental rationality that Nussbaum disdains, but neither should it be mistaken for the emotions. Like any form of rationality, substantive rationality differs from emotion in its insistence on an impartial perspective. It also requires the decision maker to explain and justify the decision on publicly acceptable grounds. Emotion, on the other hand, introduces an opaqueness or arbitrariness into the judgmental process. Treating "emotions as judgments of value," to use Nussbaum's formulation, would allow you to choose one person over another simply because you love him or her, or to favor one course of conduct because it gives you greater pleasure. While rationality is discursive, emotion is a conversation stopper, and that is one reason to be wary of it as a basis for ethical judgments of a distinctly public nature, including those of a court of law.

Professor Nussbaum's argument on behalf of emotion appears to be partly tied to her views, so marvelously captured by the title of her book, about "the fragility of goodness." She believes that the good life is "vulnerable" and "fragile," always subject to luck and misfortune because the good life requires attachment to particulars. These attachments are, Nussbaum reminds us, often imbued with emotion and can be destroyed by circumstances beyond our control. I acknowledge that the good life is indeed fragile, and our attachments to particulars are one source of fragility, but, in fact, fragility arises wherever we seek to actualize a moral judgment. Living the good life, as opposed to merely deciding what it must consist of, depends on a host of fortuities that are beyond our control. Unable to actualize a judgment, we are likely to experience a measure of disappointment or frustration, or an even stronger feeling of regret, like anger, but that does not create a place for emotion as one of the sources of judgment itself.

At various points in her work, particularly in *The Fragility of Goodness*, Nussbaum presents emotion more as a perceptual instrument than as a source or basis for judgment. Without passion we may miss the most salient and important features of a situation and thus deliberate poorly.[11] "We . . . see," she writes, "the passional reaction . . . as itself a piece of practical recognition or perception, as at least a partial constituent of the character's correct understanding of his situation."[12] Of Agamemnon, and his decision to kill his daughter in order to save the fleet, Nussbaum writes, "because in his emotions [and] his imagination . . . he does not acknowledge [Iphigenia,] . . . he doesn't *really know* that she is his daughter."[13]

Proper deliberation requires recognition of the underlying social reality, and thus Nussbaum is certainly correct in insisting that Agamemnon acknowledge his tie to Iphigenia and appreciate all that she means to him. He would be a fool to deny that tie, the loss he would suffer for her death, and what it would mean for a man to kill his own daughter. But there is a crucial difference between insisting that Agamemnon fully recognize, understand, or acknowledge the situation he is confronting and Nussbaum's further claim that the acknowledgment of that situation "in his emotions" should influence or be a basis of Agamemnon's judgment. The "passional reaction" Nussbaum calls for might be of some therapeutic value to the individual involved and might delineate a certain type of person, but it is not clear why that person might be the ideal leader or why a "passional reaction" to a situation should be necessary for, or even conducive to, proper deliberation about issues of state. In fact, such a reaction might have blinded or confused Agamemnon, preventing him from making the right decision and doing the right thing, which Nussbaum acknowledges might have been to kill his daughter.

Nussbaum realizes that the emotions might blind or mislead, but she insists that they do so no more than reason. Reason, she points out, is also fallible. What Nussbaum does not recognize, however, is that we value emotion—especially the passion she accuses Agamemnon of lacking—as part of the human personality even when it is wrong, even when it clouds or confuses the situation. To devalue passion when it misleads would not only be to neglect its actual place in our lives, but, more significantly, it would transform it into something else, something akin to reason. Indeed, Nussbaum acknowledges that, for her, "emotion is a kind of thought."[14] The emphasis on emotion is not, she writes, intended to promote "surrender to gusts of blind feeling, but [to identify] an intelligent and discriminating way of being rational."[15]

This concession might be sufficient to avoid the obvious dangers of treating "emotions as judgments of value," but it leads me to wonder whether we have arrived at almost the same point we did in our analysis of

MacIntyre—that of a return of reason. In MacIntyre, the deracinated reason of the Enlightenment reappears as the mechanism for choosing between traditions, as a safeguard against relativism. Nussbaum's problem is not relativism; rather, it is to avoid the obvious dangers—the blindness and arbitrariness—inherent in judgment based on or informed by passion or the emotions in general. To solve this problem, her argument takes a turn that parallels MacIntyre's, inasmuch as emotion becomes a kind of thought. Reason seems almost irrepressible.

Having arrived at that conclusion, one might well be tempted to declare a victory for the Enlightenment. But when we reflect on the later work of John Rawls and compare it to his work in 1971, or at least to how that work was received, we find the situation more complicated.[16] We have not a victory but something of a convergence, for starting in the mid-1980s Rawls himself has redefined or clarified his project in such a way as to qualify his commitment to the conception of reason associated with the Enlightenment.

In this work Rawls presents the "original position" and the "veil of ignorance" not as a description of social reality but as heuristic devices. He disclaims any interest in universal principles of justice but sees these devices as a way of locating the "overlapping consensus" present in American society. Thus, while MacIntyre and Nussbaum may have found it necessary to turn back to reason, even in its deracinated form, it appears that Rawls's principles of justice are not as universal as we first believed and that reason can never be purely abstract or ahistorical.

Could it be that we are not—thank God—living through a post-Enlightenment era but that we are finally coming to understand what enlightenment means?

14

Bush v. Gore and the Question of Legitimacy

Since the 1970s the coverage of law by the mass media has increased significantly. The national newspapers have assigned more reporters to cover legal affairs, and an increasing number of reporters have been trained in the law. Law also became the subject of a number of successful television dramas. Some of the most famous criminal trials of our day have been televised daily.

The public appreciation of law increased in new and dramatic ways when, in 1987, President Ronald Reagan nominated Robert Bork to the Supreme Court. In 1971 Bork had published an article in the *Indiana Law Journal* criticizing both the privacy and free speech decisions of the Warren Court, and for the next sixteen years it seemed as though conservative groups were grooming him for the Supreme Court. He had been a professor at Yale, was appointed Solicitor General by President Richard Nixon, and later was placed on the U.S. Court of Appeals by President Reagan. Liberal forces in the Senate and beyond fiercely contested his nomination to the Supreme Court, and, as a result, his confirmation hearing became a riveting public spectacle. Bork's constitutional views, as well as the accumulated doctrine of the Supreme Court, entered everyday conversation. Some law professors appeared on the evening news programs. Others found themselves at dinner parties expounding on the *Indiana Law Review* article, Bork's decisions on the Court of Appeals, the jurisprudence of the Warren Court, and the theoretical underpinnings of *Roe v. Wade*. As the hearings wore on, the nation was turned into a seminar on constitutional law.

That seminar was once again convened—for the second time in my lifetime—in the aftermath of Election 2000. Shortly before 9:00 P.M. Eastern Time on Election Day (November 7, 2000), the networks predicted that Vice President Al Gore, the Democratic candidate, would win Florida, thereby giving him the electoral votes needed for election. The Republican candidate, George W. Bush, then governor of Texas, cautioned against premature conclusions. As it turned out, he was right. As the night wore on, it became increasingly clear that, in terms of electoral votes, Florida would be the pivotal state. When the nation awoke the next morning, it was reported that Bush had edged Gore out in Florida.

Florida law provides ample opportunities to challenge election results, and the Gore camp took full advantage of those means of redress. Objections were raised about the confusing nature of the ballots provided to voters in Palm Beach County (a Democratic stronghold). A good number of ballots were thrown out in that county because many voters had indicated two very contradictory choices—Al Gore and the right-wing independent candidate Pat Buchanan. Black voters also voiced complaints. They claimed they had been discriminated against, especially through the administration of a Florida law that denied the ballot to those with felony convictions. In addition, objections were raised against the procedure used to tabulate absentee ballots. For the most part, however, the Democratic challenge focused on the failure of punch card machines to register the choice of voters adequately, because the punch did not fully perforate the card.

The proceedings to contest the election were fully covered in the press, and the oral arguments in the Florida courts were televised. Law professors once again turned into "talking heads" and, as in the Bork hearings, the nation became their classroom. Often we were asked whether the Supreme Court might intervene, and we blithely assured the questioner: "No chance. The contest will most likely be resolved by the Florida courts." Although the Bush camp had begun to instigate federal lawsuits to stop Florida courts and to preserve the declared victory, they seemed to have little chance of success. The federal claims did not seem especially compelling; the Constitution allocates considerable power to the states to govern elections, even federal ones, and the Rehnquist Court seemed fully committed to a doctrine of state sovereignty that enlarges the autonomy of states.

The first sign that the Supreme Court was of another mind was its decision to grant certiorari in a case the Bush camp had launched in federal court in Florida to stop the challenges that Gore had brought in the state court. As most law professors had predicted, the District Court summarily dismissed the Bush suit, and the U.S. Court of Appeals affirmed the dismissal. Some commentators were startled by the grant of certiorari by the Supreme Court, but the naïve, myself included, viewed it as a more ambiguous sign, not as an indication of how the Court viewed the merits of the case but rather as a gesture of respect. We conjectured that perhaps the Justices had regarded a dispute over a presidential election far too serious a matter to be resolved summarily by the denial of the writ of certiorari. The Court's subsequent decision to remand the case for clarification on some issues was reassuring on that score, and even more comforting was the Court's unanimity.

There was nothing ambiguous, however, about the Supreme Court's next decision staying an order of the Florida Supreme Court requiring a hand count to correct for machine malfunctioning. This was the decisive moment in the litigation, for it revealed a determination by the Court to intervene in the election and foreshadowed the likely outcome. I wrote as much in an article in the *Hartford Courant* on December 14, 2000, entitled "The Supreme Court at the Bar of Politics." The Florida court had handed down its decision on Friday, December 8. The Supreme Court's stay was issued on Saturday afternoon, and I learned about it as I was on Chapel Street in downtown New Haven, running the usual Saturday afternoon errands. I vividly recall being stopped by neighbors and friends, who expressed their shock and surprise at the Court's action. "What is a stay?" they wondered. "What could possibly justify it? What is the federal claim?" While these conversations and others that ensued reminded me of the public discussions surrounding the Bork nomination, at stake now was the integrity of the Court itself, not just an appointment to it. On the next Tuesday, December 12, at 10:00 p.m., the Court spoke, and by the next evening Gore had abandoned all his challenges to Election 2000.

Long before Election 2000 I had been invited to present a paper at a symposium held at the Whitney Humanities Center in honor of the Tercentennial Celebration of Yale University. The symposium was to be held on March 30-31, 2002, and my assigned topic was "Epistemology and Uncertainty in the Sciences and Humanities." I shared the platform with scientists, historians, philosophers, and literature professors. Not knowing whether law was regarded as a "science" or as a "humanity" (or maybe both), I thought it was appropriate to use the decision in *Bush v. Gore*— still at the center of public controversy—to give the audience an insight into the law's claim to reason. The original title of the essay was "The Fallibility of Reason," and Yale University Press first published it in June 2002 in a book edited by Bruce Ackerman. I borrowed the title of that book for the purpose of reprinting the essay here.

ADJUDICATION is the process through which the values embodied in authoritative legal texts are elaborated and rendered concrete. It requires the judge to listen to the presentation of facts and the law, to decide who has the best argument, and then to justify his decision. In this endeavor the judge is not free to rely on any reason. He cannot invoke some reasons that might be wholly acceptable to legislators—for example, party loyalty—but instead is limited by a set of rules imposed on him by the professional community to which he belongs. The reason of the judge is thus constrained, or, as Lord Edward Coke put it, "artificial," but reason itself remains the source of the judge's authority. The judge stands before the community as an instrument of public reason, and his work is judged accordingly. The correctness of a judicial decision depends on the judge's capacity to justify that decision on the basis of reason embodied in legal principle.

Judges have made mistakes and will no doubt do so in the future. Like all things human, judges and the public reason they embody are fallible. Indeed, in the United States the process of criticizing judicial decisions and pointing to the errors they contain might fairly be called the cornerstone of our legal culture. Lawyers commonly point to mistakes in prior judicial opinions when arguing cases, and the recognition of those mistakes changes the law. Criticizing judicial opinions is also the central work of law professors. Through the so-called Socratic method, we initiate students into the profession by encouraging them to criticize prominent judicial decisions for failing to comport with publicly acceptable reasons.

Thus, finding error, even grave error, in a judicial decision is standard practice for American lawyers. However, many wish to place *Bush v. Gore*[1] on an entirely different plane. Not only did the Court err, they claim, but the decision put the authority of law in question and caused a crisis of legitimacy. Writing in the January 8, 2001, issue of *The Nation*, Professor Sanford Levinson of the University of Texas Law School reported that *Bush v. Gore* triggered "the deepest intellectual crisis—at least for people who profess to take law seriously—in decades."[2]

In making this claim, Professor Levinson and a number of other critics place *Bush v. Gore* in a world apart from other recent, controversial, and politically charged Supreme Court decisions. The Court has drastically limited preferential treatment programs for racial minorities;[3] has curbed the power of Congress to protect civil rights;[4] has permitted the imposition of the death penalty;[5] and, on the other side of the political divide, has limited the power of the American states to regulate abortions.[6] All these decisions have been criticized as lacking adequate justification, some with good reason, but none have been accused of offending the law or causing a crisis of legitimacy. The question is whether *Bush v. Gore* is truly unique and, if so, whether this uniqueness compromises the authority of the law.

At issue in *Bush v. Gore* was a decision of the Florida Supreme Court that ordered a manual recount of thousands of ballots in several Florida counties in order to correct for deficiencies of machine counting. The focus was on punch card technology and the failure of those machines, in a large number of cases, to register any vote at all. The overall tabulation gave the Republican presidential candidate, George W. Bush of Texas, an edge, and, on that basis, the State Elections Commission certified a slate of Republican electors. Although the Florida governor, the younger brother of the Republican candidate, had recused himself from any participation in the proceedings of the commission, once the commission acted he signed the certificate required by federal statute and transmitted it to Washington. The manual recount the Florida Supreme Court ordered might have changed the outcome of the state popular vote in favor of Vice President Gore, the Democratic candidate, and thus required the certification of a slate of electors pledged to him.

The U.S. Supreme Court first stayed and then finally set aside the Florida court's order requiring a hand count, thereby leaving in force the machine count and thus the slate of electors the governor had certified. The Florida Supreme Court had issued its order on Friday, December 8; that order was stayed by the Supreme Court on Saturday, December 9, and set aside at 10:00 P.M. on Tuesday, December 12. On Wednesday evening, December 13, Vice President Gore conceded defeat. Although he narrowly won the popular vote nationwide (by 500,000 out of 100 million votes cast), the Constitution makes electoral votes, allocated on a state-by-state basis, decisive. With the Florida electoral votes, Governor Bush had 271, and Vice President Gore had 266.

Clearly some of the uniqueness of *Bush v. Gore* derives from the fact that it involved the presidency, that singularly visible and powerful political office. Some critics go so far as to accuse the Supreme Court of having, in effect, determined who would occupy that office for the next four years. Such a charge, however, presupposes that the manual recount the Florida court ordered would have produced a popular victory for Gore in Florida, but the factual basis of that assumption, though held by many at the time of the Supreme Court's decisions, is far from clear.

Following the Court's decision, various media organizations reviewed the Florida ballots in dispute. They wanted to see what would have happened if the Florida Supreme Court's decision had gone into effect and the manual recount had been conducted. Because of the hypothetical nature of the inquiry, the newspapers had to make a conjecture about the standards local officials would have used had they actually conducted the manual recount. Would the local officials, for example, have counted a dimpled chad as a vote?

One group of newspapers (the *Miami Herald* and *USA Today*) made a prediction about the standards most likely to be used, and, based on that prediction and subsequent tabulations, they found that Bush still would have won.[7] Another study, conducted by researchers paid by the *New York Times* and the *Washington Post*, used a more extensive method of analysis, comparing all ballots and suggesting results under a variety of different counting standards. Yet this study reached the same conclusion.[8] Under a wide range of standards officials might have used to tabulate marks that expressed a person's intention to vote for a particular candidate but that failed to register on a voting machine—the so-called undervotes, which the Gore campaign had asked the Florida court to recount—the study found that Bush would have won.

These studies equivocated in their conclusion. The *USA Today* and *Miami Herald* study suggested that, under a set of recount standards different from the one they deemed most likely to be used, Gore might have won. Similarly the *New York Times* and *Washington Post* study noted that if "overvotes"—ballots on which votes for two candidates were marked but one was clearly preferred—were included in a recount, Gore might have won. Ironically, in the litigation before the Florida Supreme Court the

Gore campaign did not ask for a recount of overvotes, and the Florida court required only the counting of undervotes. It is possible, however, that local Florida officials would have interpreted the recount order to include overvotes as well.

Given these speculations, we should regard the principal conclusion of these media studies—that Bush would have won had the hand recount been allowed—with a measure of caution. That prediction may well be mistaken. Yet it would be wrong to turn that cautionary statement around to lend credence to the claim that Gore would have won had the hand count been allowed. The balance of the evidence indicates that Bush would have won even if the hand count had been allowed to go forward. A measure of doubt surrounds that conclusion, and always will, but there is no factual basis for accusing the Supreme Court of having determined the outcome of Election 2000, and on that ground to argue that *Bush v. Gore* represents a special kind of judicial failing.

Nor is *Bush v. Gore* special simply because it revolves around the presidency and had significant consequences for that office. Although the presidency is a unique office and is at the center of democratic politics in America, it is often the subject of constitutional decisions. Consider the Court's decision in the *Youngstown* case,[9] setting aside the president's order to seize the nation's steel mills during the Korean War; or the Pentagon Papers Case,[10] refusing the president an injunction that would prevent the publication of a Department of Defense study, classified as "Top Secret," of U.S. military involvement in Vietnam; or *United States v. Nixon*,[11] which, during the Watergate scandal, denied President Nixon the right to maintain the confidentiality of recordings of conversations in his office. All these decisions, and many others, directly involved the presidency.

Some of these decisions may have had even greater consequences for the presidency than *Bush v. Gore*, particularly once we take account of its indeterminate practical consequences. One example is the rejection of the claim of executive privilege in *United States v. Nixon* and the Court's insistence on the disclosure of previously suppressed recordings of conversations between the president and his aides. This decision made the impeachment of President Nixon and his removal from office a near certainty. It almost immediately led to his resignation. No one would say, however, that merely because the Supreme Court's decision affected the presidency in such a decisive way that it caused an intellectual crisis in the law or threw the legitimacy of the entire enterprise into question. Whatever affront to the law *Bush v. Gore* might present must stem not from the consequences of the decision or the fact that it involved the presidency but rather from the content of the decision itself.

The Court rested its decision on the ground that the manual recount the Florida Supreme Court ordered threatened to violate the Equal Protection Clause of the Fourteenth Amendment. The Florida Supreme Court had directed those responsible for the manual recount to ascertain the intent of each voter, but a majority of the Justices of the U.S. Supreme Court thought that the risk of inconsistency in applying that standard across and within different counties offended the constitutional principle guaranteeing the equal treatment of voters. Immediately after stating that conclusion, the Court added, "Our consideration is limited to the present circumstances, for the problem of equal protection in election processes generally presents many complexities."[12]

Some critics, among them Judge Guido Calabresi, see this sentence as a willful refusal by the Court to abide by principle.[13] By restricting the application of its reasoning to the case before it, the Justices sought, according to these critics, to avoid the discipline that inevitably comes from treating a decision as binding precedent—that is, from having to apply the rule announced in one case to the next. This, the critics charge, distinguishes *Bush v. Gore* from other controversial decisions, such as those involving affirmative action or the death penalty, and contradicts the most elemental understanding of the rule of law.

Such a reading of the decision seems overwrought. The opinion in *Bush v. Gore* constitutes a sustained attempt by the majority to defend the result on the basis of equal protection jurisprudence. The offending sentence does not repudiate that effort; rather, it acknowledges the Court's understandable concern that the opinion—written, by necessity, with haste— might unwittingly disturb settled bodies of law. Such disclaimers are often found in common law decisions. They do not disavow principle but, instead, warn against extending the principle articulated too far.

There is a question in my mind, moreover, of whether the Court even possesses the capacity to free itself from the disciplining force of precedent, which arises not from what the Court wills but from the structure of the law itself. In the very act of giving a reason for its decision—that hand counts threaten equal protection—the Court established a principle that it and other courts will have to confront. It cannot escape from its own ruling. Indeed, immediately after the decision was handed down, lawyers began laying the foundation for lawsuits resting on the equal protection theory articulated in *Bush v. Gore*. Granted, in future cases, the Court might seek to constrain the application of the theory and treat *Bush v. Gore* as truly exceptional, almost idiosyncratic. Whether the Court will, in fact, seek to cabin the decision in this way is uncertain, but even if it does such a strategy will reflect more adversely on the new decisions than on *Bush v. Gore*, for it is those decisions that will contravene established law.

Although I disagree with those who read *Bush v. Gore* as a disavowal of principle, I join those who criticize the Court for the principle it did apply. Its equal protection holding has no constitutional warrant. Undoubtedly hand counts introduce a risk of treating voters inconsistently, but that kind of disparate treatment has never been nor should be deemed a violation of the Equal Protection Clause. Although that constitutional provision declares, in general terms, that no state shall "deny to any person within its jurisdiction the equal protection of the laws," it has been primarily construed to guard against classifications such as those based on race, ethnicity, or gender, that systematically disadvantage various social groups.[14] Hand counting neither employs such a forbidden classification nor threatens to disadvantage in a systematic or predictable way any cognizable social group.

A more individualistic conception of equal protection can be found in the apportionment decisions of the Supreme Court, however, particularly in the rule announced in *Reynolds v. Sims* requiring one person, one vote.[15] In that case, the Court held that a state could not aggregate more voters in one district than another, because that would dilute the voting power of certain citizens. In so ruling the Court seemed to affirm the moral equality of citizens. This principle might well be offended by the risk of disparate treatment that hand counts invariably entail. One person's vote may be counted while another's is not, even though there is no morally relevant difference between the two, only a difference in who happened to be doing the counting.

Such a theory might be thought to rest on the guarantee of "fundamental fairness" more than that of "equal protection"; in the context of *Bush v. Gore*, however, that distinction is of little moment since the Court invokes both phrases, at times almost interchangeably. Of greater concern, the theory fails to account for the fact that every method of tabulation—even one employing machines—has a certain incidence of error built into it, and thus cannot avoid the arbitrariness that might well have offended the Court. The arbitrariness was inevitable. In contrast, the arbitrariness of the electoral practice condemned by *Reynolds v. Sims*—aggregating more voters in one electoral district than another—had no quality of inevitability.

The moral equality of citizens it affirmed could be achieved by establishing electoral districts that contained an equal number of persons.

The rule of *Bush v. Gore* favors the exclusive use of machines, but there is no indication that the risk of error in hand counting is any greater than that introduced by the use of different types of machines in different counties or different precincts. In fact, it might even be less. Modern electronic systems—optical scanning of paper ballots (as used in standardized tests) or touch screen voting (as used in ATMs)—are better than the much-maligned punch card ballots, but even they have considerable incidence of errors. As Justice Stevens complained, "The percentage of nonvotes in this election in counties using a punch card system was 3.92%; in contrast, the rate of error under the more modern optical-scan system was only 1.43%."[16]

The Florida court conceived of a hand count as a way to correct for machine-counting errors. Hand counting was to supplement the machine count, and the Florida decision achieved much of its appeal from this fact. The court's decree enabled an official to ascertain the intent of a voter when a machine failed to do so. But hand counting introduces a threat to the integrity of the democratic process—the risk of partisan bias—not present in machine counting. The fear of such bias may have informed the Supreme Court's decision. The appropriate remedy for the risk of partisan bias, however, is not to bar hand counting altogether, as the Supreme Court did, but rather to establish procedural rules that would minimize that risk. It might have been stipulated, for example, that the hand counting was to be done by a committee that included representatives of all parties.

Because American elections are matters of state law, the Supreme Court could not implement such safeguards alone. Constructing these safeguards would have required a remand to the Florida Supreme Court. Like Justices Rehnquist, Scalia, Thomas, Kennedy, and O'Connor, Justices Souter and Breyer believed that inconsistency in recounting threatened to deprive voters of equal protection. Souter and Breyer, however, sought a remand so that the Florida court could construct procedural rules that would prevent or minimize such inconsistency, but the other five Justices, citing insufficient time, refused to allow a remand. In this action the majority also erred.

The majority justified its refusal to remand on the ground that when the Florida court ordered the recount on December 8, it had indicated its desire to take advantage of a "safe-harbor provision" of federal election law. The safe-harbor statute provides that if a state certifies a panel of electors six days prior to the states' general meeting of presidential electors,

Congress must accept that slate, thus (in theory) limiting contentious intervention by Congress in the presidential election process.[17] That deadline in Election 2000 was Tuesday, December 12—the day the Supreme Court handed down its decision.

Admittedly, in its decision of Friday, December 8, the Florida court expressed concern with the safe-harbor deadline, but only indirectly, by way of explaining why the recount had to begin immediately. Once the Supreme Court's stay made the commencement of the hand count impossible, the Constitution's allocation of power required the Supreme Court, after its final decision on the merits, to remand the case to the Florida court. This remand would have enabled the Florida court not only to devise mechanisms for curbing the risk of inconsistent tabulation or the introduction of partisan bias but also to decide whether it wished this more fully standardized hand recount to go forward even though doing so would have meant that Florida would not be able to take advantage of the safe-harbor provision. Deciding not to take advantage of this provision would not have been unprecedented. Quite often states are unable to do so. In Election 2000 itself, only twenty-nine states and the District of Columbia had certified their electors before the safe-harbor deadline.

Not only was the refusal to remand an error on its own terms, it compounded the error the Court had committed earlier in issuing its stay of the Florida court's recount order on Saturday, December 9. The Supreme Court declared that there was no time left for a remand, when it itself had prevented the recount from going forward in a timely manner, through the issuance of an improper stay. The stay was improperly granted because the applicant—Governor George W. Bush—did not show, as was legally required, that absent the stay he would have suffered irreparable harm. In order for a court to issue a stay, typically issued on the papers and without any opportunity for an evidentiary injunction hearing or even an argument about the law, a party must show that absent the stay he or she would suffer irreparable harm. Such irreparable harm is found in only very rare circumstances. Justice Scalia defended the stay on the theory that, if on completion the hand count gave Gore an edge and later, on consideration of the merits, the hand count was declared illegal, it might cast a "cloud" over the legitimacy of the election.[18] Although such a "cloud" might have some relevance for politics, it had none for the law, for whatever "cloud" might have been created would disappear if the Supreme Court eventually ruled that the method which had given Gore the edge was unconstitutional.

I thus heartily subscribe to the view that the Court in *Bush v. Gore* erred in issuing the stay on December 9, in deeming the hand count a violation of equal protection, and in refusing to remand the case to the Florida Supreme Court on December 12 to minimize whatever danger of arbitrariness might lie in hand counting. These errors make *Bush v. Gore* wrong as a matter of law, but they do not place it on a different moral plane than the recent decisions regarding, for example, limiting affirmative action or the ability of Congress to protect civil rights. Those cases, too, involve gross errors. Although some may perceive the errors in *Bush v. Gore* with an exceptional clarity, those errors are not qualitatively different from those in many other recent controversial decisions. In all such cases the errors stem from the fact that the Court's decision lacks adequate basis in defensible principles of law rooted either in the Constitution, in statutes, or in consistent and wise practice governing such lesser matters as the issuance of stays.

Some contend, however, that *Bush v. Gore* is especially destructive of the authority of the law not only because its errors are so stark but also because they are a product of bad faith. This charge, voiced by Professor Levinson in particular, assumes that some members of the majority, maybe all of them, were moved by a desire to make certain that Governor Bush would win the election.[19] Although Justices Stevens and Souter, both appointed by Republican presidents, dissented, the majority had all been appointed by Republican presidents and had taken positions on the bench most closely identified with policies advanced by Governor George Bush.

This charge of vulgar partisanship is fueled by many factors. Some are rank gossip—for example, news stories based on some off-hand comment made by Justice O'Connor's husband at a social gathering. He allegedly said that Justice O'Connor was anxious to retire and would not feel comfortable doing so if Gore were elected. Months later, the press officer of the Supreme Court had to issue a bizarre public announcement, denying that Justice O'Connor had any plans to retire in the immediate future.

More substantial factors, however, do lend credence to the charge of partisanship. One is that some of the dissenting Justices—they should know—scolded the majority for their lack of impartiality and complained of the damage the majority were doing to the prestige of the Court. Another is that the Justices who constituted the majority had to contravene principles that they had affirmed on many other occasions—especially the principle strengthening the power of the states at the expense of the federal government. Indeed, the support within the Court for this principle of state sovereignty had grown so much in recent years that, at the outset of the litigation, it was inconceivable to most law professors that the Court would perceive any merit to federal constitutional challenges to the Florida Supreme Court's interpretation and implementation of Florida law. The lower federal courts confirmed this speculation when, at the outset of the litigation, they summarily dismissed Bush's challenges.

Although I acknowledge some basis for a charge of rank partisanship, that charge can never rise beyond the level of suspicion. We may never shake ourselves free of that suspicion, but neither can we validate it. Nor can we preclude a more benign and much less condemnatory understanding of what moved some or even the entire majority—a desire to provide closure to the 2000 election. The majority may have feared, for example, that remanding to the Florida court would have only prolonged the uncertainty of the outcome or, even worse, led to an impasse. The Justices might have feared that the manual recount could have resulted in the Florida court ordering the governor to certify a Democratic slate of electors, with the governor, acting in concurrence with the Republican-controlled state legislature, refusing to acquiesce and adhering to his earlier certification of the Republican slate of electors.

Still, this more benign explanation fails to convince. In our system the Supreme Court sits to apply the Constitution and other laws of the United States. It is not charged with managing elections, even national ones, or avoiding impasses in the electoral process. The Constitution and various federal statutes provide the necessary mechanisms for resolving such disputes. They require the Senate and House of Representatives to meet in Washington on January 6, to receive the ballots from the States.[20] If there are conflicting slates of electors for any state and the two chambers cannot agree on which one to accept, the president of the Senate is directed by the statute to accept the slate of electors certified under seal by "the executive" of the state.

Admittedly some difficulties or awkwardness may have arisen in applying these statutory directives—for example, the president of the Senate was Vice President Gore, the Democratic candidate, and the attorney general of Florida, a Democrat who supported the Florida court's recount order, arguably could be considered part of "the executive" of Florida. In the face of such conflicts, recourse would have had to be made to the wisdom and imagination of political actors and their willingness to improvise and bargain; it was no part of the job of the Supreme Court to speculate about the difficulties that might be encountered in such a process and to end Election 2000 at the time and in the way that five Justices thought appropriate. Contrary to the views Judge Richard Posner has advanced, I do not believe that the Court is charged with supervising national elections.[21] It is not authorized to make the pragmatic judgments necessarily entailed in the discharge of such a managerial function nor does it have the capacity necessary to do so. Thus I would insist that even if the Court could be credited with achieving an orderly closure to Election 2000, *Bush v. Gore* would be unjustified as a matter of law. On the other hand, a desire to achieve such a pragmatic result—a prompt and orderly closure—might stand as a plausible explanation of what moved the Justices, or at least some of the five.

Although we will never know what moved the members of the majority (indeed, perhaps they themselves are not fully aware of their motivation), the more fundamental point is that, from the law's perspective, it doesn't really matter. The motives of the majority are irrelevant. They do not change the character of the Court's errors or magnify their significance. As I have argued throughout this book, most notably in "Objectivity and Interpretation" (chapter 9), the strength of a judicial decision, its authoritative character, and its claim for respect stem not from the motives of the Justices but from their capacity to justify the decision on the basis of publicly articulated reasons. Judges are the persons through whom the law fulfills its purposes, which are embodied in reason alone.

Although motivation has no bearing on the justifiability of a decision—an error is an error—it may reflect on the character of those who rendered the decision. To say, as Levinson and others do, that the majority was moved by vulgar partisanship is to assail the character of those who sit on the bench. It is to say that those Justices were moved by considerations that should have no place in judicial decisions. Such an accusation implies a corruption of office almost akin to accepting bribes. Such a charge, if it could ever be substantiated, which, of course, seems unlikely, would clearly undermine the authority of these judges. It might even justify impeachment and, by extension, mar the institution of which they are a part and at the moment control. However, it would not undermine the authority of the law, nor would it cause "an intellectual crisis in the law." Law belongs not to any judge or even the Supreme Court but to history or society in general.

Law is an idea. It seeks to vindicate public values through a process of reasoned elaboration. It may sometimes be faulted because the process by which reason is elaborated cannot prevent partisan manipulation of the type some suspect was at work in *Bush v. Gore*. Public reason, like all things human, is imperfect, but no more so than any other institution. We have turned to the law, and placed our store in the process of reasoned elaboration known as adjudication, because it reflects our collective wisdom as to how best to pursue justice and to give concrete meaning to our constitutional values. We will continue to do so, with almost undiminished confidence, even after *Bush v. Gore*.

Afterword

The Second Reconstruction—the inspiration for this book and much of my work—refers to a period of American history dedicated to the eradication of the social structures that had been used for almost a century to perpetuate the subjugation of blacks. At the center of this reconstructive enterprise was the Supreme Court, which spurred, legitimated, and sometimes even managed the reforms. The Court, however, did not act alone, and many achievements of that period of history can be traced to the involvement of the other branches of government and society in general. The Court drew on this involvement and, in fact, did all that it could to nourish it.

An important body of decisions was created by the Warren Court to serve this purpose, but Chief Justice Rehnquist and his colleagues have attacked those decisions, as they have the Second Reconstruction itself. In this endeavor the Rehnquist Court seems to have been swept up by grandiose conceptions of its authority and has confronted Congress in a way that defines the present moment in constitutional law, perhaps even more so than *Bush v. Gore*.

In rendering its decision in *Brown v. Board of Education*, the Supreme Court obviously reflected the many social forces then prevalent in America. Yet that decision represented a break with history and put the law on the side of equality. *Brown* became the benchmark of ordinary citizens—some white, but most black—who together formed the Civil Rights Movement and took to the streets to challenge existing social practices. They sought to make *Brown*, in the words of the Little Rock case, a living reality. These individuals were the foot soldiers of the Court. They aided the judiciary in its efforts to implement *Brown* and at the same time deepened the judiciary's own understanding of equality. The Court did what it could to shelter civil rights workers threatened by local officials and unruly mobs.

The national legislature and executive also responded to *Brown*'s call and the protest activities then afoot. In the Civil Rights Act of 1957, Congress established the U.S. Civil Rights Commission and, even more significantly, the Civil Rights Division of the Department of Justice. The Civil Rights Act of 1960 enlarged the powers of the Executive to safeguard the right to vote on a nondiscriminatory basis. Of even greater significance was the Civil Rights Act of 1964. That measure greatly enhanced the authority of the Department of Justice to initiate or participate in all manner of equal protection suits, including those to desegregate the schools. It prohibited the federal government from funding programs that discriminated on the basis of race. The 1964 Act also extended the ban on racial discrimination wrought by *Brown* to private employers and those offering public accommodations.

During this period the Executive forcefully used the power at its disposal to implement *Brown*. President Dwight D. Eisenhower sent in paratroopers and federalized the Arkansas National Guard in order to desegregate the Little Rock schools. President John F. Kennedy deployed federal troops to quell the riots that erupted when James Meredith, acting pursuant to a court order, sought to register at Ole Miss. In the early 1960s the Department of Justice began an extensive litigation program to implement the Fifteenth Amendment prohibition against discrimination in voting. As soon as the 1964 Act was passed, school desegregation suits were filed and, by 1967, the Department had added employment cases to its portfolio. Soon enough, the Department of Justice emerged as a leading force in civil rights litigation.[1]

The Department of Justice also sponsored and devised key civil rights statutes, not just the Civil Rights Act of 1964 but also the Voting Rights Act of 1965. As one of the most remarkable pieces of legislation during this entire period, the 1965 Act sought to implement the Fifteenth Amendment in bold and dramatic ways: It suspended the use of literacy tests and other devices that had been used in southern states to prevent blacks from voting; it required that all new voting laws in these jurisdictions be cleared by the Department of Justice; and it authorized the appointment of federal officials to register people to vote.

The Court responded to all these initiatives by the Executive and Congress in the most generous fashion. The civil rights statutes were sustained without reservation and, in fact, during the 1965 Term—when I was clerking for Justice Brennan—a majority of the Court virtually invited the other branches to participate in the reconstruction. In these decisions the Court was careful to preserve its supremacy—the political branches were not to diminish any of the rights the Court had articulated—yet Congress was told that it could build on the rights declared by the judiciary and extend equal protection beyond the judicially declared parameters. The overriding theme of the Second Reconstruction was not the separation, but rather the coordination, of powers.

In taking this stance the Supreme Court was, of course, driven by its substantive commitments—it was anxious to enlist whatever power was available to remake the world in the image of *Brown*. The Court understood that *Brown* could only become a living reality if all the branches partook in such an endeavor. I also believe, however, that the Court acted out of a genuine respect for the coordinate branches of government. The Court fully appreciated the other branches' distinctive powers and ways of proceeding and sought to create the space in which they might act. The Executive and Congress responded accordingly.

In two cases handed down during the 1965 Term—*United States v. Guest* and *Katzenbach v. Morgan*—a majority of the Justices made it clear that Congress had the power under Section 5 of the Fourteenth Amendment to reach certain forms of private activity—violence based on race and discrimination in housing—that had not yet been covered by the civil rights laws it had recently enacted.[2] In the Civil Rights Act of 1968, signed into law on April 11, 1968, a week after the assassination of Martin Luther King, Congress took up the invitation the Court extended and exercised the power the Court said it had. Not surprisingly the Court immediately, though obliquely, upheld the housing provisions of the Civil Rights Act of 1968—perhaps the most controversial. In *Jones v. Alfred H. Mayer Co.*, handed down in June 1968, the Court declared that a statute that had been enacted during the First Reconstruction in fact banned discrimination in private housing and that such an exercise of congressional power was constitutional.

In 1968 Richard Nixon was elected president, and history took a new turn. He ran against the Warren Court, and within his first term in office he was able to make a number of crucial appointments—Warren Burger, William Rehnquist, Lewis Powell, and Harry Blackmun—that were intended to further this goal. By the mid-1970s the Supreme Court had handed down *San Antonio Independent School District v. Rodriguez, Milliken v. Bradley, Washington v. Davis*, and *Moose Lodge v. Irvis* and, through these rulings, made it abundantly clear that it had no ambition to continue, let alone extend, the Second Reconstruction. The Court denied that poverty was a suspect classification; insulated the suburbs from the reach of desegregation orders; insisted that equal protection be measured in terms of intent rather than effect; and put all forms of private discrimination beyond the reach of the Constitution. These decisions accorded with the policy of the White House during the 1970s and 1980s, which, save for the Carter intermezzo, was controlled by the Republican Party. Presidents Reagan and Bush were able to further their policies through the appointment of Antonin Scalia, Anthony Kennedy, Sandra Day O'Connor, and Clarence Thomas.

For much of the late 1970s and 1980s, and then on to the early 1990s, Congress played a leading role in maintaining the civil rights agenda in the face of a hostile Court and White House.[3] Now and then Congress broke new ground, as with the passage of the Americans with Disabilities Act (1990) and the Violence Against Women Act (1994). The first measure, building on a 1971 Supreme Court decision prohibiting practices that have a disparate impact on blacks, required reasonable accommodation for those with physical or mental disabilities. The other, responding to the egalitarian movement that gained great salience during the 1970s, after the Civil Rights Movement had collapsed, gave women who have been assaulted because of their sex a right to sue their attackers in federal court.

For the most part, however, the interventions by Congress during the 1970s, 1980s, and early 1990s, as exemplified by the Pregnancy Disability Act of 1978, the Voting Rights Act of 1982, and the Civil Rights Act of 1991, were defensive. Responding to particular decisions of the Burger and Rehnquist Courts, Congress had no grander ambition in these measures than to restore the rights that had been repudiated and return the law to the point where it had been during the halcyon days of the Second Reconstruction.

In 1992 Bill Clinton, a Democrat, was elected president. His commitment to civil rights appeared earnest enough, but in November 1994, soon after his presidency began, politics took a sharp turn to the Right. The Newt Gingrich Congress was elected. In January 1995 Republicans obtained control of both the Senate and the House, and announced a brazen and stringent program—the "Contract with America"—that attacked government intervention in all its forms and made any semblance of reconstruction unthinkable. By 1996 Congress passed, and, to the dismay of many, President Clinton signed into law, a number of statutes that signaled the final collapse of the Second Reconstruction.

Among these enactments was the Prison Reform Litigation Act of 1996, which placed new curbs on the use of the structural injunction to reform prison practices. The welfare reform act passed in August 1996, declared that welfare was no longer an entitlement, denied immigrants any form of welfare, placed a five-year lifetime limitation on the receipt of federal welfare benefits, and greatly enlarged the discretion of the states in the administration of welfare. The anti-terrorism law of September 1996 focused on many of the reforms of the criminal process effectuated by the Warren Court. It curbed the use of habeas corpus, limited certain procedural rights of the accused, and enlarged the grounds for the imposition of the death penalty.

Many of the decisions of the Court during the era of retrenchment were justified in terms of state sovereignty: The rights being withdrawn were not criticized directly, as unworthy of protection, but rather because of the inevitable restrictions they imposed on the autonomy of the states.[4] At first this doctrine of state sovereignty was used primarily to limit the exercise of the federal judicial power, but by the late 1990s and early 2000s the Court put itself in conflict with Congress—a body then controlled by Republicans and which itself had been responsible for such restrictive measures as the Prison Litigation Reform Act and new welfare reforms. In the name of state sovereignty, a majority of the Justices then invalidated a number of statutes that had been enacted to provide equal rights.

Among the most notable decisions of this character was *United States v. Morrison* (2000), which struck down a provision of the Violence Against Women Act that gave women a federal judicial remedy against gender-based violence inflicted by private actors. It was soon followed by *Kimel v. Florida Board of Regents* (2001), in which the Court held that Congress could not hold states liable for damages when they discriminated against elderly employees. Similarly, in *Board of Trustees of the University of Alabama v. Garrett* (2001) the Court denied that Congress had the power to make states liable for discrimination based on disability. These decisions were of great practical significance in their own right, because they invalidated important statutory guarantees of equal rights. Even more, they gave further force to the principle of state sovereignty and thereby threw *Brown* and many of the achievements of the civil rights era into doubt.[5]

Bush v. Gore, the subject of the last chapter and taken by many as the hallmark of the present Court, is hard to reconcile with the principle of state sovereignty. Indeed, some have pointed to the conflict between state sovereignty and the result in that case and have used it as a basis for accusing the Court of vulgar partisanship in resolving Election 2000. From another perspective, however, *Bush v. Gore* can be seen as consistent with decisions such as *Morrison, Kimel,* and *Garrett,* for it too manifests unwillingness to respect the actions of a coordinate branch of the national government and thus represents an exercise in institutional arrogance. Although the coordination of powers that so marked the Second Reconstruction had been replaced in the early 1970s by a doctrine emphasizing the separation of powers, that doctrine at least had the benefit of enabling Congress to defend, in some limited fashion, the civil rights achievements of an earlier era. By 2000, however, separation had hardened into distrust, and the Court put itself in conflict with the legislature. The Court transformed its final authority over the articulation of constitutional rights into an exclusive authority. The familiar principle of judicial supremacy had turned into one of judicial exclusivity.[6]

The Court in *Bush v. Gore* did not justify its holding in terms of judicial exclusivity. Ironically it offered a theory of equal protection that, as we saw in the last chapter, was woefully deficient. Yet the most ardent defender of the Court's decision, Judge Richard Posner, spoke in terms more consonant with *Morrison*, *Kimel*, and *Garrett*. When pushed to explain why the resolution of Election 2000 could not be left to Congress, as indeed the Constitution and federal statutes require, he saw the national legislature as nothing more than an instrument "for raw exercises of political power."[7] Congress, he elaborated, "is a large, unwieldy, undisciplined body (actually two bodies), unsuited in its structure, personnel, and procedures to legal dispute resolution."[8]

Given the weakness of the Court's stated equal protection rationale, there is reason to suspect that Posner's disparaging view of Congress underlies *Bush v. Gore* and, for that matter, the whole line of decisions represented by *Morrison*, *Kimel*, and *Garrett*. This would be most unfortunate, however, because the theory of judicial exclusivity that might explain these decisions does violence to our constitutional structure. Such a theory is also at odds with the principle of coordination of powers that gave so much life to the Second Reconstruction and offends the most elemental understanding of how law is best made and defended in this republic.[9]

Throughout this book I have portrayed the Court as the instrument of public reason. Such a view allows the Court a measure of authority on constitutional questions but, as emphasized from the very beginning, not the last word—much less the only word. We all have a say, and the Court should listen. The task of giving meaning to the values embodied in the Constitution is the prerogative, indeed the responsibility, of every citizen, including those citizens who wield the power of the other branches of government.

Notes

CHAPTER 1. THE FORMS OF JUSTICE

1. 347 U.S. 483 (1954); 349 U.S. 294 (1955).

2. See, for example, *Lee v. Macon County Bd. of Educ.*, 267 F.Supp. 458 (M.D. Ala.) (per curiam) (three-judge court), aff'd per curiam sub nom. *Wallace v. United States*, 389 U.S. 215 (1967); *United States v. Jefferson County Bd. of Educ.*, 372 F.2d 836 (5th Cir. 1966), aff'd per curiam, 380 F.2d 385 (5th Cir.) (en banc), cert. denied, 389 U.S. 840 (1967).

3. *Green v. County School Board*, 391 U.S. 430, 438 (1968).

4. *Rizzo v. Goode*, 423 U.S. 362 (1976).

5. *Hutto v. Finney*, 437 U.S. 678 (1978). On other occasions, the Court has been more ambivalent toward judicial review of prison conditions. Compare *Bounds v. Smith*, 430 U.S. 817 (1977) (obligation to provide law libraries or legal assistance); *Wolff v. McDonnell*, 418 U.S. 539 (1974) (minimum standards required for disciplinary proceedings); and *Procunier v. Martinez*, 416 U.S. 396 (1974) (mail censorship regulations invalidated), with *Jones v. North Carolina Prisoners' Labor Union*, 433 U.S. 119 (1977) (regulations prohibiting prisoners from soliciting other inmates to join union sustained); *Meachum v. Fano*, 427 U.S. 215 (1976) (no right to fact-finding hearing when prisoner is transferred); and *Pell v. Procunier*, 417 U.S. 817 (1974) (prohibition on press and other media interviews upheld).

6. See *Hills v. Gautreaux*, 425 U.S. 284 (1976) (public housing); *Gerstein v. Pugh*, 420 U.S. 103 (1975) (pretrial detention); *Spomer v. Littleton*, 414 U.S. 514 (1974) (prosecutor's office); *O'Shea v. Littleton*, 414 U.S. 488 (1974) (state court system); *Gilligan v. Morgan*, 413 U.S. 1 (1973) (National Guard).

7. 304 U.S. 144, 152 n. 4 (1938).

8. See Michel Foucault, *Discipline and Punish: The Birth of the Prison*, ed. Alan Sheridan (New York: Pantheon, 1977); Erving Goffman, *Asylums: Essays on the Social Situation of Mental Patients and Other Inmates* (Garden City, N.Y.: Anchor Books, 1961), 3–124.

9. See, generally, William A. Niskanen Jr., *Bureaucracy and Representative Government* (Chicago: Atherton, 1971); William A. Niskanen, "Bureaucrats and Politicians," *Journal of Law and Economics* 18 (December 1975): 617–43; Julius Margolis, "Comment," *Journal of Law and Economics* 18 (December 1975): 645–59; see also

Graham T. Allison, *Essence of Decision: Explaining the Cuban Missile Crisis* (Boston: Little, Brown, 1971).

10. Professor Ely's we-they theory was intended to explain the asymmetry of the theory of legislative failure in the racial area and why strict scrutiny is appropriate for measures to help blacks but not for those that hurt them; but it may have applicability beyond that sphere. See John Hart Ely, "The Constitutionality of Reverse Racial Discrimination," *University of Chicago Law Review* 41 (summer 1974): 723–41. For my critique of the theory, see Owen Fiss, "Groups and the Equal Protection Clause," *Philosophy and Public Affairs* 5, no. 2 (1976): 107–77, reprinted in Marshall Cohen, Thomas Nagel, and Thomas Scanlon, eds., *Equality and Preferential Treatment* (Princeton, N.J.: Princeton University Press, 1977), 84–154.

11. Fiss, "Groups," 131. See also Terrance Sandalow, "Judicial Protection of Minorities," *Michigan Law Review* 75 (April-May 1977): 1184.

12. See Ronald Dworkin, "No Right Answer?" in *Law, Morality, and Society: Essays in Honour of H.L.A. Hart*, ed. P.M.S. Hacker and J. Raz (Oxford: Clarendon, 1977), 58; Ronald Dworkin, *Taking Rights Seriously* (Cambridge, Mass.: Harvard University Press, 1977).

13. At one point the theory of market failure, much like the theory of legislative failure, was monolithic in its prescription in cases of failure (market failure inexorably led to government regulation), though today it has a broader, more pluralistic vision. See Oliver E. Williamson, *Markets and Hierarchies: Analysis and Antitrust Implications* (New York; Free Press, 1975); Ronald H. Coase, "Discussion," *American Economic Review* 54, no. 3 (May 1964): 194–97 (Papers and Proceedings of the Seventy-sixth Annual Meeting of the American Economic Association, May 1964); Ronald H. Coase, "The Problem of Social Cost," *Journal of Law and Economics* 3 (October 1960): 1–47.

14. The example is inferred from the citations *Stromberg v. California*, 283 U.S. 359 (1931), and *Lovell v. City of Griffin*, 303 U.S. 444 (1938), two Hughes Court decisions heralding a new era for free speech. In discussing the theory of specificity the footnote speaks of the entire Bill of Rights, giving us a further insight into what that Court actually meant by textual specificity. The entire discussion of this branch of *Carolene Products* reads: "There may be narrower scope for operation of the presumption of constitutionality when legislation appears on its face to be within a specific prohibition of the Constitution, such as those of the first ten amendments, which are deemed equally specific when held to be embraced within the Fourteenth" (304 U.S. at 152 n. 4). Then followed the citation to *Stromberg* and *Lovell*.

15. In the case of the textually specific prohibitions, it would seem that the preferences of the framers, rather than those of the people or judges, would control. The authors of *Carolene Products* seemed prepared to respect the preferences of that particular social group, and yet some Progressives appeared intent on discrediting those preferences; see, for example, Charles A. Beard, *An Economic Interpretation of the Constitution of the United States* (New York: Macmillan, 1913).

16. These examples are all taken from a single but protracted case involving the Arkansas prison system, sustained in some particulars by the Supreme Court in *Hutto v. Finney*, 437 U.S. 678 (1978). For a collection of all the decisions in the Arkansas litigation, see Owen Fiss and Doug Rendleman, *Injunctions*, 2d ed. (Mineola, N.Y.: Foundation Press, 1984), chap. 9, 528. See also Bruce Jackson, *Killing Time: Life in the Arkansas Penitentiary* (Ithaca, N.Y.: Cornell University Press, 1977); M. Kay Harris and Dudley P. Spiller, *After Decision: Implementation of Judicial Decrees in Correctional Settings* (Washington D.C.: Government Printing Office, 1976).

17. In understanding the role of the objective perspective in adjudication I have been particularly helped by two essays of Thomas Nagel dealing with objectivity in ethics: "Subjective and Objective," in *Mortal Questions* (Cambridge: Cambridge University Press, 1979), 196; and "The Limits of Objectivity" in Sterling M. McMurrin, ed., *The Tanner Lectures on Human Values*, vol. 1 (Cambridge: Cambridge University Press, 1980), 75. See also Thomas Nagel, *The View from Nowhere* (Oxford: Oxford University Press, 1986).

18. See Herbert Wechsler, "Toward Neutral Principles of Constitutional Law," *Harvard Law Review* 73 (November 1959): 1–35.

19. Michel Crozier, *The Bureaucratic Phenomenon* (Chicago: University of Chicago Press, 1964), 187–98.

20. Two of the most spectacular instances of the transformation are Judge Henley's decade-long struggle with the Arkansas prison system (see note 16, above) and Judge Weinstein's attempt to reorganize the Mark Twain School in Coney Island (see Robert M. Cover, Owen Fiss, and Judith Resnik, *Procedure* [Westbury, N.Y.: Foundation Press, 1988], 227). See also James J. Fishman, "The Limits of Remedial Power: *Hart v. Community School Board 21*," in *Limits of Justice: The Courts' Role in School Desegregation*, ed. Howard I. Kalodner and James J. Fishman (Cambridge, Mass.: Ballinger, 1978), 115–65; Curtis J. Berger, "Away from the Court House and Into the Field: The Odyssey of a Special Master," *Columbia Law Review* 78 (May 1978): 707–38; James E. Rosenbaum and Stefan Presser, "Voluntary Racial Integration in a Magnet School," *School Review* 86 (February 1978): 156–86; Lesley Oelsner, "New York's Best Public Schools Defy Racial Stereotyping," *New York Times*, 23 January 1978, B1.

21. Abram Chayes, "The Role of the Judge in Public Law Litigation," *Harvard Law Review* 89 (May 1976): 1290.

22. The "pattern or practice" concept plays a pervasive role in structural litigation. Sometimes it is used as an evidentiary requirement, as a necessary predicate for structural relief (only a series of acts that amount to a "pattern or practice" will justify such thoroughgoing relief); sometimes it is used as a technique for marshaling the resources of the executive branch (the Department of Justice should sue only when there is a "pattern or practice" of discrimination); sometimes it is even used as a basis for inferring intent. See, generally, *International Bhd. of Teamsters v. United States*, 431 U.S. 324 (1977).

23. See, generally, Fiss, "Groups"; see also Note, "Antidiscrimination Class Actions Under the Federal Rules of Civil Procedure: The Transformation of Rule 23(b)(2)," *Yale Law Journal* 88 (March 1979): 868–91.

24. See Derrick A. Bell Jr., "Serving Two Masters: Integration Ideals and Client Interests in School Desegregation Litigation," *Yale Law Journal* 85 (March 1976): 470–516; cf. Stephen C. Yeazell, "Group Litigation and Social Context: Toward a History of the Class Action," *Columbia Law Review* 77 (October 1977): 866–96 (describing the origins of class-action suits in terms of more cohesive social groups).

25. See, for example, *Estelle v. Justice*, 426 U.S. 925 (1976) (Rehnquist, J., dissenting from denial of certiorari); *Rizzo v. Goode*, 423 U.S. 362 (1976).

26. See, generally, Marc Galanter, "Why the 'Haves' Come Out Ahead: Speculations on the Limits of Legal Change," *Law and Society Review* 9 (fall 1974): 95–160; Christopher D. Stone, "Should Trees Have Standing?—Toward Legal Rights for Natural Objects," *Southern California Law Review* 45 (spring 1972): 450–501.

27. Having reached that conclusion, the court may now redefine the victim group so that it is coextensive with the beneficiary—the victim of police brutality is all the people of the city, not just the racial minority—but that post hoc redefinition does not seem useful or necessary.

28. See *Holt v. Sarver*, 309 F. Supp. 362, 365 (E.D. Ark. 1970), aff'd, 442 F.2d 304 (8th Cir. 1971) ("This case, unlike earlier cases . . . which have involved specific practices and abuses alleged to have been practiced upon Arkansas convicts, amounts to an attack on the System itself"); *Talley v. Stephens*, 247 F. Supp. 683, 691 (E.D. Ark. 1965) ("The Court does not think that it should bring this opinion to a close without stating that nothing said herein should be construed as a claim that the respondent personally is an evil, brutal, or cruel man or that he personally approves of all long standing practices of the penitentiary system.").

29. See, generally, Owen Fiss, *The Civil Rights Injunction* (Bloomington: Indiana University Press, 1978). Other factors, such as the insensitivity of state bureaucracies to market incentives and the decentralized system of initiation, might also help to explain the preeminence of the injunction in structural reform. It should be noted that some other remedies (e.g., declaratory judgments, conditional habeas corpus) have many of the same qualities as the injunction, for example, its prospectivity, and such remedies could be expected to be found in structural suits.

30. For an attempt to address the problems of harmonizing the criminal law with bureaucratic reality, see Note, "Decisionmaking Models and the Control of Corporate Crime," *Yale Law Journal* 85 (July 1976): 1091–1129.

31. See *Lee v. Macon County Bd. of Educ.*, 221 F. Supp. 297 (M.D. Ala. 1963); Owen Fiss, *Injunctions* (Mineola, N.Y.: Foundation Press, 1972), 618–19, 626–28; see also note 2, above.

32. In a dissent from denial of certiorari, three Justices objected to the United States having party status. *Estelle v. Justice*, 426 U.S. 925 (1976) (Rehnquist, J., with whom Burger, C.J., and Powell, J., join, dissenting from denial of certiorari) (inter-

venor). See also *United States v. Solomon*, 563 F.2d 1121 (4th Cir. 1977) (plaintiff). A law was subsequently passed to remove any doubts about the authority of the United States as a litigant. See *Civil Rights of Institutionalized Persons Act of 1980*, 42 U.S.C. 1997(c).

33. See Geoffrey E. Aronow, "The Special Master in School Desegregation Cases: The Evolution of Roles in the Reformation of Public Institutions Through Litigation," *Hastings Constitutional Law Quarterly* 7 (spring 1980): 742.

34. See Theodore Eisenberg and Stephen C. Yeazell, "The Ordinary and the Extraordinary in Institutional Litigation," *Harvard Law Review* 93 (January 1980): 465–517.

35. Fiss, *Civil Rights Injunction*, 31.

36. For a sympathetic use of the town meeting metaphor, using it as a predicate for expanding the possibilities of intervention, see Stephen C. Yeazell, "Intervention and the Idea of Litigation: A Commentary on the Los Angeles School Case," *UCLA Law Review* 25 (August 1977): 244–60.

37. See, for example, Richard A. Posner, "A Theory of Negligence," *Journal of Legal Studies* 1 (January 1972): 29–96; Guido Calabresi, *The Costs of Accidents: A Legal and Economic Analysis* (New Haven: Yale University Press, 1970).

38. Martin Shapiro, "Courts," in *Handbook of Political Science: Governmental Institutions and Processes*, vol. 5, ed. Fred I. Greenstein and Nelson W. Polsby (Reading, Mass.: Addison-Wesley, 1975), 321–71.

39. See William M. Landes and Richard A. Posner, "Adjudication as a Private Good," *Journal of Legal Studies* 8 (March 1979): 235–84. When a court acts as a background institution, it is giving expression to the public value favoring the peaceful resolution of disputes, which is quite different from resolving the dispute itself.

40. Mediation is also a dispute resolution process but is distinguished from arbitration or adjudication by its subjective quality: The correct result is defined as that which the parties accept. See, generally, Martin P. Golding, *Philosophy of Law* (Paramus, N.J.: Prentice Hall, 1975), 106–25; Melvin Aron Eisenberg, "Private Ordering Through Negotiation: Dispute-Settlement and Rulemaking," *Harvard Law Review* 89 (February 1976): 637–81.

41. See Julius G. Getman, "Labor Arbitration and Dispute Resolution," *Yale Law Journal* 88 (April 1979): 916, 920–22 (describing the incipient departures from this established practice).

42. The dynamics of co-optation in the administrative field may be especially tied to the linkage of specialized jurisdiction and short-term appointments (the administrator develops an expertise that has a limited market). As such, the loss of independence of the regulator from the regulatee may be more severe in the administrative domain than in the judicial, and less curable.

43. Chayes, "Role of the Judge," 1281. For a parallel and important account of contemporary civil litigation, see Kenneth E. Scott, "Two Models of the Civil Process," *Stanford Law Review* 27 (February 1975): 937–50.

44. Eisenberg and Yeazell, "Institutional Litigation." See also Fiss, *Injunctions*, 325–414; Chayes, "Role of the Judge," 1303.

45. Lon L. Fuller, "The Forms and Limits of Adjudication," *Harvard Law Review* 92 (December 1978): 353–409.

46. During this twenty-year period the essay did not lie dormant: It was used in Professor Fuller's courses at Harvard, it received a wide "underground" circulation in mimeographed form, it was widely cited, and portions appeared in two articles by Fuller—"Adjudication and the Rule of Law," *Proceedings of the American Society of International Law* 54 (1960): 1–7; and "Collective Bargaining and the Arbitrator," *Wisconsin Law Review* (January 1963): 3–46.

47. Michael Polanyi, *The Logic of Liberty: Reflections and Rejoinders* (London: Routledge, 1951).

48. Fuller, "Forms and Limits," 403.

49. In discussing another example, wage and price controls in a socialist regime, Fuller gives a more complete explanation of the source of the problem:

It is simply impossible to afford each affected party a meaningful participation through proofs and arguments. It is a matter of capital importance to note that it is not merely a question of the huge number of possibly affected parties, significant as that aspect of the thing may be. A more fundamental point is that [each possible solution] would have a different set of repercussions and might require in each instance a redefinition of the "parties affected." (Ibid., 394–95)

50. But compare Melvin Aron Eisenberg, "Participation, Responsiveness, and the Consultative Process: An Essay for Lon Fuller," *Harvard Law Review* 92 (December 1978): 427.

51. *Holt v. Sarver*, 309 F. Supp. 362, 373–76 (E.D. Ark. 1970), aff'd, 442 F.2d 304 (8th Cir. 1971). See also note 45, above.

52. See, generally, Max Weber, *The Theory of Social and Economic Organization*, ed. Talcott Parsons, trans. A. M. Henderson (New York: Oxford University Press, 1947), 329–41; Williamson, *Markets and Hierarchies*.

53. This model of adjudication has a relevance that extends even beyond the state bureaucracy; it may be used to safeguard public values from the threats posed by the so-called private bureaucracies, such as the corporation or union. See, for example, Christopher D. Stone, "Controlling Corporate Misconduct," *Public Interest*, no. 48 (summer 1977): 55–71; Note, "Monitors: A New Equitable Remedy?" *Yale Law Journal* 70 (November 1960): 103–25.

54. This claim has its counterpart in earlier times, though then it was primarily used as part of a criticism of the activism of the newly formed Warren Court, see, for example, Henry M. Hart Jr., "The Time Chart of the Justices," *Harvard Law Review* 73 (November 1959): 84–125; for a spirited reply, see Thurman Arnold, "Pro-

fessor Hart's Theology," *Harvard Law Review* 73 (May 1960): 1298–1317. The claim of overwork often appears as the rock-bottom defense of a Supreme Court practice that seems very much in tension with the competency-giving process, the failure of the Court to explain its choice of cases. See Gerald Gunther, "The Subtle Vices of the 'Passive Virtues'—A Comment on Principle and Expediency in Judicial Review," *Columbia Law Review* 64 (January 1964): 1–25.

55. *Lankford v. Gelston*, 364 F.2d 197 (4th Cir. 1966). For the decree actually entered on remand, see Fiss, *Injunctions*, 116.

56. *United States v. Swift & Co.*, 286 U.S. 106 (1932). See, generally, Note, "Flexibility and Finality in Antitrust Consent Decrees," *Harvard Law Review* 80 (April 1967): 1303–27.

57. See, for example, *Hutto v. Finney*, 437 U.S. 678, 711–14 (1978) (Rehnquist, J., dissenting); Archibald Cox, *The Role of the Supreme Court in American Government* (New York: Oxford University Press, 1976), 97.

58. These issues, plus the problem of uncertainty, are explored more fully in Owen Fiss, "The Jurisprudence of Busing," *Law and Contemporary Problems* 39 (winter 1975): 194–216.

59. The competency-giving processes of the judge, dialogue and independence, have a conceptual connection to those subsidiary considerations of the remedial process that have a more normative character, for example, evenhandedness. The problem I perceive relates to strategic considerations, so important to the success of the remedy.

60. Perhaps this explains one of the most striking features of opinions in structural cases: the failure to discuss the remedy with any specificity at all. This silence is probably more a function of embarrassment than an absence of self-awareness of the factors that shaped the decree.

61. Compare Professor Bickel's account of the remedial function, suggesting it is somehow tied to the duty of disposing of concrete controversies:

> The Court does not sit to make precatory pronouncements. It is not a synod of bishops, nor a collective poet laureate. It does not sit, Mr. Freund has remarked, "to compose for the anthologies." If it did, its effectiveness would be of an entirely different order; and if it did, we would not need to worry about accommodating its function to the theory and practice of democracy. The Court is an organ of government. It is a court of law, which wields the power of government in disposing of concrete controversies. (Alexander Bickel, *The Least Dangerous Branch* [Indianapolis: Bobbs-Merrill, 1962], 246–47 [footnote omitted])

62. Compare Chayes, "Role of the Judge," 1298–1302, who, adopting a consent theory of legitimacy, celebrates the so-called negotiated quality of the decree, to the point of exaggerating the consensual element in the remedial process. A

structural suit can be settled at the remedial stage in the same sense that it can be settled at the liability stage, but neither type of settlement is consensual in the same way that a bilateral transaction might be.

63. *Bush v. Orleans Parish School Bd.*, 204 F. Supp. 568, supplemented, 205 F. Supp. 893 (E.D. La.), modified, 308 F. 2d 491 (5th Cir. 1962). See also Robert Crain, *The Politics of School Desegregation: Comparative Case Studies of Community Structure and Policy-Making* (Chicago: Aldine, 1968).

CHAPTER 2. THE SOCIAL AND POLITICAL FOUNDATIONS OF ADJUDICATION

1. Lon L. Fuller, "The Forms and Limits of Adjudication," *Harvard Law Review* 92 (December 1978): 353–409.

2. John Hart Ely, *Democracy and Distrust: A Theory of Judicial Review* (Cambridge, Mass.: Harvard University Press, 1980).

3. Donald L. Horowitz, "The Judiciary: Umpire or Empire?" *Law and Human Behavior* 6, no. 2 (September 1982): 140–41.

4. The phrase is from Robert Nozick, *Anarchy, State, and Utopia* (New York: Basic Books, 1974).

CHAPTER 3. THE RIGHT DEGREE OF INDEPENDENCE

1. See Bruce Allen Murphy, *The Brandeis/Frankfurter Connection: The Secret Political Activities of Two Supreme Court Justices* (New York: Oxford University Press, 1982); Bruce Allen Murphy, "Elements of Extrajudicial Strategy: A Look at the Political Roles of Justices Brandeis and Frankfurter," *Georgetown Law Journal* 69 (October 1980): 101–32. Justice Fortas's continuing involvement as President Johnson's adviser was one factor that damaged his candidacy for the chief judgeship. See Laura Kalman, *Abe Fortas: A Biography* (New Haven: Yale University Press, 1990), 293–357; Bruce A. Murphy, *Fortas: The Rise and Ruin of a Supreme Court Justice* (New York: Morrow, 1988), 234–68.

2. For threats of impeachment stemming from the obscenity decisions of the 1960s, see Edward de Grazia, *Girls Lean Back Everywhere: The Law Of Obscenity and the Assault on Genius*, chap. 27 (New York: Random House, 1991).

3. *United States v. Will*, 449 U.S. 200 (1980).

4. See *Equal Educational Opportunities Act of 1974* (20 U.S.C. § 1705). By way of background, see Theodore Eisenberg, "Congressional Authority to Restrict Lower Federal Court Jurisdiction," *Yale Law Journal* 83 (January 1974): 498–533; Lawrence Gene Sager, "Congressional Limitations on Congress' Authority to Regulate the Jurisdiction of the Federal Courts," *Harvard Law Review* 95 (November 1981): 17–89; Robert H. Bork, *Constitutionality of the President's Busing Proposals* (Washington, D.C.: American Enterprise Institute, 1972).

5. *Prison Litigation Reform Act* (1996), 18 U.S.C. § 3626 (1994 ed., and Supp.IV).

6. For a description of the incident, see generally William E. Leuchtenburg, *The Supreme Court Reborn: The Constitutional Revolution in the Age of Roosevelt* (New York: Oxford University Press, 1995), 132.

7. This statement is attributed to President Jackson, who was venting his disgust at the Supreme Court's ruling in *Worcester v. Georgia.* See Kathleen Sullivan and Gerald Gunther, eds., *Constitutional Law,* 14th ed. (New York: Foundation Press, 2001), 23.

CHAPTER 4. THE BUREAUCRATIZATION OF THE JUDICIARY

1. For a discussion of federalism as a coordinate system, see Robert M. Cover and T. Alexander Aleinikoff, "Dialectical Federalism: Habeas Corpus and the Court," *Yale Law Journal* 86 (May 1977): 1035–1102; Robert M. Cover, "The Uses of Jurisdictional Redundancy: Interest, Ideology, and Innovation," *William and Mary Law Review* 22 (summer 1981): 639–82.

2. For a discussion of the impact of committee-like relationships on the judicial process, see Owen Fiss, "Dombrowski," *Yale Law Journal* 86 (May 1977): 1103–64.

3. See Michel Crozier, *The Bureaucratic Phenomenon* (Chicago: University of Chicago Press, 1964), 145–74 (identifying dynamics leading to divergence of real and formal power).

4. See Mirjan Damaska, "Structures of Authority and Comparative Criminal Procedure," *Yale Law Journal* 84 (January 1975): 495 (only in "narrow area of binding lower courts . . . on the remand" is there real control of lower court behavior).

5. In 2002 Congress modified the system for judicial investigation and sanction that it had put in place in 1980. However, the substance of possible sanctions for judicial misbehavior remains the same. The Judicial Improvements Act of 2002, Pub. L. No. 107–273, § 11042(a), 116 Stat. 1848 (to be codified at 28 U.S.C. §§ 351–64), provides a partial catalogue of appropriate sanctions for Article III judges: (1) certifying the disability of a judge; (2) requesting that a judge voluntarily retire; (3) ordering temporarily that no new cases be assigned to a judge; and (4) censuring or reprimanding a judge, either publicly or privately. In addition, the judicial council may refer any complaint to the Judicial Conference of the United States, which may, if it determines that impeachment may be warranted, refer the matter to the House of Representatives (ibid., §§ 354–55).

6. See John B. Oakley and Robert S. Thompson, *Law Clerks and the Judicial Process: Perceptions of the Qualities and Functions of Law Clerks in American Courts* (Berkeley: University of California Press, 1980) (empirical study of clerks in federal and California courts). Much of the widespread interest in law clerks stems from Bob Woodward and Scott Armstrong, *The Brethren: Inside the Supreme Court* (New York: Simon and Schuster, 1979).

7. On the role of staff attorneys, see Donald P. Ubell, Report on Central Staff Attorneys' Offices in the United States Courts of Appeals, 87 *Federal Rules Decisions* 253 (February 19, 1980), 254–309. Some circuit courts also have "settlement counsel" who try to facilitate, encourage, and maybe even pressure the parties into settlement. Sometimes persons called "screening clerks" or "pro se clerks" perform the function of staff attorneys. The Supreme Court does not formally have staff attorneys, barring a position known as the "administrative assistant" who serves the Chief Justice, but a comparable institution has evolved through the establishment of a pool of law clerks to screen certiorari petitions. See also Judith Resnik "Trial as Error, Jurisdiction as Injury: Transforming the Meaning of Article III," *Harvard Law Review* 113 (February 2000): 953–1037.

8. See Chester A. Newland, "Personal Assistants to Supreme Court Justices: The Law Clerks," *Oregon Law Review* 40 (June 1961): 301–3.

9. See, for example, Geoffrey E. Aronow, "The Special Master in School Desegregation Cases: The Evolution of Roles in the Reformation of Public Institutions Through Litigation," *Hastings Constitutional Law Quarterly* 7 (spring 1980): 742; Curtis J. Berger, "Away from the Court House and Into the Field: The Odyssey of a Special Master," *Columbia Law Review* 78 (May 1978): 707–38; Joel B. Harris, "The Title VII Administrator: A Case Study in Judicial Flexibility," *Cornell Law Review* 60 (November 1974): 53–74; David L. Kirp and Gary Babcock, "Judge and Company: Court-Appointed Masters, School Desegregation, and Institutional Reform," *Alabama Law Review* 32 (winter 1981): 313–97; Michael G. Starr, "Accommodation and Accountability: A Strategy for Judicial Enforcement of Institutional Reform Decrees," *Alabama Law Review* 32 (winter 1981): 399–440; Comment, "Equitable Remedies: An Analysis of Judicial Utilization of Neoreceiverships to Implement Large Scale Institutional Change," *Wisconsin Law Review*, no. 4 (1976): 1161; Note, "'Mastering' Intervention in Prisons," *Yale Law Journal* 88 (April 1979): 1062–91.

10. See Albro Martin, "Railroads and the Equity Receivership: An Essay on Institutional Change," *Journal of Economic History* 34 (September 1974): 688.

11. The magistrate system was first established in 1968, and over the next decade or so Congress intervened twice—once in 1976 and again in 1979—to strengthen the system and enlarge the duties of magistrates. Judicial Conference of the United States, *The Federal Magistrates System: Report to the Congress by the Judicial Conference of the United States* (Washington D.C.: The Judicial Conference, 1981), 1–8. For a critical assessment of this trend, see Note, "Article III Constraints and the Expanding Civil Jurisdiction of Federal Magistrates: A Dissenting View," *Yale Law Journal* 88 (April 1979): 1023–61 (arguing that trial by magistrate impermissibly delegates Article III power).

12. Max Weber, "Bureaucracy," in *From Max Weber: Essays in Sociology*, ed. H. H. Gerth and C. Wright Mills (New York: Oxford University Press, 1946), 196, 220–21.

13. See Lloyd I. Rudolph and Susanne Hoeber Rudolph, "Authority and Power in Bureaucratic and Patrimonial Administration: A Revisionist Interpretation of Weber on Bureaucracy," *World Politics* 31 (January 1979): 196–200.

14. Weber, "Bureaucracy," 216.

15. Hannah Arendt, *Eichmann in Jerusalem: A Report on the Banality of Evil*, rev. and enl. ed. (New York: Viking, 1965). Arendt discusses bureaucracy as a Rule by Nobody in Hannah Arendt, "On Violence," in *Crises of the Republic* (New York: Harcourt Brace Jovanovich, 1972), 103, 137–38; Hannah Arendt, *The Human Condition* (Chicago: University of Chicago Press, 1958), 40, 44–45. Other dimensions of bureaucratization are discussed in Hannah Arendt, "Lying in Politics," in *Crises of the Republic*, 1; and Hannah Arendt, *The Origins of Totalitarianism* (New York: Harcourt Brace Jovanovich, 1973), 375, 398–409.

16. Hannah Arendt, *The Life of the Mind*, 1 vol. ed. (New York: Harcourt Brace Jovanovich, 1978), 185.

17. Arendt, *Eichmann in Jerusalem*, 287 (emphasis omitted).

18. See Harry T. Edwards, "A Judge's View on Justice, Bureaucracy, and Legal Method," *Michigan Law Review* 80 (December 1981): 261–66, 268–69.

19. *Morgan v. United States*, 298 U.S. 468, 481 (1936).

20. The phrase is from Dennis F. Thompson, "Moral Responsibility of Public Officials: The Problem of Many Hands," *American Political Science Review* 74 (December 1980): 905–16.

21. See Christopher D. Stone, *Where the Law Ends: The Social Control of Corporate Behavior* (New York: Harper and Row, 1975), 35–59; Christopher D. Stone, "The Place of Enterprise Liability in the Control of Corporate Conduct," *Yale Law Journal* 90 (November 1980): 1–77; Developments in the Law, "Corporate Crime: Regulating Corporate Behavior Through Criminal Sanctions," *Harvard Law Review* 92 (April 1979): 1227–1375; Note, "Structural Crime and Institutional Rehabilitation: A New Approach to Corporate Sentencing," *Yale Law Journal* 89 (1979): 353–75.

22. *Michigan Law Review* 80 (December 1981): 258.

23. See Wade H. McCree, "Bureaucratic Justice: An Early Warning," *University of Pennsylvania Law Review* 129 (April 1981): 793–97. Several Supreme Court Justices also have spoken publicly about bureaucratization, linking it to burgeoning caseloads. Justice Rehnquist, "Are the True Old Times Dead?" *MacSwinford Lecture*, University of Kentucky (September 23, 1982) (on file at the Public Information Office, Supreme Court of the United States); Justice Powell, "Remarks to the American Bar Association," *Division of Judicial Administration* (August 9, 1982) (on file at the Public Information Office, Supreme Court of the United States).

24. Henry J. Friendly, *Federal Jurisdiction: A General View* (New York: Columbia University Press, 1973), 55. Judge Friendly concludes his effort to pare down the jurisdiction of the federal courts with a recognition of all that must remain:

We would expect the district courts and the courts of appeals to devote themselves to the great work for which they are uniquely equipped—assuring protection of rights guaranteed by the Constitution, enforcing civil rights legislation, dealing with controversies between the citizen and the federal government, applying the federal criminal law, interpreting and applying acts of Congress that furnish protection, both old and new, to consumers, investors and the environment, dealing with federal labor and antitrust legislation as well as such traditional federal specialties as admiralty, bankruptcy and copyright, and controlling the states so that congressional policy will not be impeded either by too niggardly or too expansive local requirements. (Ibid., 197–98)

25. The number of summary dispositions and bench decisions has grown steadily. See, generally, Resnik, "Trial as Error." At the 1982 Second Circuit Judicial Conference, Justice Marshall pointed to a similar trend on the Supreme Court and condemned the "growing and inexplicable readiness on the part of the current Court to dispose of cases summarily." See Remarks of Justice Marshall, Second Circuit Judicial Conference, 4 (September 9, 1982) (on file at the Public Information Office, Supreme Court of the United States). Justices Stevens and Brennan have also criticized this same trend. See *Board of Educ. v. McCluskey*, 458 U.S. 966, 971–73 (1982) (Stevens, J., dissenting, joined by Brennan, J., and Marshall, J.).

26. Alvin B. Rubin, "Bureaucratization of the Federal Courts: The Tension Between Justice and Efficiency," *Notre Dame Lawyer* 55 (June 1980): 654–55. Richard Hoffman, a clerk of the Court of Appeals for the District of Columbia, also emphasizes the need to separate managerial and adjudicatory duties, but he reports less-than-satisfactory experiences with the performance of circuit executives and, instead, urges an expanded use of circuit councils. See Richard B. Hoffman, "The Bureaucratic Spectre: Newest Challenge to the Courts," *Judicature* 66 (August 1982): 65–66, 68–69, 72.

27. 377 U.S. 533 (1964). According to John Ely, the Court found itself with no alternative to the one person, one vote standard "precisely because of considerations of administrability." John Hart Ely, *Democracy and Distrust: A Theory of Judicial Review* (Cambridge, Mass.: Harvard University Press, 1980), 124 (emphasis omitted). He was speaking about the difficulties a court might have in applying a more nuanced standard in some particular case, but the point carries over to the difficulties one court might encounter in supervising the application of such a standard by another court.

28. See, for example, *Dayton Bd. of Educ. v. Brinkman*, 443 U.S. 526, 542 (1979) (Rehnquist, J., dissenting); *Columbus Bd. of Educ. v. Penick*, 443 U.S. 449, 519–24 (1979) (Rehnquist, J., dissenting); *Dayton Bd. of Educ. v. Brinkman*, 433 U.S. 406, 418–21 (1977); *Rizzo v. Goode*, 423 U.S. 362, 373–81 (1976). For a discussion of the problem of control by appellate courts over "disobedient" judges in another era,

see Note, "Judicial Performance in the Fifth Circuit," *Yale Law Journal* 73 (November 1963): 90–133 (discussing recalcitrance of southern district judges in civil rights cases); see also Jack Bass, *Unlikely Heroes: The Dramatic Story of the Southern Judges of the Fifth Circuit Who Translated the Supreme Court's* Brown *Decision into a Revolution for Equality* (New York: Simon and Schuster, 1981) (role of Fifth Circuit in desegregation cases).

29. Some have suggested that United States trustees, who would be located in the executive or, more particularly, in the Department of Justice, could perform the role of special masters. See Hoffman, "Bureaucratic Spectre," 71. There is an irony to this suggestion, since the institution of the special master arose in response to the withdrawal of the Department of Justice from structural litigation in the late 1960s. See Aronow, "Special Master in School Desegregation," 746–47.

30. This may already be the established rule. See *La Buy v. Home Leather Co.,* 352 U.S. 249, 256–57 (1957); see also Federal Rule of Civil Procedures 53(b) ("A reference to a master shall be the exception and not the rule.") However, there has been far greater acceptance of the role played by magistrate judges. See, for example, the Federal Magistrates Act of 1968; *Matthews v. Weber,* 423 U.S. 261 (1976). In June 2002 the Advisory Committee on the Federal Rules of Civil Procedure proposed some changes to the role of the special master and they were approved by the Supreme Court in March 2003.

31. See Patrick E. Higginbotham, "Bureaucracy—The Carcinoma of the Federal Judiciary," *Alabama Law Review* 31 (winter 1980): 6–72.

32. Rehnquist, "Old Times," 15–16. Judge Posner recommends freezing the number of district court judges as a means of containing appellate caseloads and thereby avoiding an increase in the number of appellate court judges. Richard A. Posner, "Will the Federal Courts of Appeals Survive Until 1984? An Essay on Delegation and Specialization of the Judicial Function," *Southern California Law Review* 56 (March 1983): 763–67. He, too, seems to believe that maintaining the special status of federal (appellate) judges is critically linked to limiting their number. Later in the same article, he suggests that increasing the number of federal appellate judges may be a "positive step," since it would reduce the concentration of federal power (ibid., 790). See also his more recent *Federal Courts: Challenge and Reform* (Cambridge, Mass.: Harvard University Press, 1996).

33. *Northern Pipeline Constr. Co. v. Marathon Pipe Line Co.,* 458 U.S. 50, 115 (1982) (White, J., dissenting).

34. See, for example, *United States v. Hubbard,* 686 F.2d 955 (D.C. Cir. 1982) (per curiam) (ordering no disclosure of Church of Scientology documents); *United States v. Hinckley,* 672 F.2d 115 (D.C. Cir. 1982) (per curiam) (ruling on suppression motions in trial of person charged with attempt to assassinate the president). A similar use of the anonymous edict appears on the Supreme Court. See, for example, *Maryland v. United States,* 460 U.S. 1001 (1983) (summary affirmance of provisions of AT&T antitrust decree); *Buckley v. Valeo,* 424 U.S. 1 (1976)

(per curiam) (invalidating portions of federal campaign finance statute); *Bush v. Gore* 531 U.S. 98 (2000).

CHAPTER 5. AGAINST SETTLEMENT

1. Derek Bok, "A Flawed System," *Harvard Magazine* 85, no. 5 (May-June 1983): 38–45, reprinted in *New York State Bar Journal* 55, no. 6 (October 1983): 8–16, and *New York State Bar Journal* 55, no. 7 (November 1983): 31–36; excerpted in *Journal of Legal Education* 33 (December 1983): 570–85.

2. Ibid., 45.

3. Ibid.

4. See, for example, Warren E. Burger, "Isn't There a Better Way?" *American Bar Association Journal* 68 (March 1982): 274–77; Warren E. Burger, "Agenda for 2000 A.D.—A Need for Systematic Anticipation," Keynote Address of the National Conference on the Causes of Popular Dissatisfaction with the Administration of Justice, April 7–9, 1976, published in 70 *Federal Rules Decisions* 83, 93–96 (1976).

5. Federal Rules of Civil Procedure, Rule 16 (1983 Amendment). This is where language referring to ADR was first introduced into the Federal Rules of Civil Procedure. The language was slightly modified with the 1993 Amendments, "settlement and the use of special procedures to assist in resolving the dispute when authorized by statute or local rule." For a discussion of the problems that arise when judges become deeply involved in pre-trial attempts to facilitate settlement, see Judith Resnik, "Managerial Judges," *Harvard Law Review* 96 (December 1982): 374–448.

6. See Richard A. Posner, "An Economic Approach to Legal Procedure and Judicial Administration," *Journal of Legal Studies* 2 (June 1973): 399–458; George L. Priest, "Regulating the Content and Volume of Litigation: An Economic Analysis," *Supreme Court Economic Review* 1 (1982): 163–83; Steven Shavell, "Suit, Settlement, and Trial: A Theoretical Analysis under Alternative Methods for the Allocation of Legal Costs," *Journal of Legal Studies* 11 (January 1982): 55–81.

7. In a case challenging conditions in the Texas state prison system, for example, Judge Justice ordered the United States to appear as an amicus curiae "in order to investigate the facts alleged in the prisoners' complaints, to participate in such civil action with the full rights of a party thereto, and to advise (the) court at all stages of the proceedings as to any action deemed appropriate by it." *In re Estelle*, 516 F.2d 480, 482 (5th Cir. 1975) (quoting unpublished district court order), cert. denied, 426 U.S. 925 (1976). The decree that was eventually entered found systemic constitutional violations and ordered sweeping changes in the state's prisons. See Owen Fiss and Judith Resnik, *Adjudication and Its Alternatives* (New York: Foundation Press, 2003), chap. 3.

8. In *Glazer v. J.C. Bradford & Co.*, 616 F.2d 167 (5th Cir. 1980), for example, the court held that the plaintiff was bound by his attorney's offer of settlement

simply because he had earlier instructed his attorney to investigate the possibility of settling the case.

9. According to Judge Gilbert Merritt, in the early 1980s almost half the cases in the Sixth Circuit involved suits against government agencies or officials. See Gilbert S. Merritt, "Owen Fiss on Paradise Lost: The Judicial Bureaucracy in the Administrative State," *Yale Law Journal* 92 (July 1983): 1469–77.

10. *Antitrust Procedures & Penalties Act*, Pub. L. No. 93–528, § 2, 88 Stat. 1706, 1707 (codified at 15 U.S.C. § 16(e) (1982)). In pertinent part, the Act provides:

> Before entering any consent judgment proposed by the United States under this section, the court shall determine that the entry of such judgment is in the public interest. For the purpose of such determination, the court may consider—
> (1) the competitive impact of such judgment, including termination of alleged violations, provisions for enforcement and modification, duration or relief sought, anticipated effects of alternative remedies actually considered, and any other considerations bearing upon the adequacy of such judgment;
> (2) the impact of entry of such judgment upon the public generally and individuals alleging specific injury from the violations set forth in the complaint including consideration of the public benefit, if any, to be derived from a determination of the issues at trial.

11. In *Maryland v. United States*, 460 U.S. 1001 (1983), the Supreme Court summarily affirmed the district court's approval of a consent decree proposed by the government in the AT&T antitrust case. In dissent, Justice Rehnquist, joined by the Chief Justice and Justice White, questioned the constitutionality of § 16(e). The District Court had interpreted § 16(e) to mean that the proposed consent decree should be accepted "if it effectively opens the relevant markets to competition and prevents the recurrence of anticompetitive activity, all without imposing undue and unnecessary burdens upon other aspects of the public interest" (*United States v. American Tel. & Tel. Co.*, 552 F. Supp. 131, 153 [D.D.C. 1982], aff'd sub nom. *Maryland v. United States*, 460 U.S. 1001 [1983]). Justice Rehnquist, however, said: "It is not clear to me that this standard, or any other standard the District Court could have devised, admits of resolution by a court exercising the judicial power established by Article III of the Constitution" (460 U.S. at 1004). He continued:

> The question whether to prosecute a lawsuit is a question of the execution of the laws, which is committed to the executive by Article II. There is no standard by which the benefits to the public from a "better" settlement of a lawsuit than the Justice Department has negotiated can be balanced against the risk of an adverse decision, the need for a speedy resolution of the case,

the benefits obtained in the settlement, and the availability of the Department's resources for other cases. (Ibid., 1006)

12. "A class action shall not be dismissed or compromised without the approval of the court, and notice of the proposed dismissal or compromise shall be given to all members of the class in such manner as the court directs" (Federal Rules of Civil Procedure, Rule 23(e)). The amendment to this rule approved by the Supreme Court in March 2003 is not much better, though it permits an opt-out for those who object to the settlement.

13. Domestic relations cases form the largest subject-matter category of cases on state court dockets. See United States National Criminal Justice Information and Statistics Service, *State Court Caseload Statistics: The State of the Art* (Washington D.C.: Government Printing Office, 1978), 53. Much of this litigation occurs after the entry of initial decrees. See J. Thomas Oldham, review of *The Marriage Contract*, by Lenore Weitzman, *University of Colorado Law Review* 54 (spring 1983): 478–80.

14. *United States v. Swift & Co.*, 286 U.S. 106, 119 (1932).

15. See *United States v. Swift & Co.*, 189 F. Supp. 885, 904, 910–12 (N.D. Ill. 1960), aff'd 367 U.S. 909 (1961). For a history of the Meat Packers' consent decree over a fifty-year period, see Owen Fiss, *Injunctions* (Mineola, N.Y.: Foundation Press, 1972), 325–99.

16. See the Prison Litigation Reform Act of 1996, 18 U.S.C. § 3626 (2000). The Act recognizes the difficulty of administering consent decrees given the fact that circumstances are always changing, and there is no standard by which to judge whether any particular changes are sufficient to warrant a modification of the decree.

17. *New York State Ass'n for Retarded Children v. Carey*, 631 F.2d 162, 163–64 (2d Cir. 1980) (court unwilling to hold governor in contempt of consent decree when legislature refused to provide funding for committee established by court to oversee implementation of decree). The First Circuit explicitly acknowledged limitations on the power of courts to enforce consent decrees in *Brewster v. Dukakis*, 687 F.2d 495, 501 (1st Cir. 1982), and *Massachusetts Ass'n for Retarded Citizens v. King*, 668 F.2d 602, 610 (1st Cir. 1981).

18. In *United States v. Board of Educ.*, 717 F.2d 378, 384–85 (7th Cir. 1983), the Court of Appeals found that the district court had acted too hastily in ordering the United States to provide additional financial support for Chicago's voluntary desegregation program pursuant to the consent decree that the federal government and the school board had entered into with the plaintiffs. The Seventh Circuit instead instructed the district court to give the federal government time to comply voluntarily with its obligations.

19. Some observers have argued that compliance is more likely to result from a consent decree than from an adjudicated one. See "The Allure of Individualism"

(chapter 6). But increased compliance may well be due to the fact that a consent decree asks less of the defendant, rather than because it creates a more amicable relationship between the parties. See Craig A. McEwen and Richard J. Maiman, "Mediation in Small Claims Court: Achieving Compliance Through Consent," *Law and Society Review* 18, no. 1 (1984): 11–49.

20. See Alexander Bickel, *The Least Dangerous Branch* (Indianapolis: Bobbs-Merrill, 1962), 111–99 (discussing "the passive virtues"). For an analysis of the doctrines of vagueness and overbreadth as techniques for avoidance, see Note, "The Void-for-Vagueness Doctrine in the Supreme Court," *University of Pennsylvania Law Review* 109 (November 1960): 67–116.

21. Bok, "A Flawed System," 42.

22. Ibid., 41. As to the validity of the comparisons and a more subtle explanation of the determinants of litigiousness, see John Owen Haley, "The Myth of the Reluctant Litigant," *Journal of Japanese Studies* 4 (summer 1978): 389 ("Few misconceptions about Japan have been more widespread or as pernicious as the myth of the special reluctance of the Japanese to litigate"); see also Marc Galanter, "Reading the Landscape of Disputes: What We Know and Don't Know (And Think We Know) About Our Allegedly Contentious and Litigious Society," *UCLA Law Review* 31 (October 1983): 57–59 (paucity of lawyers in Japan due to restrictions on number of attorneys admitted to practice rather than to non-litigousness).

Chapter 6. The Allure of Individualism

1. 490 U.S. 755 (1989).

2. *Gomez v. United States Dist. Ct.*, 503 U.S. 653 (1992); *Vasquez v. Harris*, 503 U.S. 1000 (1992); *McCleskey v. Zant*, 499 U.S. 467 (1991); see also Steven G. Calabresi and Gary Lawson, "Equity and Hierarchy: Reflections on the Harris Execution," *Yale Law Journal* 102 (October 1992): 255–79; Evan Caminker and Erwin Chermerinsky, "The Lawless Execution of Robert Alton Harris," *Yale Law Journal* 102 (October 1992): 225–54; Stephen Reinhardt, "The Supreme Court, The Death Penalty, and the *Harris* Case," *Yale Law Journal* 102 (October 1992): 205–23.

3. See, for example, Douglas Laycock, "Due Process of Law in Trilateral Disputes," *Iowa Law Review* 78 (July 1993): 1011–28; Susan P. Sturm, "The Promise of Participation," *Iowa Law Review* 78 (July 1993): 981–1010; Samuel Issacharoff, "When Substance Mandates Procedure: *Martin v. Wilks* and the Rights of Vested Incumbents in Civil Rights Consent Decrees," *Cornell Law Review* 77 (January 1992): 189–253.

4. See, generally, Robert G. Bone, "Rethinking the 'Day in Court' Ideal and Nonparty Preclusion," *New York University Law Review* 67 (May 1992): 193–295.

5. 42 U.S.C. § 2000e-2 (Supp. III 1991).

6. 291 U.S. 431, 441 (1934) ("The law does not impose upon any person

absolutely entitled to a hearing the burden of voluntary intervention in a suit to which he is a stranger. . . . Unless duly summoned to appear in a legal proceeding, a person not a privy may rest assured that a judgment recovered therein will not affect his legal rights.").

7. *Martin v. Wilks*, 490 U.S. at 762.

8. See also Owen Fiss, "Justice Chicago Style," *University of Chicago Legal Forum* (1987): 1–17.

9. That is why Professor Susan Sturm, who favors negotiated decrees out of consideration for efficacy, takes almost as inclusive a view toward participation as does Justice Rehnquist, though she stresses the importance of participation at the liability stage and would not equip those who are to be heard at that stage with all the procedural rights that we tend to associate with the adversarial process—just enough to co-opt them. See Sturm, "Promise," 981; Susan Sturm, "A Normative Theory of Public Law Remedies," *Georgetown Law Journal* 79 (June 1991): 1357–1446; and Susan Sturm, "Resolving the Remedial Dilemma: Strategies of Judicial Intervention in Prisons," *University of Pennsylvania Law Review* 138 (January 1990): 805–912.

10. *Martin v. Wilks*, 759.

11. Ibid., 767.

12. Ibid., 759.

13. Professors Sturm and Laycock, building on the work of Samuel Issacharoff, argue that the employer will welcome a preferential promotion program as a way of minimizing liability for back pay. See Issacharoff, "Substance Mandates Procedure," 241–47. But they never consider the possibility that employees who were the victims of past discrimination have an intense interest in fighting for back pay. Pressing for their interest might correct for the imperfection in the representational structure due to the alleged conflict between employer-employee interests.

14. Sturm, "Promise," 991–92.

15. Stephen C. Yeazell, "Intervention and the Idea of Litigation: A Commentary on the Los Angeles School Case," *UCLA Law Review* 25 (August 1978): 244–60.

16. 410 U.S. 113 (1973).

17. See Lon L. Fuller, "The Forms and Limits of Adjudication," *Harvard Law Review* 92 (December 1978): 365–67.

18. See, for example, László Bruszt and David Stark, "Remaking the Political Field in Hungary: From the Politics of Confrontation to the Politics of Competition," *Journal of International Affairs* 45 (summer 1991): 201, 234–37.

19. 339 U.S. 306 (1950).

20. Professor Laycock recognizes this aspect of *Mullane*, but rather than trying to harmonize both holdings into a single theory as I do—one founded on the right of representation—he keeps them distinct. He views the willingness of the *Mullane* Court to dispense with the requirement of individual notice regarding certain

categories of beneficiaries as an exception or, as he puts it, a "second-best solution when individual notice is impractical." He writes:

> Perhaps the point on which Professor Fiss and I disagree is the relationship between the two holdings in *Mullane*. He seems to see a general rule of discretion and reasonableness, with adequate representation as the essence of due process, and with the particular result that on the facts of *Mullane*, identifiable claimants should be individually notified. I see individual notice to identifiable claimants as the general rule and the essence of due process, and adequate representation as a second-best solution when individual notice is impractical. (Laycock, "Due Process," 1020)

Of course, individual notice to beneficiaries whose address is unknown is not "impractical" but only more expensive, because it requires the expense of a search or investigation to determine the whereabouts of these beneficiaries. In that respect, it stands on the same footing as individual notice to beneficiaries whose addresses are known, which differs from that allowed by the state (newspaper publication) in terms of expense. The amounts may differ but the metric is the same. Similarly, in order to deal with the contingency of a letter going astray in the mail, the Court might have required certified mail or personal service—once again, not "impractical" but only more expensive. In any event, Professor Laycock fails to explain why the Court should ever tolerate "second-best solutions" when constitutional rights are at stake. If, as Professor Laycock claims, individual notice is the essence of due process, then the Court should have given the trustee the burden of spending more on notice to make sure due process is afforded or, alternatively, hold that the settlement of accounts is not binding on those individuals who did not actually receive notice.

21. *Mullane*, 339 U.S. at 314.

22. Ibid., 319.

23. *Martin v. Wilks*, 490 U.S. at 762 n. 2.

24. The right to opt out, provided in Rule 23, might be seen as giving expression to a right of participation, but the opt-out right is only provided in one category of class actions and presumably is not based on due process. See Mark W. Friedman, "Constrained Individualism in Group Litigation: Requiring Class Members to Make a Good Cause Showing Before Opting Out of a Federal Class Action," *Yale Law Journal* 100 (December 1990): 745–63.

25. 417 U.S. 156 (1974).

26. Ibid., 163–64 n. 4, 177 n. 14.

27. Professor Laycock insists that my fears are exaggerated, and he proposes a scheme that promises to be faithful to *Martin v. Wilks* and to protect structural injunctions, at least in the employment context (Laycock, "Due Process," 1026–28). In truth, however, that scheme, consisting of a combination of the class action

device—individual notice to all incumbent employees, an opportunity to organize themselves into separate classes, and the appointment of a guardian ad litem for future unknown employees—rests on the right of representation, not the right of participation affirmed by *Martin v. Wilks*.

Chapter 7. The Political Theory of the Class Action

1. See Sherman Act, 15 U.S.C. §§ 1–7 (1994); *Mugler v. Kansas*, 123 U.S. 623, 672–73 (1887) (affirming that proceedings in equity brought by an attorney general are appropriate alternatives to criminal proceedings to curb nuisances).

2. *Alyeska Pipeline Serv. Co. v. Wilderness Soc'y*, 421 U.S. 240, 271 (1975) (holding that respondents could not recover attorney's fees based on a "private attorney general" approach because only Congress can authorize such exception to the American rule). This result was changed by the *Civil Rights Attorney's Fees Awards Act of 1976*, Pub. L. No. 94–559, 90 Stat. 2641 (amending 42 U.S.C. § 1988 [1970]). On the state level, see *Serrano v. Unruh*, 652 P.2d 985, 997 (Cal. 1982) (holding that attorney's fees can be awarded under the "private attorney general" theory).

3. Judith Resnik, Dennis E. Curtis, and Deborah R. Hensler, "Individuals Within the Aggregate: Relationships, Representation, and Fees," *New York University Law Review* 71 (April/May 1996): 296–391.

4. See, generally, Jack Greenberg, *Crusaders in the Courts: How a Dedicated Band of Lawyers Fought for the Civil Rights Revolution* (New York: Basic Books, 1994); Samuel Walker, *In Defense of American Liberties: A History of the ACLU* (Carbondale: Southern Illinois University Press, 1999).

5. Harry Kalven Jr. and Maurice Rosenfield, "The Contemporary Function of the Class Suit," *University of Chicago Law Review* 8 (June 1941): 713.

6. *Eisen*, 417 U.S. at 173 (quoting Federal Rule of Civil Procedure 23(c)(2) for the proposition that the court is required to direct to class members "the best notice practicable under the circumstances, including individual notice to all members who can be identified through reasonable effort").

7. See Amendments to the Federal Rules of Civil Procedure, 85 *Federal Rules Decisions* 521, 521 n. 1 (1980) (Powell, J., dissenting). In registering a caveat about the process in which the rules are promulgated, Justice Powell, who only a few years earlier wrote *Eisen*, noted that the:

> Court's role in the rulemaking process is largely formalistic. Standing and advisory committees of the Judicial Conference make the initial studies, invite comments on their drafts, and prepare the Rules . . . Congress should bear in mind that our approval of proposed Rules is more a certification that they are the products of proper procedures than a considered judgment on the merits of the proposals themselves.

CHAPTER 8. THE AWKWARDNESS OF THE CRIMINAL LAW

1. *Lankford v. Gelston*, 364 F.2d 197 (4th Cir. 1966).

2. Susan Wolf, "The Legal and Moral Responsibility of Organizations," in *NOMOS XXVII: Criminal Justice*, ed. J. Roland Pennock and John W. Chapman, 267–86 (New York: New York University Press, 1985).

3. *Miranda v. Arizona*, 384 U.S. 436 (1966).

4. See Paul Gewirtz, "Remedies and Resistance," *Yale Law Journal* 92 (March 1983): 585–681.

5. 18 U.S.C. §§ 241, 242 (1994).

6. Ibid., § 245 (1994).

7. Hannah Arendt, *Eichmann in Jerusalem: A Report on the Banality of Evil*, rev. and enlarged ed. (New York: Viking, 1963).

8. Michael R. Belknap, *Federal Law and Southern Order* (Athens: University of Georgia Press, 1987).

CHAPTER 9. OBJECTIVITY AND INTERPRETATION

1. See Charles Taylor, "Interpretation and the Sciences of Man" *Review of Metaphysics* 25 (September 1971): 3–51; see also Charles Taylor, "Understanding in Human Science," *Review of Metaphysics* 34 (September 1980): 25–38.

2. Clifford Geertz, *Negara: The Theatre State in Nineteenth-Century Bali* (Princeton, N.J.: Princeton University Press, 1980); see also Clifford Geertz, "Deep Play: Notes on the Balinese Cockfight," in *The Interpretation of Cultures: Selected Essays* (New York: Basic Books, 1973), 412–53.

3. See, for example, Paul Brest, "The Fundamental Rights Controversy: The Essential Contradictions of Normative Constitutional Scholarship," *Yale Law Journal* 90 (April 1981): 1063–1109; Sanford Levinson, "Law as Literature," *Texas Law Review* 60 (March 1982): 373–403; see also Michael Walzer, "Philosophy and Democracy," *Political Theory* 9 (August 1981): 379–99.

4. See, for example, Harold Bloom et al., *Deconstructionism and Criticism* (New York: Seabury, 1979). For a spirited review of this book, revealing the many strands within the Deconstruction Movement, see Denis Donoghue, "Deconstructing Deconstruction," *New York Review of Books*, 12 June 1980, 37–41. For the more philosophic aspirations of deconstructionism, see Jacques Derrida, *Of Grammatology*, trans. G. C. Spivak (Baltimore: The Johns Hopkins University Press, 1976). See also J. M. Balkin, "Deconstructive Practice and Legal Theory," *Yale Law Journal* 96 (March 1987): 743–86.

5. See, for example, John Hart Ely, *Democracy and Distrust: A Theory of Judicial Review* (Cambridge, Mass.: Harvard University Press, 1980). Professor Grey also understands interpretation in this narrow fashion. See Thomas C. Grey, "Origins

of the Unwritten Constitution: Fundamental Law in American Revolutionary Thought," *Stanford Law Review* 30 (May 1978): 843–93; Thomas C. Grey, "Do We Have an Unwritten Constitution?" *Stanford Law Review* 27 (February 1975): 703–18.

6. Isaiah Berlin, "Two Concepts of Liberty," in *Four Essays on Liberty* (Oxford: Oxford University Press, 1969), 118–72.

7. The bounded quality of the interpretive method is suggested by the idea of the hermeneutic circle, which denotes the parameters within which an interpretation achieves its validity and is based on the assumption that, at some point, an interpretation must make an intuitive appeal to common understandings. The idea of the hermeneutic circle is discussed in Taylor "Interpretation," 6–13, and is vividly described in Geertz, *Negara*, 103, as "a dialectical tacking." David Hoy draws a parallel between the idea of the hermeneutic circle and John Rawls's notion of reflective equilibrium. See David Hoy, "Hermeneutics," *Social Research* 47 (Winter 1980): 649–71, 666.

8. See Thomas Kuhn, *The Essential Tension*, enlarged 2d ed. (Chicago: University of Chicago Press, 1977); Thomas S. Kuhn, *The Structure of Scientific Revolutions*, enlarged 2d ed. (Chicago: University of Chicago Press, 1970).

9. Taylor, "Understanding," 33–37.

10. The phrase belongs to Justice Holmes, *Southern Pacific Co. v. Jensen*, 244 U.S. 205, 222 (1917) (dissenting opinion) ("The common law is not a brooding omnipresence in the sky but the articulate voice of some sovereign"), and it is often used to mock the idea of objectivity.

11. See Stanley Fish, *Is There a Text in This Class? The Authority of Interpretive Communities* (Cambridge, Mass.: Harvard University Press, 1980). Professor Fish acknowledges the creative relationship between reader and text, but he sees the reader as a member of an interpretive community whose institutions shape or structure his view of the world. He argues that those who happen to share the same values and thus belong to the same interpretive community can judge the correctness of an interpretation, though the standards may change as the community does. The question for literature, however, is whether the interpretive community possesses the necessary authority to confer on what I have called the disciplining rules. For an illuminating review of this important book, see Gerald Graff, "Culture and Anarchy," review of *Is There a Text in This Class?* by Stanley Fish, *The New Republic*, 14 February 1981, 36–38.

12. Gerald Gunther, "Too Much a Battle with Straw Men?" review of *Government by Judiciary: The Transformation of the Fourteenth Amendment*, by Raoul Berger, *Wall Street Journal*, 25 November 1977, 4.

13. See, generally, Paul Brest, "The Misconceived Quest for the Original Understanding," *Boston University Law Review* 60 (March 1980): 204–38.

14. 163 U.S. 537 (1896).

15. Ludwig Wittgenstein, *On Certainty*, ed. G.E.M. Anscombe and G.H. von

Wright, trans. Denis Paul and G.E.M. Anscombe, §§ 74, 156 (New York: J. & J. Harper, 1969).

16. Alexis De Tocqueville, *Democracy in America* (London, 1838), 123–32.

17. This tradition is explored in the articles of Professor Grey, referred to in note 5 above, and also in Robert M. Cover, *Justice Accused: Antislavery and the Judicial Process* (New Haven: Yale University Press, 1975).

18. See W. Phillips, ed., *The Constitution: A Pro-Slavery Compact*, enlarged 2d ed. 1845, 1st ed. 1844 (The Anti-Slavery Examiner No. 11).

19. See Charles A. Beard, *An Economic Interpretation of the Constitution of the United States* (New York: Macmillan, 1913).

20. This is the essential insight of Professor Lon Fuller and his attempt to reformulate the natural law tradition in procedural terms. See Lon L. Fuller, *The Morality of Law*, rev. ed. (New Haven: Yale University Press, 1969).

21. John Rawls, *A Theory of Justice* (Cambridge, Mass.: Harvard University Press, Belknap Press, 1971). A similar perspective is found in Thomas Nagel's *The View From Nowhere* (Oxford: Oxford University Press, 1986). Earlier Nagel spoke of the individual struggling to stand outside himself and the world as a way of achieving an objective perspective. Thomas Nagel, "Subjective and Objective," in *Mortal Questions* (Cambridge: Cambridge University Press, 1979), 196–213.

22. John Austin, *The Province of Jurisprudence Determined*, ed. Wilfrid E. Rumble (Cambridge: Cambridge University Press, 1995).

23. See, generally, Robin Higham, ed., *Bayonets in the Streets: The Use of Troops in Civil Disturbances* (Lawrence: University Press of Kansas, 1969). The history of the efforts to desegregate the University of Mississippi is also detailed in *United States v. Barnett*, 330 F.2d 369 (5th Cir. 1963).

24. H.L.A. Hart, *The Concept of Law* (Oxford: Clarendon, 1961).

25. Hans Kelsen, *General Theory of Law and State*, trans. Anders Wedberg (Cambridge, Mass.: Harvard University Press, 1945).

26. 369 U.S. 186 (1962).

27. 358 U.S. 1 (1958).

28. See *Milliken v. Bradley*, 418 U.S. 717 (1974).

Chapter 10. Judging as a Practice

1. See Ludwig Wittgenstein, *Philosophical Investigations*, trans. G.E.M. Anscombe (New York: Macmillan, 1960). Saul Kripke, *Wittgenstein on Rules and Private Language* (Cambridge, Mass.: Harvard University Press, 1982). *Conventionalism* is a term more commonly used in the philosophy of science for the view that scientific laws are not imposed by nature but, rather, are conventions we choose from among the various ways of describing the world. The origin of conventionalism is usually traced to Henri Poincaré, *Science and Hypothesis*, trans. George

Bruce Halsted (New York: Science Press, 1905), although it is probably better known today through the work of Thomas Kuhn, *The Structure of Scientific Revolutions*, enlarged 2d ed. (Chicago: University of Chicago Press, 1970).

2. Stanley Fish, "Fish v. Fiss," *Stanford Law Review* 36 (July 1984): 1325–47; all quotes by Fish, unless otherwise indicated, are to this article in the *Stanford Law Review*. See also Stanley Fish, "Interpretation and the Pluralist Vision," *Texas Law Review* 60 (March 1982): 495–505; Stanley Fish, "Working on the Chain Gang: Interpretation in Law and Literature," *Texas Law Review* 60 (March 1982): 551–67.

3. John Hart Ely, *Democracy and Distrust: A Theory of Judicial Review* (Cambridge, Mass.: Harvard University Press, 1980), 1–41.

4. See Michael Perry, *The Constitution, the Courts, and Human Rights* (New Haven: Yale University Press, 1982).

5. Paul Brest first coined the term *originalism* in "The Misconceived Quest for the Original Understanding," *Boston University Law Review* 60 (March 1980): 204–38.

6. Perry, *Constitution*, 66–75.

7. Ronald Dworkin, "The Forum of Principle," *New York University Law Review* 56 (May/June 1981): 499–500.

8. Stephen R. Munzer and James W. Nickel, "Does the Constitution Mean What It Always Meant?" *Columbia Law Review* 77 (November 1977): 1037–41.

9. Earlier the same impulse could be found in the work of Thomas C. Grey, "Do We Have an Unwritten Constitution?" *Stanford Law Review* 27 (February 1975): 703–18. Like Perry, Grey has begun to retreat from his early deterministic account of interpretation. See Thomas C. Grey, "The Constitution as Scripture," *Stanford Law Review* 37 (November 1984): 1–25.

10. Ely, *Democracy and Distrust*, 88.

11. Perry, *Constitution*, 11.

12. Ibid., 123. Perry seizes on Raoul Berger's research into the framers' intent on school segregation with a relish that makes one suspect that he is not trying to find a proper basis for *Brown* but is, instead, trying to use *Brown* as a way to legitimate this more controversial theory of judicial review (67–75). See also Michael Perry, review of *Government by Judiciary: The Transformation of the Fourteenth Amendment*, by Raoul Berger, *Columbia Law Review* 78 (April 1978): 685–705.

13. Ely, *Democracy and Distrust*, 1–9; Perry, *Constitution*, 1–8.

14. Alexander M. Bickel, *The Least Dangerous Branch* (New Haven: Yale University Press, 1962), 16–23.

15. See Sanford Levinson, "Law as Literature," *Texas Law Review* 60 (March 1982): 373–403.

16. I use the term *rules* interchangeably with *norms*, *standards*, and *principles*, and the term is meant to suggest, as Fish understands, a generalized assertion about what should be done.

17. Fish, "Pluralist Vision."

18. Levinson, "Law as Literature," 385 (quoting Richard Rorty, "Nineteenth-Century Idealism and Twentieth-Century Textualism," in *Consequences of Pragmatism* [Minneapolis: University of Minnesota Press, 1982], 151).

19. Wittgenstein himself wrote, "Any interpretation still hangs in the air along with what it interprets, and cannot give it any support. Interpretations by themselves do not determine meaning" (*Philosophical Investigations*, § 198, 80e).

20. Lest you think I am unfair in attributing to Fish this picture of the judge as basketball player, let me quote the critical passage:

> [The judge] is already filled with and constituted by the very meanings that on Fiss's account he is dangerously free to ignore. This amounts finally to no more, or less, than saying that the agent is always and already situated, and that to be situated is not to be looking about for constraints, or happily evading them (in the mode, supposedly, of nihilism) but to be constrained already. To be a judge or a basketball player is not to be able to consult the rules (or, alternatively, to be able to disregard them) but to have become an extension of the "know how" that gives the rules (if there happen to be any) the meaning they will immediately and obviously have.

21. The distinction between "knowing how" and "knowing that" is presented in greater detail in Gilbert Ryle, *The Concept of Mind* (London: Hutchinson, 1949).

22. Elsewhere he puts the point a little more provocatively. He describes the president appointing someone to the bench who has no previous judicial and legal experience and who, on being appointed, is handed a rule book:

> What would happen? The new judge would soon find that she was unable to read the rules without already having a working knowledge of the practices they were supposed to order, or, to put it somewhat more paradoxically, she would find that she could read the rules that are supposed to tell her what to do only when she already knew what to do.

23. Fish writes, in an effort to allay my fears about a new form of nihilism, "On my analysis, the Constitution cannot be drained of meaning, because it is not a repository of meaning; rather, meaning is always being conferred on it by the very political and institutional forces Fiss sees as threats."

24. Wittgenstein, *Philosophical Investigations*, §§ 23–24, 11e-12e.

25. Ibid., § 66, 31e.

26. One can only wonder what he means by "in general."

CHAPTER 11. THE DEATH OF LAW?

1. Louis Menand, "Radicalism for Yuppies," *The New Republic*, 17 March 1986,

20–23; Jerry Frug, "Henry James, Lee Marvin, and the Law," *New York Times,* 16 February 1986, § 7, 1; Richard Lacayo, "Critical Legal Times at Harvard," *Time,* 18 November 1985, 87; Calvin Trillin, "A Reporter at Large: Harvard Law," *New Yorker,* 26 March 1984, 53–83.

2. Paul D. Carrington, "Of Law and the River," *Journal of Legal Education* 34 (June 1984): 222–28. For correspondence addressing the article by Carrington, see Peter W. Martin, "'Of Law and the River,' and of Nihilism and Academic Freedom," *Journal of Legal Education* 35 (March 1985): 1–26.

3. Richard A. Posner, *Economic Analysis of Law* (Boston: Little, Brown, 1972).

4. On close inspection, the "law as efficiency" hypothesis does not even hold up in the one area in which it seems plausible. See Michael J. Trebilcock, *The Common Law of Restraint of Trade: A Legal and Economic Analysis* (Toronto: Carswell, 1986).

5. Richard A. Posner, "A Theory of Negligence," *Journal of Legal Studies* 1 (January 1972): 29–96.

6. George L. Priest, "The New Scientism in Legal Scholarship: A Comment on Clark and Posner," *Yale Law Journal* 90 (April 1981): 1291–92.

7. Richard A. Posner, "Wealth Maximization and Judicial Decision-Making," *International Review of Law and Economics* 4 (December 1984): 131–32.

8. Richard A. Posner, "The Ethical and Political Basis of the Efficiency Norm in Common Law Adjudication," *Hofstra Law Review* 8 (spring 1980): 505.

9. Ibid.

10. R. H. Coase, "The Problem of Social Cost," *Journal of Law and Economics* 3 (October 1960): 1–44.

11. Harold Demsetz, "When Does the Rule of Liability Matter?" *Journal of Legal Studies* 1 (January 1972): 13–28.

12. Roberto Mangabeira Unger, "The Critical Legal Studies Movement," *Harvard Law Review* 96 (January 1983): 561–675; published as a book by Harvard University Press in 1986. For two general collections of material on Critical Legal Studies, see David Kairys, ed., *The Politics of Law: A Progressive Critique* (New York: Pantheon, 1982); Critical Legal Studies Symposium, *Stanford Law Review* 36 (January 1984): 1–673.

13. See, generally, Owen Fiss, "What Is Feminism?" *Arizona State Law Journal* 26 (summer 1994): 413–28.

14. Indeed, Professor Frug refers to Feminism as only a "source" of Critical Legal Studies. See Frug, "Henry James," 1.

15. Duncan Kennedy, "Distributive and Paternalist Motives in Contract and Tort Law, with Special Reference to Compulsory Terms and Unequal Bargaining Power," *Maryland Law Review* 41, no. 4 (1982): 638–49. For a fuller and more recent account of Kennedy's views on adjudication, see his *A Critique of Adjudication: Fin De Siecle* (Cambridge, Mass.: Harvard University Press, 1997).

16. Marc Granetz, "Duncan the Doughnut," *The New Republic,* 17 March 1986, 22.

17. Unger, "Critical Legal Studies."

18. Duncan Kennedy, "The Structure of Blackstone's Commentaries," *Buffalo Law Review* 28 (spring 1979): 209–382. For his second thoughts on the "fundamental contradiction," see Peter Gabel and Duncan Kennedy, "Roll Over Beethoven," *Stanford Law Review* 36 (January 1984): 1–54.

19. Frug, "Henry James," 28.

20. Sanford Levinson, "Law as Literature," *Texas Law Review* 60 (March 1982): 373–403. For the response, see Stanley Fish, "Interpretation and the Pluralist Vision," *Texas Law Review* 60 (March 1982): 495–505. See also Richard H. Weisberg, "Text into Theory: A Literary Approach to the Constitution," *Georgia Law Review* 20 (summer 1986): 939–94.

21. This occurred in the course of a discussion of his article, "Justification (and Justifiability) of Law in a Contradictory World," in *Nomos XXVIII: Justification,* ed. J. Roland Pennock and John Chapman, 71–99 (New York: New York University Press, 1986).

22. Frank I. Michelman, "The Meanings of Legal Equality," in Canadian Institute for Advanced Legal Studies, *The Cambridge Lectures 1985,* ed. Frank E. McArdle, 85–102 (Montreal: Les Editions Yvon Blais, 1987).

23. Robert H. Bork, "Neutral Principles and Some First Amendment Problems," *Indiana Law Journal* 47 (fall 1971): 10.

24. Owen Fiss, "What Is Feminism?" *Arizona State Law Journal* 26 (summer 1994): 413–28.

CHAPTER 12. REASON VS. PASSION

1. 397 U.S. 254 (1970).

2. Hannah Arendt, *The Life of the Mind,* one vol. edition (New York: Harcourt Brace Jovanovich, 1978), 185.

3. Ronald Dworkin, "The Forum of Principle," *New York University Law Review* 56 (May/June 1981): 469–518.

4. 424 U.S. 319 (1976).

5. Richard A. Posner, "An Economic Approach to Legal Procedure and Judicial Administration," *Journal of Legal Studies* 2 (June 1973): 441–42.

6. 424 U.S. at 334–35.

7. Jerry L. Mashaw, "The Supreme Court's Due Process Calculus for Administrative Adjudication in *Mathews v. Eldridge*: Three Factors in Search of a Theory of Value," *University of Chicago Law Review* 44 (fall 1976): 48.

8. William J. Brennan Jr., "Reason, Passion, and 'The Progress of the Law,'" The Forty-Second Annual Benjamin N. Cardozo Lecture, *The Record of the Association*

of the Bar of the City of New York 42 (1987): 948–77, reprinted in *Cardozo Law Review* 10 (October/November 1988): 3–23.

9. Ibid., 21.

10. Ibid.

11. Ibid., 5.

12. See, for example, Derrick Bell, "The Civil Rights Chronicles," *Harvard Law Review* 99 (November 1985): 4–83; Richard Delgado, "Storytelling for Oppositionists and Others: A Plea for Narrative," *Michigan Law Review* 87 (August 1988): 2411–41; Patricia Williams, "Spirit-Murdering the Messenger: The Discourse of Fingerpointing as the Law's Response to Racism," *University of Miami Law Review* 42 (September 1987): 127–57.

13. See, for example, Martha L. Minow and Elizabeth V. Spelman, "Passion for Justice," *Cardozo Law Review* 10 (October/November 1988): 37–76. Some read Carol Gilligan, *In a Different Voice: Psychological Theory and Women's Development* (Cambridge, Mass.: Harvard University Press, 1982), in these terms, but I do not. She has been meticulous in presenting her position as an enrichment of reason.

14. See, for example, Paul Gewirtz, "Aeschylus' Law," *Harvard Law Review* 101 (March 1988): 1043–55.

15. Roberto Mangabeira Unger, *Passion: An Essay on Personality* (New York: Free Press, 1984). Duncan Kennedy's "fundamental contradiction" had been framed in terms of passions—the love of others and the fear of others. See Duncan Kennedy, "The Structure of Blackstone's Commentaries," *Buffalo Law Review* 28 (spring 1979): 205–382.

16. Here I especially have in mind the work of Martha Nussbaum, *The Fragility of Goodness: Luck and Ethics in Greek Tragedy and Philosophy* (Cambridge: Cambridge University Press, 1986).

17. See Delgado, "Storytelling."

18. See Stephen Wizner, "Passion in Legal Argument and Judicial Decision-making: A Comment on *Goldberg v. Kelly*," *Cardozo Law Review* 10 (October/November 1988): 179–92.

19. Brennan, "Reason, Passion," 12.

20. Ibid., 4.

21. In *Goldberg v. Kelly*, Brennan disposed of the issue in these terms: "Thus, the interest of the eligible recipient in uninterrupted receipt of public assistance, coupled with the State's interest that his payments not be erroneously terminated, clearly outweighs the State's competing concern to prevent any increase in its fiscal and administrative burdens" (397 U.S. at 266).

22. Edward de Grazia, "Humane Law and Humanistic Justice," *Cardozo Law Review* 10 (October/November 1988): 29.

23. Minow and Spelman speak of "non-arbitrary passion," in "Passion for Justice," 47, but that strikes me as an oxymoron.

24. Brennan, "Reason, Passion," 17 (emphasis added).

25. Ibid., 10 (emphasis added).
26. Ibid., 21.
27. The use of storytelling as a strategy of debunking the idea of truth is explicit in Delgado, "Storytelling."

CHAPTER 13. THE IRREPRESSIBILITY OF REASON

1. See, for instance, Stuart Hampshire, "A New Philosophy of the Just Society," review of *A Theory of Justice* by John Rawls, *New York Review of Books*, 24 February 1972, 34–39.
2. Alasdair MacIntyre, *After Virtue: A Study in Moral Theory* (Notre Dame: University of Notre Dame Press, 1986).
3. Nussbaum, *The Fragility of Goodness.*
4. As he puts it, "there are . . . rationalities rather than rationality" (Alasdair MacIntyre, *Whose Justice? Which Rationality?* [Notre Dame: University of Notre Dame Press, 1988], 9).
5. See, generally, Julia Annas, "MacIntyre on Traditions," *Philosophy and Public Affairs* 18 (autumn 1989): 388–404.
6. For a criticism of the relativism in MacIntyre, see Thomas Nagel, "Agreeing in Principle," review of *Whose Justice? Which Rationality?* by Alasdair MacIntyre, *Times Literary Supplement*, 8–14 July 1988, 747–48. For a general statement of Nagel's views, see Thomas Nagel, *The View From Nowhere* (Oxford: Oxford University Press, 1986).
7. MacIntyre, *After Virtue*, 246–55.
8. MacIntyre, *Whose Justice?* 395.
9. Martha Nussbaum, "Emotions as Judgments of Value," *Yale Journal of Criticism* 5 (spring 1992): 201–12.
10. In "Emotions as Judgments of Value," Martha Nussbaum writes:

The preference that economic Utilitarianism, for example, has had for a certain sort of reasoning (detached, cool, calculative, concerned with quantitative measurement), and its tendency to erect this preference into a norm, so that Reason and the Rational get defined in terms of it, and everything that lies outside is branded as mere irrationality—all this has certainly had a large influence on the rhetoric of our public life and, at a deeper level, on the ways in which political and economic deliberations are actually conducted. (*Yale Journal of Criticism* 5 [spring 1992]: 201–2)

11. Nussbaum, *Fragility of Goodness*, 45.
12. Ibid.
13. Ibid., 45–46.
14. Nussbaum, "Emotions as Judgments of Value," 209.

15. Ibid., 211.

16. See, for example, John Rawls, "Justice as Fairness: Political not Metaphysical," *Philosophy and Public Affairs* 14 (summer 1985): 223–51; John Rawls, "The Idea of an Overlapping Consensus," *Oxford Journal of Legal Studies* 7 (spring 1987): 1–25; John Rawls, "The Priority of Right and Ideas of the Good," *Philosophy and Public Affairs* 17 (autumn 1988): 251–76. These essays have been compiled in John Rawls, *Collected Papers* ed. Samuel Freeman (Cambridge, Mass.: Harvard University Press, 1999). Some of this work—especially "Justice as Fairness"—was specifically conceived as a response to the criticism of Michael J. Sandel, *Liberalism and the Limits of Justice* (New York: Cambridge University Press, 1998), and of Michael Walzer, "Philosophy and Democracy," *Political Theory* 9 (August 1981): 379–99.

CHAPTER 14. *BUSH V. GORE* AND THE QUESTION OF LEGITIMACY

1. 531 U.S. 98 (2000).

2. Sanford Levinson, "Return of Legal Realism," *The Nation*, 8 January 2001, 8.

3. See, for example, *Adarand Constructors, Inc. v. Pena*, 515 U.S. 2000 (1995).

4. See, for example, *United States v. Morrison*, 529 U.S. 598 (2000).

5. See, for example, *Gregg v. Georgia*, 428 U.S. 153 (1976); *McCleskey v. Kemp*, 481 U.S. 279 (1987).

6. *Roe v. Wade*, 410 U.S. 113 (1973); *Planned Parenthood of Southeastern Pennsylvania v. Casey*, 505 U.S. 833 (1992).

7. Martin Merzer "Review Shows Ballots Say Bush but Gore Backers Have Some Points to Argue," *Miami Herald* (National News), 4 April 2001, 1A.

8. Ford Fessenden and John M. Broder, "Examining the Vote: The Overview; Study of Florida Ballots Finds Justices Did Not Cast the Deciding Vote," *New York Times,* 12 November 2001, A1.

9. *Youngstown Sheet & Tube Co. v. Sawyer*, 343 U.S. 579 (1953).

10. *New York Times Co. v. United States*, 403 U.S. 713 (1971).

11. 418 U.S. 683 (1974).

12. 531 U.S. 98, 109.

13. See Guido Calabresi, "In Partial (but not Partisan) Praise of Principle," in *Bush v. Gore: The Question of Legitimacy,* ed. Bruce Ackerman (New Haven: Yale University Press, 2002), 67–83.

14. Owen Fiss, "Groups and the Equal Protection Clause," *Philosophy and Public Affairs* 5, no. 2 (1976): 107–77.

15. 377 U.S. 533, 563–69 (1964).

16. 531 U.S. at 126 n.4.

17. 3 U.S.C. § 5 (2000).

18. 531 U.S. 1046, 1047 (2000).

19. Levinson, "Legal Realism"; see also Jack M. Balkin and Sanford Levinson, "Legal Historicism and Legal Academics: The Roles of Law Professors in the Wake of *Bush v. Gore*," *Georgetown Law Journal* 90 (November 2001): 173–97.

20. See U.S. Constitution, amendment 12, and 3 U.S.C. §§ 15–18 (2000).

21. See Richard A. Posner, *Breaking the Deadlock: The 2000 Election, The Constitution, and the Courts* (Princeton, N.J.: Princeton University Press, 2001).

AFTERWORD

1. See, generally, Brian K. Landsberg, *Enforcing Civil Rights: Race Discrimination and the Department of Justice* (Lawrence: University Press of Kansas, 1997).

2. See Archibald Cox, "Constitutional Adjudication and the Promotion of Human Rights," *Harvard Law Review* 80 (November 1966): 91–122.

3. See William N. Eskridge Jr., "Reneging on History? Playing the Court/Congress/President Civil Rights Game," *California Law Review* 79 (May 1991): 613–84.

4. See Owen Fiss and Charles Krauthammer, "The Rehnquist Court: A Return to the Antebellum Constitution," *The New Republic*, 10 March 1982, 14–21.

5. See Jack M. Balkin, "History Lesson," *Legal Affairs* 1 (July/August 2002): 44–49.

6. See, generally, Larry D. Kramer, "We the Court," *Harvard Law Review* 115 (November 2001): 4–169.

7. See Richard A. Posner, *Breaking the Deadlock: The 2000 Election, The Constitution, and the Courts* (Princeton, N.J.: Princeton University Press, 2001), 145.

8. Ibid., 250.

9. See, generally, Robert C. Post and Reva B. Siegel, "Equal Protection by Law: Federal Antidiscrimination Legislation after *Morrison* and *Kimel*," *Yale Law Journal* 110 (December 2000): 441–260.

Index

Acknowledgments

The classroom is my workshop. The essays collected in this volume have been shaped in decisive ways by the classes I offered at the Yale Law School over the last twenty-five years. Sometimes I shared the podium with colleagues—notably Bruce Ackerman, Robert Burt, Anthony Kronman, Jerry Mashaw, and George Priest—and I learned a great deal from them. I am also grateful to the students in my classes. Their hopes for the law were always an inspiration; their reflections and sometimes passionate criticism helped me better understand what I believe and, surprisingly, the very lessons I was trying to teach.

Three students—Theodore Sampsell-Jones, Nicholas Daum, and Elizabeth Kendall— assisted me in collecting, organizing, and editing the essays presented in this volume. With extraordinary insight and almost boundless dedication, they enabled me to define the unifying themes and helped me to understand what value a book such as this might have in the sad and sorry era of retrenchment through which we are now living. Many other friends, students, and colleagues made significant contributions to specific essays and to this book in general. I gladly and warmly acknowledge their contributions: Geoffrey Aronow, Deborah Ashford, Lynn Baker, Eric Beckman, Joel Beckman, Eric Bentley Jr., Ryan Bergsieker, Alexandra Block, Jennifer Brown, Marcel Bryar, Joanna Calne, Stuart Chinn, Rodrigo Correa Gonzales, Robert Cover, Lawrence Douglas, William Duker, Richard Dunville, Michael Fitts, Jordan Flyer, Stephen Fuzesi, Stephen Garvey, Julius Getman, Paul Gewirtz, Brandt Goldstein, Joseph Halpern, Jane Harden, Robert Ihne, Pamela Karlan, Robert Katzmann, Alvin Klevorick, Martin Klotz, Christopher Kutz, Michael Laudor, Matthew Lindsay, Burke Marshall, William Michael, Martha Minow, Robert Rabin, Judith Resnik, Jeremy Rossman, Kevin Russell, Eric Sapp, Robert Schapiro, Reva Siegel, Michael Starr, Irwin Stotzky, Holly Thomas, Anne Wallwork, and Gerson Zweifach.

Lorraine Nagle has been my secretary for these twenty-five years. Fiercely dedicated to her work, yet imbued with the kindest of dispositions, she helped bring into being all the essays in this book and did so with a professionalism and sympathy that are truly exemplary.

About the Author

Owen Fiss is Sterling Professor of Law at Yale University.